Contributions to Economics

The series *Contributions to Economics* provides an outlet for innovative research in all areas of economics. Books published in the series are primarily monographs and multiple author works that present new research results on a clearly defined topic, but contributed volumes and conference proceedings are also considered. All books are published in print and ebook and disseminated and promoted globally. The series and the volumes published in it are indexed by Scopus and ISI (selected volumes).

Cristina Peicuti

A Monetary and Economic History of France since 1944

From Francs to Euros

Springer

Cristina Peicuti
ESCP Business School
Paris, France

ISSN 1431-1933 ISSN 2197-7178 (electronic)
Contributions to Economics
ISBN 978-3-032-17595-3 ISBN 978-3-032-17596-0 (eBook)
https://doi.org/10.1007/978-3-032-17596-0

Translation from the French language edition: "Histoire monétaire et économique de la France de 1944 à nos jours" by Cristina Peicuti, © Editions Eyrolles 2024. Published by Editions Eyrolles. All Rights Reserved.

This Springer imprint is published by the registered company Springer Nature Switzerland AG
The registered company address is: Gewerbestrasse 11, 6330 Cham, Switzerland

38e prix
Turgot
MENTION D'HONNEUR
38ème EDITION
25 Mardi mars 2025

"Everyone must come to the realization that one day you have to pay"[1]
Charles de Gaulle, 1963

[1] Charles de Gaulle at Cabinet meeting held on 7 May 1963.
Peyrefitte, Alain (2002), *C'était de Gaulle*, Quarto Gallimard, p. 920.

Foreword

Cristina Peicuti's *A Monetary and Economic History of France since 1944, From Francs to Euros* offers us a tightly argued, deeply informed narrative that does a superb job at both chronicling and clarifying the post-WWII monetary and economic trajectory of a major nation-state—fourth among the world's G7—in the modern world. It is of great interest to those of us outside France who want to understand it but have a hard time seeing in. And it is of great interest to those of us who want to understand the post-WWII monetary and economic trajectory of the North Atlantic, and indeed of the world.

France is both a key part of the whole trajectory of and also a key benchmark to use in assessing individual country trajectories. I see Peicuti's volume as both an essential case study and a challenge to our broader narratives. Her meticulous account of dirigisme, inflation, Europeanization, crisis, and monetary union reveals a nation both exemplary and idiosyncratic. Peicuti neither genuflects before nor declaims against the state's economic power, and its role in France's post-WWII transformation and development. Rather, she anatomizes it. The book's structure—from the inflationary dirigisme of the post-war period, through the wrenching adjustments towards Maastricht and the euro, to the recent return of dirigisme amid crisis—is an elegant frame for a tumultuous subject.

It is easy to forget that my teacher David Landes made his initial reputation as a France pessimist: he argued that France's familial capitalism made it culturally impossible for its economy to catch up to or even keep pace with the more capitalist, more organized, more transaction-focused economies across the Rhine and the Channel, let along the United States. Yet he was wrong.

It is easy to forget that as recently as 1986, France remained substantially a polity of administratively set prices. Again, one that lacked the capitalist economic flexibility that the then-preachers of Neoliberal doctrine taught was essential for prosperity. Yet they were wrong.

It is easy to dismiss the European Monetary System as a technocratic footnote. Yet its collapse, in the end, provoked a huge shift towards a much more integrated economic Europe—albeit one integrated in a particularly and peculiarly fraught way.

Peicuti makes these moments vivid, showing how they were lived as political turning points, for their implications for macroeconomic aggregates were in reality changing and shaping the lives of tens of millions. One sees in these pages the shadow of the Rueff Plan, the embers of May '68, the conditionalities of EU integration, and the reverberations of sovereign debt markets. One hears the voices of street protesters and shopkeepers as well as technocrats and ministers.

France's history oscillates so vividly between grand aspiration and administrative reality. It aspires to a form of national greatness tied to state-led industrial policy and full employment. It has had to repeatedly come to terms with constraints imposed by inflation and voters' strong dislike for it, by capital mobility and the need to mobilize societal wealth for national development purposes, and European integration alongside the maintenance of national peculiarities. France's post-WWII monetary and economic history is that of oscillation.

The monetary history of France, from the Fourth Republic through to Macron's handling of the COVID-19 and Ukraine shocks, is a key part of global political economy. It covers the triumph and victories followed by the long twilight of the post-war Keynesian settlement, the rise of neoliberalism, and the ambivalent consolidation of the eurozone. To tell such a story requires command of macroeconomics, institutional detail, political theory, and—perhaps above all—historical sensibility. Peicuti demonstrates all of these with clarity and conviction.

I can say that the future we now face—in France and elsewhere—will be much more intelligible to those who have read this book.

Author of *Slouching Towards Utopia: An Economic History of the Twentieth Century*

J. Bradford DeLong
Professor of Economic History,
Finance, and Macroeconomics
University of California
Berkeley, United States

About This Book

The French state has historically been dirigiste, which is incompatible with a democratic system and market economy. Moreover, by its very nature, dirigisme is inflationary. It was European Union integration that forced the French government to loosen its stranglehold and open up the country's economy. The ordinance on the freedom of pricing and competition only dates back to December 1, 1986, repealing the ordinance of June 30, 1945, that introduced price controls. But the COVID-19 pandemic has seen dirigisme rise from the ashes, along with inflation, which is impoverishing the French people and providing a breeding ground for the extremes. Will France get back on the straight and narrow, returning to inclusive growth, or will it sink into the quicksand of public debt and dirigisme?

Contents

About the Author

Cristina Peicuti foresaw the 2008 crisis, which was the subject of her thesis, "The Subprime Mortgage Crisis and the Credit Channel" (Paris, Panthéon-Assas University, 2006–2009). A professor and the scientific director of a research chair at the École Supérieure de Commerce de Paris (ESCP BS), she is a senior economist at one of the world's thirty globally systemic banks (G-SIBs). Cristina is the author of several books: *A Monetary and Economic History of France since 1944*, *Of Banks and Crises* (2024), *Decoding Economic Crises* (2023), and *Credit, Destabilisation and Crises* (2010).

Chapter 1
Introduction

Could anyone in France in the nineteenth century have foreseen the country's socio-economic evolution over the next hundred years? In 1863, the 35-year-old Jules Verne took up the challenge by writing *Paris au XXe siècle*. His publisher Pierre-Jules Hetzel's refusal to publish the manuscript was definitive and edifying: "My dear Verne, [...] you have undertaken an impossible task and, like your predecessors in such matters, you have not been able to pull it off. It is a hundred feet below the level of your *Five Weeks in a Balloon*. [...] It is tabloidish, and the topic is ill-chosen."[1]

Jules Verne predicts the evolution of Paris, its economy, and society in the twentieth century. The forecasts of economists have been proved wrong for as long as the profession has existed. Despite the development of econometrics and big data, the economic forecasts produced by central and commercial banks, rating agencies, and other research institutes have struggled to come about. They remain hopelessly wrong. But Jules Verne is a visionary like no other. In this book, he not only imagines Paris in the twentieth century, but also what will become of the city in the following century. He envisions transportation without noise and air pollution, the kind of transportation that will ultimately be the transportation of the twenty-first century. He describes a city crisscrossed by hydrogen-powered buses, cars, and "glittering trains, which seemed to furrow the air with fantastic speed."[2]

> "These various improvements were certainly suited to this feverish century, during which the pressure of business permitted no rest or delay. [...] No doubt he would have been astonished; but the men of 1960 were no longer lost in admiration of such marvels; they exploited them quite calmly, without being any the happier, for, from their hurried gait, their peremptory manner, their American 'dash,' it was apparent that the demon of wealth impelled them onward without mercy or relief."[3]

---

[1] Verne, Jules (2002), *Paris au XXe siècle*, Le livre de poche, p. 14.

[2] Verne, Jules, translated by Howard, Richard (2002), *Paris in the Twentieth Century: The Lost Novel*, Del Rey, p. 26.

[3] Ibid, p. 26.

C. Peicuti, *A Monetary and Economic History of France since 1944*, Contributions to Economics, https://doi.org/10.1007/978-3-032-17596-0_1

These modes of transport "seemed to unite all the virtues of rapidity, facility, and comfort",[4] heralding the advent of an American economic vision of the world that would appear after 1945, making very little inroads at first due to Charles de Gaulle's efforts to counter this influence, but then spreading at full tilt with the development of the Internet and the financialization of the economy:

> '"But who dreams of being entertained? Let's bore one another to death! That's our ruling principle today!"
>
> 'And you can't see any remedy for it?' Michel asked.
>
> 'None, so long as finance and machinery prevail! And it's really machinery that's doing the mischief.'"[5]

Nevertheless, from 1945 onward, the "demon of wealth" would gradually replace the French *douceur de vivre*, until the ecological transition of the twenty-first century, when the French began to aspire to a return to the ways of old.

Jules Verne describes the concentration of the economy and population in modern megacities, envisioning a Greater Paris with its 5 million inhabitants: "the delimitation of the present capital was marked by the forts of Mont Valérien, Saint-Denis, Aubervilliers, Romainville, Vincennes, Charenton, Vitry, Bicêtre, Montrouge, Vanves, and Issy; […] It had devoured the entire Department of the Seine."[6]

In Jules Verne's vision, the walls protecting Paris have disappeared, replaced by a first ring of railroad tracks that more or less encircle the city. The book depicts a globally wealthier society that has enjoyed spectacular technical progress, but even so fiscal pressures on the lowest-income households and poverty are no less. There are murmurs of discontent, summarized in this euphonious verse: "Le mur murant Paris rend Paris murmurant."[7] The Yellow Vests movement would bear this out.

Jules Verne describes the happy outcome of globalization, for "the links of commerce are drawing nations ever closer! The British, the Russians, the Americans all have their banknotes, their rubles, their dollars invested in our commercial enterprises."[8] He describes a country where the British are gradually becoming the great landowners, taking their revenge on William the Conqueror. And he goes on "for it's the century's profession of faith: with Montaigne and maybe Rabelais it was what do I know? In the nineteenth century, it was what does it matter to me? And nowadays we say: how much does it earn? Well, the day a war earns as much as an industrial investment, then there'll be wars."[9]

The book depicts a Parisian society where "by dint of multiplying university branches, lycées, primary and secondary schools, Christian seminaries, cramming

---

[4] Ibid, p. 20.

[5] Verne, Jules, translated by Howard, Richard (2002), *Paris in the Twentieth Century: The Lost Novel*, Del Rey, p. 91.

[6] Ibid, p. 18.

[7] Verne, Jules (2002), *Paris au XXe siècle*, Le livre de poche, p. 38.

[8] Verne, Jules, translated by Howard, Richard (2002), *Paris in the Twentieth Century: The Lost Novel*, Del Rey, p. 83–84.

[9] Ibid, p. 84.

establishments, as well as the various asylums and orphanages, some sort of instruction had filtered down to the lowest layers of the social order. If no one read any longer, at least everyone could read, could even write."[10] French has been relegated to the rank of an "ancient language," much like Latin and Greek that "were not only dead languages but buried as well",[11] and at prize-giving orations "a Chinese speech replaced [French] to great advantage."[12]

Fast forward to 2024 and economic history is at this very crossroads, where American domination is at risk of being replaced by Chinese domination. What has slowed China's inexorable ascent to becoming the most powerful economy in the world has been its totalitarian zero-COVID management of the health crisis.

When France dominated the world, the economic theories of the country's physiocrats resonated throughout the world, employing French; then it was the turn of English and American economists, employing English. Will it soon be the turn of the Chinese language, as Jules Verne predicted?

Jules Verne was both a visionary and a futurist. In the book, "the civil service developed in every possible way, shape, and form",[13] the main character to bemoan that "there are ten million of them in France; figure the chances of advancement, and take your place in line!"[14] According to the French national office for statistics INSEE, at the end of 2019, 5.66 million persons, or one in five employed persons, worked in the French civil service,[15] compared with one in nine in Germany. Admittedly, this is far less than predicted by Jules Verne, but he was right in his prediction that "government jobs" would multiply, and they still are. In France, the number of civil servants increased by 36.3% between 1980 and 2007, by comparison with which the number of employed persons increased by 16.4% over the same period. In other countries, it was the exact opposite, notably in Germany.

As foreseen by Jules Verne, globalization can be interrupted by wars. These exogenous shocks to the economy see the war industry prosper and ultimately enable the world's dominant power to consolidate its position. On the other hand, it is not clear much is gained by the original belligerents. The Second World War marked a halt to the happy-go-lucky globalization underway since the 1920s. The war in Ukraine is a harbinger of further disruptions to globalization, which is no longer a given now that climate change has further heightened awareness among young people that we are all in the same boat.

---

[10] Ibid, p. 4.

[11] Ibid, p. 7.

[12] Ibid, p. 7.

[13] Verne, Jules, translated by Howard, Richard (2002), *Paris in the Twentieth Century: The Lost Novel*, Del Rey, p. 4.

[14] Ibid, p. 170.

[15] https://www.insee.fr/en/statistiques/5346161.

Part I
Inflationary Dirigisme from 1945 to 1973

The period from 1945 to 1973, known in France as the *Glorious Thirty*, marked the transition from a protectionist rural economy to a modern economy, with the dynamic development of the services sector and a gradual opening to the world.

Inflation in France was higher than that of most Western countries as it was mainly the result of "inflationary dirigisme," an expression that entered French economic history with René Mayer. For him, it was "an evil born of war." He used the expression to encapsulate a Keynesian-inspired economic policy that based the evolution of purchasing power on a permanent imbalance in the nation's accounts, notably through public deficits and debt, intended to guarantee strong growth thanks to public investments, which in reality turned out to be costly and of little use, and which accepted to sacrifice the currency and savings as a result of galloping inflation to correct the induced imbalances. What would have been the extent of the Glorious Thirty if France had ended price controls as early as 1945? What would France's place on the world stage have been without its 41 years of inflation and economic distortion?

The almost three decades from 1945 to 1973 became known as the "*Trente Glorieuses*" in France, an expression coined by French economist Jean Fourastié [1907–1990], and the title of the book he authored.[1] This expression refers to the Revolution of July 27, 28, and 29, 1830, in French the "*Trois Glorieuses*," depicted by Eugène Delacroix in his painting entitled *La Liberté guidant le peuple*. For Jean Fourastié, this was a pivotal moment, the overthrow of King Charles X marking France's transition from the Ancient Regime, with the replacement of the principle of hereditary right by that of popular sovereignty, opening the way to a modern democracy. In the same way, the Glorious Thirty marked the transition from a protectionist rural economy to a modern economy, with the dynamic development of the services sector and a gradual opening to the world. From less than 15% at the end of the 1960s, the aggregate value of imports and exports came to account for more than 21% of the country's gross domestic product at the end of 1970. In stark contrast

[1] Fourastié, Jean (1970), *Les Trente Glorieuses: Ou la révolution invisible de 1946 à 1975*, Fayard.

to the July Revolution, the economic revolution of the Glorious Thirty was "invisible," as pointed out in the subtitle of Jean Fourastié's book, and lasted almost three decades.

Nevertheless, as indicated above, the immediate aftermath of the Second World War was a very trying period for the French population. At the time, no one would have described these first few years as "glorious." So while 1945 was not the start proper of the Glorious Thirty, 1973, the year of the oil crisis, did truly bring this period to an end.

Between 1949 and 1974, France's economy grew at an average annual rate of 5.3%, compared with 2.93% for the United Kingdom, 3.93% for the United States, 5.5% for Italy, 5.68% for West Germany, and 9.29% for Japan. The twelve countries that later formed the European Community recorded average annual growth of 4.6% during the Glorious Thirty. After the oil crisis, from 1974 to 2007, France's gross domestic product in real terms declined by 2.2% a year on average.

The margin rate of nonfinancial corporations, which hovered around 28% in the 1950s and 1960s, slumped to −3.4% in 1975. This was partly because wages were indexed to what was then galloping inflation, while businesses were prevented from passing on the increases in payroll and production costs in full to customers. The margin rate bounced back and set a new normative low at 23.1% in 1982, before recovering thanks to a policy of competitive disinflation. On the other hand, the investment rate of nonfinancial corporations, which averaged 23% in the 1950s and 1960s, fell sharply during the first oil crisis and would never again reach the heights set during the Glorious Thirty. The same applies to unemployment, which had reached less than 3% in France, and would never again fall that low.

The first significant public deficit was incurred in 1975. It was the result of the various stimulus measures implemented by the government after the first oil crisis, as well as the fall in tax receipts due to the recession.

In his book, Jean Fourastié wondered whether, after the oil shock and the ensuing recession, France's growth trajectory would recover to what it was during the Glorious Thirty. In the final chapter, entitled *The End of Easy Times*, Fourastié is skeptical, citing four factors: the oil crisis, protectionist temptations, the disorganization of the international monetary system, and the challenges responding to the rise of emerging countries. He concluded that, despite these external factors, if France did implement an effective economic policy, it could renew with its dynamism of old. As it turned out, because economic policy was not sufficiently well directed and calibrated after the 1973 oil shock, there was no return to the growth trajectory of the Glorious Thirty.

The price ordinance 45-1483 of June 30, 1945 (*Ordonnance n°45-1483 du 30 juin 1945 relative aux prix*[2]) marked the start of inflationary dirigisme in France, which lasted until the text was repealed on December 1, 1986, from which date prices for goods and services were freely set by the play of competition, which led to price stability. In contrast to the failure of economic policy, the government's anti-inflationary fiscal policy after the Glorious Thirty was crowned with success.

[2] https://www.legifrance.gouv.fr/loda/id/JORFTEXT000000516237.

Monetary policy was undoubtedly effective during this period: inflation fell back and prices stabilized until the COVID-19 pandemic when the government locked down the country[3] and vowed to take all necessary measures “whatever the cost”.[4] Then came the war in Ukraine that further stoked inflation.

[3] France has been confronted by more lethal diseases of epidemic proportion before (plague, leprosy), but never did it order a nationwide lockdown like the one in 2020, which was inspired by China’s management of the health emergency.

[4] Pledge given by President Macron in his address to the French nation on March 12, 2020. Harks back to the famous “whatever it takes” uttered by Mario Draghi on July 26, 2012, which ended the European sovereign debt crisis triggered by Greece’s warning that it might default on its debt. Whereas three words from Mario Draghi nipped the crisis in the bud without costing the European Union a single euro, Emmanuel Macron’s pledge cost several tens of billions of euro.

Chapter 2
Post-war Reconstruction and Marshall Plan

In July 1944, all forty-four allied nations gathered for the United Nations Monetary and Financial Conference at the Mount Washington Hotel in Bretton Woods, New Hampshire, to regulate the international monetary and financial order. The Bretton Woods System, as it became known, lasted from 1945 to 1976, when the United States modified the system for its convenience.

In 1945, France was in ruins. Reconstructing the country posed a major logistical challenge, a situation compounded by elevated inflation and a public debt that reached 170% of gross domestic product.

At the end of the war, the French colonial empire, which unlike Metropolitan France had not been ravaged by the war, represented a formidable asset, with an area more than seven times the size of France itself spread over five continents. But on May 8, 1945, the colonies' thirst for freedom became apparent with violent clashes in Algeria. This was followed on August 16 by Ho Chi Minh's call for a general insurrection in Indochina. Shortly after, Ho Chi Minh declared the independence of the Democratic Republic of Vietnam.

The Social Security was created by the ordinances of October 4 and 19, 1945 (*Ordonnance n° 45–2250 du 4 octobre 1945 portant organisation de la sécurité sociale* and *Ordonnance n° 45/2454 du 19 octobre 1945 Régime des Assurances sociales applicable aux assurés des professions non agricoles*).

The law defining the status of France's civil servants was passed on October 19, 1946 (*Loi n° 46–2294 du 19 octobre 1946 relative au statut général des fonctionnaires*).

A formal framework was established for the country's reconstruction with the creation on January 3, 1946, of a special planning commission (*Commissariat au Plan*, the forerunner of the *Commissariat Général à la Stratégie et à la Prospective*, better known as *France Stratégie*). It defined a four-year plan aimed at modernizing the country and increasing its production capacity and productivity. The funds needed for the reconstruction came from the French Treasury but, especially, from the Marshall Plan. The objective was not to reconstruct France as it was pre-war but

C. Peicuti, *A Monetary and Economic History of France since 1944*, Contributions to Economics, https://doi.org/10.1007/978-3-032-17596-0_2

what it should be in the future. To this end, General de Gaulle [1890–1970] created the Atomic Energy Commission (*Commissariat à l'Énergie Atomique - CEA*) on December 31, 1945. France's first artificial nuclear reactor, baptized Zoé, was started up on December 15, 1948. The contours of modern France were starting to be etched out.

International Monetary System Under Construction at Bretton Woods Even Before the End of the Second World War

On July 1, 1944, some months before the surrender of the axis powers, 730 delegates from all forty-four allied nations gathered in Bretton Woods, New Hampshire, United States, to modify the British-inspired international monetary system so that it could support the new world economic order spawned by the war and the accompanying economic policy of inflation and devaluation.

France's delegate at the conference was Pierre Mendès France [1907–1982] to whom Harry Dexter White [1892–1948], who was the architect of the Bretton Woods system, would speak in French when he did not want others to understand their exchanges. Pierre Mendès France noted bitterly that French used to be the language spoken and understood by everyone at international meetings. White was so attached to France that his PhD dissertation, defended in 1930 and published by Harvard University Press in 1933, was entitled *The French International Accounts, 1880–1913*. In 1934, White joined the US Treasury and would go on to be the Director of the Division of Monetary Research, which worked on the international monetary system, at the Treasury Department.

John Maynard Keynes [1883–1946] was the star of the conference, but it was White who imposed his vision of the new international monetary system over the objections of the British economist.

Keynes wanted to get rid of the gold standard which he rightly considered deflationary. To this end, he proposed the creation of a bank of central banks, called the International Clearing Union, adding that he "would like to see the Board of the Bank composed of imaginative expansionists."[1] The intention was that it would use a special unit of account, named the bancor, and would make loans to countries in deficit to help with their turnaround. White's approach to domestic economic policy was Keynesian, but his approach to the international economy was inspired by the report on purchasing power parity by Swedish economist Gustav Cassel [1866–1945]. His view was that the solution to any current account imbalances is to devalue

[1] Keynes, John Maynard, 1945/1991, p. 194 cited in Mosley, P. (1998). *The World Bank, 'Global Keynesianism' and the Distribution of the Gains from Growth.* In Sapsford, D., Chen, Jr. (eds) Development Economics and Policy. Palgrave Macmillan, London. https://doi.org/10.1007/978-1-349-26769-9_20.

the currencies of countries in deficit, so as to lower export prices without these countries having to lower domestic prices and wages. For White, a system of fixed and adjustable exchange rates pegged to gold is viable if parity adjustments are negotiated and if an International Monetary Fund and a World Bank are created. The International Monetary Fund would be responsible for lending to countries short of currency, in exchange for these agreeing to a policy aimed at reducing their domestic demand. The World Bank would contribute to the convergence of economies and living standards by financing long-term projects. White prevailed over Keynes.

The Situation in 1945: France, a Country in Ruins

"In 1944, the French were unhappy, now they're disgruntled. That's progress."[2]
Charles de Gaulle

Paris was liberated on August 25, 1944. In December 1944, de Gaulle traveled to Russia. Even though the German Instrument of Surrender signed on May 7, 1945, was in quadruplicate, one each for the United States, Great Britain, Russia and France, it was clear that France had contributed far less to the final victory, as the French people were well aware. There was also the fact that, from 1940 to 1944, the Vichy government had collaborated with Germany. The France that emerged victorious from the First World War and then the Second World War defies comparison. Even so, the IFOP opinion poll published on July 1, 1945, showed that 80% of French people considered that France was still a great power.

Russia's human losses, both military and civilian, during the Second World War represented 10% of its population, compared with 1.5% in France's case. Asked "Which country contributed most to Germany's defeat?" in an IFOP opinion poll conducted from August, 28 to September 2, 1944, in Paris, 61% of respondents named Russia, 29.3% the United States, and 11.5% Britain. In 1945, anyone criticizing Russia or its Communist Party was suspected of having fascist sympathies. The French Communist Party (*Parti communiste français—PCF*), which stated that "France is just our country, but the USSR is our homeland," would capitalize on the disinformation of the French population. The Party quashed any dissenting opinion using a powerful, vitriolic press that it controlled, taking to task any opposition.

Yet the Soviet Union did not liberate the populations of Central Europe, instead occupying or annexing countries representing one-quarter of Europe's land mass and 28% of its population, all the while attempting to exert influence over Western Europe. While the Second World War marked the start of the end of Western colonial empires, it was the start of the Soviet colonization of Central Europe, which lasted 45 years. Despite Britain making the case for France's presence, it was not invited to the Yalta and Potsdam conferences, which confirmed the Soviet takeover of the

[2] https://www.histoire-en-citations.fr/citations/de-gaulle-en-1944-les-francais-etaient-malheureux.

countries of Central Europe. General de Gaulle was only informed of the conclusions, which he took note of, stating that he did not feel bound by provisions adopted in his absence.

Under Soviet rule, all businesses were nationalized and all farm holdings were collectivized, thinkers and entrepreneurs (some 20% of the population of these formerly prosperous and democratic republics) who opposed this being eliminated. The heavy hand of the State over the business and agricultural sectors would remain in place for 45 years until the fall of the Berlin Wall, leading to the economic and intellectual ruin of these countries.

General de Gaulle had admonished French business leaders for not joining him in London after his call of June 18, 1940. So in the spring of 1945, he had no qualms about announcing a series of nationalizations in the mining, banking, air, road and maritime transportation sectors. After being requisitioned in 1944, the plants of car manufacturer Louis Renault were taken over, becoming the Régie nationale des usines Renault in January 1945. On March 17, 1946, the country's coal mines were nationalized with the creation of Charbonnages de France. Electricity and gas companies were nationalized a few weeks later, on April 8, and then insurance companies on April 25. Nationalizations already featured in the program of the National Council of the Resistance (*Conseil national de la Résistance—CNR*) published in 1944. It was not the Communist Party that was behind these nationalizations, but it did vote with the government. It is interesting to note that the Communist Party criticized Pierre Mendès France, the Economy Minister, for not granting any privileges to nationalized companies and for demanding rigorous financial management, requiring these companies to turn a profit.

The Social Security was created by the ordinances of October 4 and 19, 1945, the aim being to establish a coordinated network of funds instead of multiple organizations. The new scheme "is the promise made to each person that no matter the circumstances, he will have the necessary means so that he and his family can live with decency."[3]

Under the Law of October 30, 1946 (*Loi n° 46–2426 du 30 octobre 1946 sur la prévention et la réparation des accidents du travail et des maladies professionnelles*), abrogating the Law of 1898 (*Loi du 9 avril 1898 sur les responsabilités des accidents dont les ouvriers sont victimes dans leur travail*), risks arising from occupational accidents were assumed by the Social Security. In addition to the payment of indemnities, the Social Security was entrusted with risk prevention.

On October 31, 1945, General de Gaulle created the Atomic Energy Commission (*Commissariat à l'énergie atomique—CEA*), laying the foundation for France to become the leading nuclear power in Europe.

In 1945, Europe lay in ruins. With just 0.2% of the total death toll, half of the world's gold reserves and the only country possessing the nuclear bomb, the United

---

[3] Translation from Chemla, Eliane (2016), *The French Social Security System*, in *The Right to Social Security in the Constitutions of the World. Broadening the Moral and Legal Space for Social Justice*, ed. M. Wujczyk, Geneva.

Original French text: https://assurance-maladie.ameli.fr/qui-sommes-nous/histoire.

States emerged as the real winner from the conflict. Its victory would drive the country's economic growth in the following century.

Economic activity in the United States reached its wartime peak in February 1945 when it became clear that the end of the war was approaching. When demobilization began, this was accompanied by a sharp decrease in government expenditures, which fell from $83 billion in 1945 to $30 billion in 1946,[4] and a rapid decline in industrial production. Inflation accelerated when price control was dropped in 1946. The wholesale price index jumped by 16.4% from January 1946 to August 1948, but this rise was substantially less than the inflation experienced by France over the same period. If one considers the period 1938 to 1952, it will be observed that inflation remained moderate in Anglo-Saxon countries having emerged victorious from the Second World War; it was middling in the Iberian Peninsula and Switzerland, which remained neutral during the conflict; and it was high in the former battlegrounds.

In 1945, France had a population of 40 million, of which 2.1 million were still in Germany, held there as prisoners of war, deportees, or sent as forced laborers under the Compulsory Work Service Scheme (*service du travail obligatoire—STO*) introduced by the Vichy government in 1943. In his speeches, by associating France with the final victory on an equal footing with the other allies, de Gaulle gave the French people the strength to rebuild their country so that it might once again take its place as a world power. Confidence in the economy being crucial, this communication strategy was what was needed. De Gaulle's attitude had another consequence, which is that France's disastrous situation in 1945 and the reconstruction effort did not attract much attention at the international level. Much of the attention was on the reconstruction effort for the vanquished, namely Germany. Yet, far more of France was laid waste than during the First World War (75 départements compared with just 15 in 1918), with 23% of buildings destroyed, more than 50% in several cities (Brest, Le Havre, Caen, Saint-Lô, Rouen, Beauvais, and Amiens).

The country's reconstruction posed a huge logistical challenge:

> "All the bridges over the Seine from Paris to the sea, over the Loire from Nevers and over the Rhône from Lyon had been blown up. With the four hundred and fifty railway bridges that had been destroyed, a total of three thousand bridges had been reduced to rubble. Ten thousand of the twelve thousand locomotives owned by the SNCF had been wrecked or otherwise taken out of service, along with 40% of the motor vehicle fleet. Of the five hundred thousand trucks in circulation in 1939, three hundred thousand were not to be found."[5]

With only four thousand trucks supplying Paris and rationing continuing after the war, Parisians went hungry. The bread rationing card was reintroduced on November 28, 1945.

Infant mortality peaked in 1945. Also, one child in three suffered serious growth problems due to malnutrition. For one thing, agricultural production in 1945 was 20% lower than in 1938. Shortages led to inflation.

---

[4] Friedman, Milton, Schwartz, Anna Jacobson (1963), *A Monetary History of the United States, 1867–1960*, National Bureau of Economic Research Publications, Princeton University Press, Chap. 10, p. 157. https://www.nber.org/system/files/chapters/c11389/c11389.pdf.

[5] Elgey, Georgette (2018), *Histoire de la IVe république, De 1945 à 1957*, éditions Robert Laffont, p. XVIII.

On January 20, 1946, de Gaulle stepped down as President of France's provisional government:

> "Peyrefitte - 'In 1946, when you stepped down, did you think that you would soon be called back?'
>
> The General paused a while before answering me. Eventually, however, he quietly said:
>
> De Gaulle - 'The party system was making a strong comeback. I knew it couldn't solve post-war problems. To tell the truth, I didn't think it would last as long as it did and that we'd have to wait until we were on the brink of civil war to put an end to it.'
>
> Peyrefitte - 'You stepped down saying that you had put France back on track. But was it really on track? Its economy was not out of the woods by a long stretch. Why did you side with Pleven against Mendès? At the same time, in Belgium, Camille Gutt[6] applied the harsh method advocated by Mendès, and it worked.'
>
> De Gaulle - 'The French are not Belgians. They are more restless and there are more of them. France is fragile. It was easier to apply draconian remedies to eight million Belgians than to forty million French.'"[7]

Between 1938 and 1944, the public debt rose fourfold, the currency in circulation fivefold. In 1939, France had 2500 tons of gold, i.e., 20% of the reserves held by the world's banks. This made it the world's leading monetary power. In 1945, France had 1700 tons of gold.[8] It had been overtaken by the United States, which held 50% of the world's reserves. The war in Europe had the effect of concentrating economic power and gold reserves on another continent.

As a result of the 1929 financial crisis, France's national income fell from FRF435 billion (€27,151 billion) in 1929 to FRF380 billion (€20,555 billion) in 1938 and FRF207 billion (€2,776 billion) in 1945. Taking into account currency erosion due to inflation, the purchasing power of 207 billion francs in 1945 is therefore the same as that of €2,776 billion in 2021, emphasizing the staggering fall in France's income over this period.

Note that during the war, "every day, Germany levied four hundred million francs in occupation costs; this daily levy was increased to seven hundred million in the summer of 1944, and half the national wealth went up in smoke, i.e., over FRF5000 billion."[9]

---

[6] Having held various ministerial positions in the Belgian government in exile, Camille Gutt [1884–1971] returned to Brussels in September 1944, and resumed his work as minister of finance until February 1945. Widely credited for having turned around the country's economic and financial situation, resorting to drastic measures such as a currency exchange (withdrawal of the existing banknotes from circulation, exchanging them up to a certain maximum value; this becoming known as the Gutt Operation).

[7] Peyrefitte, Alain (2002), *C'était de Gaulle*, Quarto Gallimard, p. 46.

[8] In 2022, France held 2,436.5 tons of gold and the United States 8,133.47 tons of gold, but its importance has changed since the end of the gold standard.

[9] Elgey, Georgette (2018), *Histoire de la IVe république, De 1945 à 1957*, Éditions Robert Laffont, p. XVIII.

The Start of Decolonization

At the end of the war, the French colonial empire was more than seven times the size of France and spanned five continents. Inspired by the liberation of France that left colonizing powers in a fragile state, the colonized peoples of Africa and Asia also began to dream of independence. On May 8, 1945, a gathering of Algerians in Sétif to celebrate the Allies' victory ended in clashes after the local French gendarmerie tried to seize banners attacking colonial rule. There ensued a series of massacres that would ultimately lead to the Algerian war for independence. On July 11, 1945, Étienne Fajon, speaking on behalf of the PCF, stated that "the killings at Sétif are the manifestation of a fascist plot, which has found agents in nationalist circles."[10] Much the same rhetoric was employed almost eighty years later by Vladimir Putin about Ukraine.

The redistribution of economic power at the global level that began with the world wars would continue to the benefit of other continents and emerging countries. In this way, France's economic and monetary history since 1945 has been shaped by the Second World War.

Conceiving a decolonization plan that would increase France's standing in the world by having it grant independence to its colonies was not an option at the end of the Second World War. After four years of occupation, France was nostalgic for its past greatness, with its colonial empire very much part of its glorious past. Also, after the defeat of 1940, the French army wanted to renew with victory, be it on distant battlefields putting down rebellious colonies. The Fourth Republic draped itself in nationalism, for victory in the Second World War owed little to France. Consequently, decolonization was not on the agenda.

Charles de Gaulle's view was that decolonization would be harder for the French than the British as in the case of France:

> "From the outset, we based our colonization on the principle of assimilation. [...] We made them recite 'Our Ancestors the Gauls'; that wasn't very clever. That's why decolonization was so much more difficult for us than it was for the British. They always recognized the differences of race and culture. They organized self-government. All they had to do to make it work was to loosen the links. We denied these differences. We wanted to be a Republic of a hundred million identical and interchangeable French people. That's why the French experienced decolonization as a wrench."[11]

Furthermore, giving independence to one country would have set off a domino effect, as all other colonized countries would also have demanded their independence. It is in this context that the First Indochina War broke out in 1946.

It was a struggle not just for liberation, but also to impose Marxism, led by Hô Chi Minh [1890–1969], Asia's foremost Communist leader, who trained for two years in Moscow, after having been a member of the French Socialist Party in 1920 and

[10] https://www.lemonde.fr/archives/article/1995/05/14/les-massacres-de-setif_3870215_1819218.html.

[11] Comments by Charles de Gaulle in the Salon Doré, Élysée Palace, October 27, 1959. Peyrefitte, Alain (2002), *C'était de Gaulle*, Quarto Gallimard, p. 68–69.

having voted for the Third International, which made him one of the founders of the French Communist Party. In 1930, he created the Indochinese Communist Party. Significantly, this came about through the transformation of the old Vietnamese Communist Party. Hô Chi Minh was first and foremost a Marxist before being Vietnamese, like all communists who saw themselves as Russian patriots before being national patriots. They accused the "imperialists" of serving foreign interests but, in fact, it is they who served the interests of foreign countries. Communist parties have always indulged in nationalist one-upmanship to win new followers. This approach was particularly appropriate for bringing Marxism to the colonies, as Stalin explained in *Marxism and the National and Colonial Question.*[12]

On August 16, 1945, Ho Chi Minh called for a general insurrection in Indochina. Shortly after, Ho Chi Minh declared the independence of the Democratic Republic of Vietnam.

France had two hundred thousand soldiers to maintain control over a vast territory.

In 1949, in an effort to stabilize the situation, France officially renounced sovereignty, granting Vietnam, Laos, and Cambodia the status of associate states within the newly created French Union (*Union française*), but for the most part, France retained effective control. The First Indochina War was played out in the context of the Cold War when China recognized the Democratic Republic of Vietnam on January 18, 1950, followed by the Soviet Union on January 31. Mao Tse-tung [1893–1976], the founder of the People's Republic of China, which he led from 1949 until his death, considered that the Chinese revolution should become the model for all colonial countries. This political recognition of Vietnam before the Soviet Union marked China's return to the international stage. It was the first in a long series of actions that would lead it to become a leading power once again. France would recognize the People's Republic of China on January 27, 1964.

The Soviet Union supplied arms and war material which transited through China (the Soviet Union and the other Communist Bloc countries would go on to establish a $500 million fund to support the Marxist war effort on March 28, 1954). General de Lattre de Tassigny (he would be posthumously elevated to the dignity of Marshal of France in 1952) toured the United States in September 1951, addressing the American people on NBC's Meet the Press notably, explaining that the war concerned all of them and that his only son had died in Vietnam to defend the free world. This, and the fact the conflict was now part of the Cold War, convinced the United States to step in and help France finance the war: "Between that time [June 1950] and the fall of Dienbienphu in May of 1954, our $2.6 billion worth of military and economic aid to the French in Vietnam paid for 80 per-cent of the cost of the war against the Vietminh."[13] In 1952, the US Military Assistance Advisory Group was established

[12] Stalin, Joseph (2021), *Marxism and the National and Colonial Question*, Foreign Language Press. Originally published in 1934, a collection of articles and speeches on the nationalities question in the Soviet Union.

https://foreignlanguages.press/wp-content/uploads/2021/11/C28-Marxism-and-the-National-and-Colonial-Question-1st-Printing.pdf.

[13] https://www.congress.gov/bound-congressional-record/1966/02/21/senate-section.

in Saigon to coordinate requisitioning, procurement, and dissemination of supplies and equipment to the French army.

The US Congress wanted the Vietnam conflict to end by 1954 at the latest. Since Roosevelt's passing, the Americans had been telling France that they would prefer it to concentrate all its efforts and resources on European reconstruction and forsake its colonial empire. The Americans did not want the war in Indochina. It was the French who gradually dragged them into this conflict through repeated demands that the United States help fund the war effort. The Americans did help the French, but on the understanding that decolonization would ensue.

In the first issue of L'Express, published on May 10, 1953, Pierre Mendès France asserted: "The only way out lies […] in negotiation. Our situation was better last year than it is now; it is probably less bad now than it will be next year."[14] Joseph Laniel [1889–1975], who was appointed President of the Council of Ministers on June 28, 1953, also considered that the independence and sovereignty of Vietnam, Laos and Cambodia should be reinforced, but since December 1946, the Viet Minh would not settle for anything less than the departure of the French and the establishment of a people's republic. At the same time, with the exception of Pierre Mendès France and a few opponents, politicians were all publicly announcing victory, yet in private were convinced of the inexorability of defeat. Was it a visionary impasse to even imagine decolonization by France? Was it a reflection of the instability and internal wrangling besetting France's political parties?

The cost of the plan put together by General Navarre, when he was appointed Commander-in-Chief in Indochina on May 8, 1953, was FRF100 billion (equivalent of €2.32 billion). Thanks to Joseph Laniel's connections (he had been hunting buddies with General Eisenhower since the Second World War, and was a close friend of Douglas MacArthur, a member of the US Embassy in Paris and General MacArthur's nephew), a financial agreement was signed on September 30, 1953, under which the United States undertook to make $385 million available to France by December 31, 1954. Once American aid had been obtained, Edgar Faure tried to convince Laniel that peace should be negotiated directly with Hô Chi Minh, but Georges Bidault [1899–1983] succeeded in convincing him otherwise. At the same time the United States was providing aid to France, so Chinese aid to the Viet Minh in the form of supplies and ammunition was being ramped up. The Americans took this increased support as a signal that China might send troops to Indochina. On September 2, 1953, Secretary of State John Foster Dulles delivered an address on Korean problems before the American Legion at St. Louis. His remarks included the following statement concerning Indochina: "A single Chinese-Communist aggressive front extends from Korea on the north to Indochina in the south."[15] The United States had come to the realization that the outcome of the conflict in Indochina would affect its own vital interests in the region.

On November 20, 1953, General Navarre wrote to the Undersecretary in charge of relations with the Associated States to inform him that he had decided to launch

---

14 https://www.gouvernement.fr/partage/10188-premiere-parution-de-l-hebdomadaire-l-express.

15 https://history.state.gov/historicaldocuments/frus1952-54v13p1/d385.

a military operation at Diên Biên Phu, setting up a fortified airhead in this basin at the crossroads between Laos, China, and Thailand. On December 27, 1953, General Giap, the Commander-in-Chief of the Vietnamese People's Army during the First Indochina War, surrounded the 12,000-strong entrenched camp. On February 7, 1954, René Pleven, Minister of National Defense, visited Saigon. He considered that the announcement of direct negotiations between France and the Viet Minh would be a disaster for France's prestige. It would be seen as a betrayal by the Vietnamese soldiers fighting alongside the French, and would likely prompt them to desert even before the end of the negotiations.

The battle of Diên Biên Phu began in earnest on March 13, 1954. The French artillery commander, distraught at his inability to silence the well-camouflaged Viet Minh batteries, would commit suicide the next day. On March 15, General Navarre told High Commissioner Dejean that the battle was lost. The message was immediately passed on to Paul Reynaud, Georges Bidault, René Pleven, Marshal Alphonse Juin, and General Paul Ely. France pinned its hopes on an intervention by the US Air Force to repulse the assailants surrounding Diên Biên Phu. However, on April 5, 1954, the US ambassador told Georges Bidault that it would need congressional approval to enter the war, but that Congress was very reluctant, as American voters had been shocked to learn that 90% of the human and financial cost of the Korean War was borne by the United States. It was therefore the wrong time to start a new war. The ambassador also explained that the US would not act alone and that it wanted to internationalize the conflict by involving Britain and the Commonwealth countries.

The battle of Diên Biên Phu all but ended on May 7, 1954. Joseph Laniel was forced to resign on June 12, 1954.

Between 1945 and 1954, losses for the French Army were high: 92,797 killed-in-action and 75 thousand wounded-in action.

Officially, between 1946 and 1954, the Indochina war cost France FRF1800 billion (equivalent of €41.8 billion), or 60% of the total cost, the rest being borne by the United States.[16] The financial cost was mainly in respect of personnel, to keep in the field an army that increased from 50 to 180 thousand men over the period. The First Indochina War consumed an increasing share of the French defense budget, reaching 45% in 1950, the year in which American aid began to be ramped up. By 1953, the United States was providing 80% of the funding for the war. In the midst of France's economic reconstruction, the cost of this war was considered outrageous.

The First Indochina War hurt French economic growth, which fell from 8.6% in 1950 to 5.8% in 1951. The intensification of the war effort amplified the slowdown: GDP increased by just 3.1% in 1952, then by just 3.5% in 1953. The end of the war in 1954 saw GDP growth recover to 5.6%. But for this war, France's reconstruction would have gotten off to a stronger start and then accelerated, leading to stronger growth, with faster economic returns.

---

16 Tertrais, Hughes (1196), *L'impact économique et financier des deux guerres d'Indochine*, Les Cahiers de l'Institut d'Histoire du Temps Présent, n°34, juin 1996. Les guerres d'Indochine de 1945 à 1975, p. 213.

https://www.persee.fr/docAsPDF/ihtp_0769-4504_1996_num_34_1_2380.pdf.

As a greater war effort was demanded of Britain than France during the Second World War, French public debt neared 170% of GDP in 1944, while that of Britain exceeded 250%. In 1946, when the Indochina war broke out, France's debt-to-GDP ratio reached 89.5%. Despite the high cost of the Indochina war, the conflict did not ruin France: its debt-to-GDP ratio in fact fell to 32.1% in 1954, at the end of the Indochina war.

On the other hand, war expenditure in Indochina had an inflationary effect that is difficult to quantify, as post-war inflation had multiple sources. Nevertheless, it can be observed that when military appropriations for Indochina reached their peak between 1948 and 1950, the French franc underwent a series of devaluations.

Reconstruction

"You speak of greatness, but today the French are small. There will only be greatness when the French are of a stature to warrant it... For this purpose, they must modernize"[17]

Jean Monnet

A formal framework was established for the country's reconstruction with the creation on January 3, 1946, of the General Planning Commission (*Commissariat au Plan—CP*). It defined a four-year plan aimed at modernizing the country and at increasing its production capacity and productivity. This approach to economic planning was reminiscent of the Soviet economic system, but has its origins in the program drawn up by the National Council of the Resistance (*Conseil National de la Résistance - CNR*), which called for "the intensification of national production along the lines of a plan drawn up by the State after consultation with all contributing to this production",[18] and owed much to Pierre Mendès France's zeal as a social planner and to the pragmatism and entrepreneurial spirit of Jean Monnet [1888–1979]. This was the first experience of central planning in a European market economy. Some 74% of the investments financed under the Plan were earmarked for nationalized companies, the remaining 26% for agriculture and private-sector industry, provided that investments were consistent with the objectives set out in the Plan.

The plan was funded not only by the French Treasury, after some tough negotiations between Jean Monnet and the Minister of Finance and Economic Affairs, but above all by the Marshall Plan, which earmarked $22.5 billion from 1948 to 1952 for the post-war recovery of Europe, the United States leaving European countries to distribute this sum among themselves. The Marshall Plan was definitively adopted on April 3, 1948, with the signing of the Foreign Assistance Act of 1948 by Harry Truman. Sixteen Western countries applied. Although offered participation, Stalin

[17] Extract from a conversation Monnet had with de Gaulle in Washington, D.C., in August 1945, a few weeks after the end of the war.
Yergin, Daniel, and Stanislaw, Joseph (1998), Commanding Heights, Simon & Schuster, Inc., N.Y. https://www.pbs.org/wgbh/commandingheights/shared/minitextlo/prof_jeanmonnet.html.

[18] https://www.crrl.fr/module-Contenus-viewpub-tid-2-pid-120.html.

refused to have the Soviet Union accept plan benefits and also blocked benefits to Eastern Bloc countries. France received 20% of the total. As the 1946 Monnet Plan was consistent with the objectives of the Marshall Plan, the entire envelope earmarked for France could be used: 22% of the total would go to Electricity of France, 13% to Coal Mining of France, and 11% to the national railway company SNCF.

The aim of France's four-year plan was to invent and build the France of tomorrow, not to rebuild the France of yesterday, destroyed by the war. Let this be a warning to those who, in the wake of the COVID-19 pandemic, wish to repatriate yesterday's activities from China to France to re-establish France's sovereignty. It should not be France's ambition, in the twenty-first century, to revive the country's steel industry, but to innovate. It is about inventing the activities of tomorrow's world, repositioning human life and activity in harmony with the planet, and halting, or at least slowing down climate disruption. In the twenty-first century, even more than after the Second World War, it is a brand new world that needs to be built.

The General Planning Commission had a staff of around thirty, supervising more than one thousand people drawn from the different sectors of the economy, selected for their skills and expertise. This organization was very modern for its time. There were eighteen modernization and equipment commissions, which were not automatically chaired by a civil servant, but by the most qualified person in the field of activity. The biggest challenge faced by the General Planning Commission was to ensure that each piece of the puzzle would fit together, namely that the work of the individual commissions would contribute to the overall plan.

The General Planning Commission was headed by Jean Monnet, the son of a brandy producer in the town of Cognac, who did not complete the baccalauréat qualification. An entrepreneur and merchant, Jean Monnet worked for three decades with Anglo-Saxons, so he was familiar with their mindset. He was a fluent English speaker and well-traveled: as his father wanted to export his cognac to the four corners of the world, his son served a commercial apprenticeship in London from the age of 16 to 18, and would spend time in Canada, the United States, and Romania selling his father's production. He would even export cognac to China. During the Second Battle of the Marne in 1918, Jean Monnet, then thirty, was in Canada selling the family's cognac to the Hudson's Bay Company: "Through the intermediary of old family friends, he proposed to the government that he negotiate a loan of 100 million gold francs from the Hudson's Bay Company in exchange for it acting as sole purchasing agent for France in Canada. It's a deal, came the reply."[19]

In 1939, then aged 51, he was in London where he chaired the Franco-British Economic Coordination Committee. Entrusted with securing supplies from North America for the British Purchasing Commission, Jean Monnet left for Washington in August 1940. After moving to Algiers in 1943 as a member of the National Liberation Committee (*Comité français de libération nationale—CFLN*), he returned to Washington as head of the French mission negotiating the Lend-Lease. The Americans demanded proof of the expenses incurred. To obtain the financing, Jean Monnet

[19] *Histoire de la IVe république, De 1945 à 1957*, Georgette Elgey, Éditions Robert Laffont, 2018, p. 311.

drew up an import plan that led to the idea of an economic plan. Moreover, even before the war, France's industrial plants and equipment were already on their last legs: in 1938, their average age was 20 years, compared with 7 years in Germany and 5 years in the United States. In 1945, industrial production was half that of 1938. Jean Monnet was aware that rapid modernization in France would require importing equipment and tools.

The plan was structural. It aimed to reverse the downward trend of the French economy. It concerned "six basic activities that condition the economy as a whole and its recovery: coal, electricity, steel, cement, farm machinery and inland transport."[20] They were a priority, as the recovery of the French economy depended for 30% on these activities. So, for example, credits earmarked for housing in the budget were first allocated to industrial reconstruction. Speed was of the essence because France could not live forever by importing on credit and using up its reserves. Jean Monnet's ambition was to balance foreign trade by 1950. In the plan, the target was for French production to be 25% higher than in 1929, which had been a record economic year for France. In short, the plan was to turn around the French economy in just four years.

The plan's general objectives were:

> "1) To increase production in Metropolitan France and the overseas territories, and their trade exchanges with the rest of the world, particularly in areas where they are most favorably positioned.
>
> 2) To raise labor productivity to the level of countries where it is highest;
>
> 3) To ensure full employment of the workforce;
>
> 4) To raise the standard of living of the population and improve housing conditions and community life."[21]

Initially, to boost productivity at a time when there were labor shortages and the equipment had not yet been modernized, Léon Blum [1872–1950] encouraged the French to work forty-eight hours a week, even though the legal working week remained forty hours.

To balance public finances, tax increases were voted twice each year in 1948 and 1949, and an exceptional levy equivalent to a year and a half of tax receipts was raised in 1948.

To curb post-war inflation, René Mayer [1895–1972], who served as Finance Minister in the Schumann government, took a series of measures ranging from the more conventional, such as cutting spending by FRF67 billion, restoration of a free market for gold and cutting the price of domestic coal by over 10%, to the more atypical, such as abolishing 5,000-franc banknotes and partially devaluing the currency against the US dollar and the Swiss franc, without changing the exchange rate between the French franc and the British pound.

---

[20] Video resource: https://enseignants.lumni.fr/fiche-media/0000000337/jean-monnet-annonce-les-objectifs-du-premier-plan.html.

[21] https://strategie-prod-renew.ext.ssl-gouv.fr/sites/strategie.gouv.fr/files/atoms/files/decret_3_janvier_1946.pdf.

The Plan's objectives were achieved when it came to coal production, electricity generation, steelmaking, and transport. As for France's agriculture, harvests recovered to their pre-war levels. The last ration coupons were abolished in 1949.

During the period covered by the plan, only 250 thousand homes were built or rebuilt. The number of dwellings per 10,000 inhabitants rose from 5.5 in 1947 to 17 in 1950 and 18.7 in 1951. By comparison, it reached 39 in England and 75 in Germany. It was not until 1952 that overall national production exceeded its level in 1929. France was rising from the ashes, but much remained to be done.

Inflation from 1944 to 1952: The Start of Inflationary Dirigisme

"Inflation is a form of taxation without representation"[22]

Milton Friedman

Created in 1914, the consumer price index (CPI) published by INSEE is "the instrument to measure inflation. It is used to estimate the average variation between two given periods in the prices of products consumed by households. It is a composite measurement of trends in the prices of products, at constant quality. It is published each month in the Official Journal."[23]

INSEE points out that "the consumer price index is not an index of the cost of living. What the consumer price index seeks to measure is the effects of price variations on the purchase cost of the products consumed by households. The cost of living index, meanwhile, seeks to measure variations in purchasing costs to maintain the standard of living of households at a specified level."[24]

The Franc germinal was established in 1803 by the then First Consul Napoléon Bonaparte. Gold and silver-based coins circulated interchangeably on the basis of a fixed ratio between the values of the two metals throughout the nineteenth century. This bimetallic standard lasted until the First World War. The war effort was financed by printing ever more money. Wars are by their very nature inflationary. In the 1920s, the French government pursued an inflationary monetary policy until the third premiership of Raymond Poincaré [1860–1934] in 1926. During this term of office, the true value of the French currency was re-established, becoming known as the Franc poincaré.

The twentieth century was much more inflationary than the 19th, even though both centuries witnessed sustained economic growth and far-reaching changes in people's living conditions through creative destruction. If the price index is set at 100 in 1820, what will be observed is that in the nineteenth century, when the gold standard was

---

[22] Friedman, Milton (1974), *Inflation, Taxation, Indexation*, in *Inflation: Causes, Consequences, Cures*, pp. 71–88; IEA Readings, no. 14, Institute of Economic Affairs., London.

[23] https://www.insee.fr/en/metadonnees/definition/c1557.

[24] Ibid.

in force, it had fallen to 76, reflecting an increase in the value of money. One franc in 1913 is worth four euros nowadays. Throughout the world, inflation accelerated during the two world wars and the energy crises. Note, furthermore, that growth was stronger than in the nineteenth century, and any semblance of a gold standard ended in 1976.

France experienced a sharp rise in general price levels compared to other Western countries. Comparing the rise in retail prices between 1914 and 1993, they were multiplied by 13.5 times in the United States and by 1650 times in France when expressed in old francs.

Inflation climbed from 8% in 1939 to 19% in 1940, then pulled back to 16% in 1941 and 1942. It then jumped to 28% in 1943, edged down to 27% in 1944, before climbing to 38% in 1945. It was at the end of the war that inflation took off spectacularly, reaching a peak of 64% in 1946, which has not been equaled since. Inflation tends to rise faster than it ebbs, and it has been said that "Inflation is like toothpaste. Once it's out, you can hardly get it back in again."[25] Inflation edged lower to 60% in 1947 and then to 58% in 1948, plunging to 3% in 1949, before recovering to 11% in 1950, 17% in 1951, and then falling back to 12% in 1952.[26]

Between 1938 and 1952, the average price index for Switzerland, West Germany, Canada, the USA, Sweden, Norway, Australia, the Netherlands, the UK, Spain, Brazil, Argentina, Austria, Finland, France, and Italy increased at an annual rate of 5.1%. Inflation in France was five times the average for these sixteen countries over this period. Only in Italy was inflation higher than in France, at almost ten times the average over the same period. Inflation was lower in Anglo-Saxon countries, which emerged victorious from the conflict, and in the Iberian Peninsula, which remained neutral. It was higher in those countries that were the battlegrounds. War is inflationary by nature. It leads to a lasting decline in the standard of living of the belligerents.

Furthermore, in 1945 and 1946, there was black-market inflation due to shortages and rationing. In 1945, black-market prices exceeded official prices by 70%. In 1946, rarer products fetched 2.5 times more on average. For example, a kilogram of coffee sold for four times the official price in 1946, and the 11 CV Citroën forward drive for three times the official price. The black market disappeared in 1948 thanks to René Mayer's efforts to liberalize the economy.

One may rightly ask why France's inflation rate was higher than that of most Western countries. The answer is that inflation after the Liberation was mainly the result of "inflationary dirigisme," an expression that entered French economic history with René Mayer. For him, it was "an evil born of war." He used the expression to encapsulate a Keynesian-inspired economic policy that based the evolution of purchasing power on a permanent imbalance in the nation's accounts, notably through

---

[25] Dr Karl Otto Pöhl, source: https://www.bundesbank.de/resource/blob/666662/cebdc3a25107a0d45060fdb36270abb4/mL/quotes-by-karl-otto-poehl-data.pdf.

[26] INSEE, *Annuaire statistique rétrospectif*, Imprimerie nationale, 1966, p. 405 et Annuaire rétrospectif de la France, 1948-1988, Imprimerie nationale, 1990, p. 286.

public deficits and debt,[27] in order to guarantee strong growth thanks to public investments, which in reality turned out to be costly and of little use, and which accepted to sacrifice the currency and savings as a result of galloping inflation so as to correct the induced imbalances.

René Mayer was the main negotiator for the nationalization of the railroads, but he represented the railway companies. The French government's management of the economy as a planned economy, through nationalizations and by controlling not only prices but also quantities via rationing, fueled galloping inflation. René Mayer tried to stabilize prices through a liberal adjustment of the economy, to have it now depend solely on the market for prices and exchange rates, while at the same time attempting to balance public finances. But the road was a long one, since it was only on December 1, 1986, that Ordinance No. 45–1483 of June 30, 1945, was repealed and the prices of goods and services were freely determined by competition. What would have been the extent of the Glorious Thirty if France had put an end to price controls as early as 1947? What would France's place on the world stage have been without its 41 years of inflation and economic distortion?

Price ordinance 45–1483 of June 30, 1945 (*Ordonnance n°45–1483 du 30 juin 1945 relative aux prix*) states that:

> "The re-establishment of republican legality on the mainland necessarily entails the adoption of general legislation on the fixing of prices [...]"[28]
>
> Decisions relating to the prices of all goods and services are taken:
>
> 1 By interministerial orders issued by the minister in charge of the national economy and the minister responsible for the goods and services on the list drawn up by decree on the proposal of the minister in charge of the national economy;
>
> 2 By decree of the minister of national economy for all other goods and services;
>
> 3 By decree of the regional commissioner of the Republic under a delegation of authority granted by decree of the minister of the national economy; the delegation decree setting out the purpose and scope of the regional commissioner's powers;
>
> 4 By order of the prefect acting on behalf of the regional commissioner of the Republic;
>
> 5 By bodies approved by the minister for the national economy acting under a delegation of powers granted by order of the minister for the national economy and, for goods and services included in the list referred to in paragraph 1 (par. 1) of this article, by order of the minister for the national economy and the minister responsible. Decrees delegating authority set out the purpose and scope of the powers of approved bodies, as well as the obligations incumbent upon them in this respect."[29]

[27] The public deficit corresponds to a negative annual balance in the general government budget. It occurs when public expenditures exceed public resources. When resources exceed expenditures, this leads to a public surplus. The deficit is based on annual flows.

At the end of the year, the public deficit is added to the public deficits of previous years, which together constitute the public debt. Public debt is a stock item. It corresponds to all the financial commitments made in the form of loans by the State, local authorities, and organizations directly dependent on them.

[28] https://www.legifrance.gouv.fr/download/securePrint?token=Md4Vp4M2SY$DxvTHmy6M.

[29] https://www.legifrance.gouv.fr/loda/id/JORFTEXT000000516237.

Chapter 2 of the ordinance, entitled "Principles of price fixing," comprises four sections: "Freezing prices," "Modifications to the freezing of prices," "New goods and services," and "Goods and services having undergone modifications." The ordinance establishes a complex pricing system. Below are three articles from this text:

> "Art. 16. Prices for all goods and services are and shall remain frozen, either at the level they reached on September 1, 1939, or at the level resulting from decisions taken since that date.
> Art. 17. Blocked prices are the prices charged by the business itself; if the business cannot provide justification for this price, or if it was not selling the goods or services in question at the time the prices were frozen, these prices shall be the prices usually charged for identical goods or services by similar businesses.
>
> Art. 18. I. The price level at the date the price is blocked is determined for goods and services whose quality has not been modified, taking into account:
>
> 1° The constituent parts determining the quantity or importance of the good or service;
>
> 2° Packaging, transportation, and other ancillary services;
>
> 3° Discounts, rebates, refunds, and bonuses of all kinds customarily granted to customers and all adjustments arising from other terms of sale and payment;
>
> 4° And, in general, all the benefits usually granted by the business in connection with transactions."[30]

René Mayer, who was elected to the National Assembly as a Radical Socialist in 1946, served as Minister for Finance and Economic Affairs for just over twelve months in the cabinets of Robert Schuman (from November 24, 1947, to July 4, 1948) and then René Pleven (from August 11, 1951, to January 20, 1952). He understood that a command economy, in which chronic shortages are often the norm, feeds inflation and corresponds more to a Soviet, totalitarian economy than to a liberal economy capable of fulfilling French republican values. He was also convinced that charging "true prices" is a prerequisite for economic and financial stability. To ensure that prices reflected market realities, during his first term in office, René Mayer increased public tariffs for energy and transport, raised salaries by 25%, withdrew the 5000-franc banknotes from circulation, reduced economic subsidies, and declared a tax amnesty that led to a repatriation of funds held abroad estimated at between $80 million and $100 million.

René Mayer pushed through a devaluation of the franc, introducing multiple exchange rates depending on the currency pair and the nature of the transactions. This devaluation did, as expected, lead to a recovery in the balance of payments. The International Monetary Fund disapproved of this approach, though it was effective, and sanctioned France, which became ineligible to use the Fund's resources until 1955, hence could no longer make drawings.

René Mayer was a convinced European. In a note addressed to General de Gaulle in Algiers in 1943, he suggested a "Federation of Western Europe." But the devaluation was seen by Stafford Crips, the British Chancellor of the Exchequer, as an attack on sterling. Relations between France and Britain became very tense, and remained so even after René Mayer's departure. Jean Monnet, who had been dreaming since

---

30 https://www.legifrance.gouv.fr/loda/id/JORFTEXT000000516237.

1940 of a Franco-British entente, with stronger ties at economic level, would step up his contacts and meetings in an effort to ease tensions.

For René Mayer, reconstruction meant increasing France's production and productivity and reducing direct aid and subsidies to the population and businesses, which were inflationary in their effects. To ensure that Marshall Plan subsidies would be channeled into essential investments, he created the appropriate administrative departments within six months: the Modernization and Equipment Fund (*Fonds de modernisation et d'équipement*) with the Law of January 7, 1948, the Autonomous Reconstruction Fund (*Caisse autonome de la reconstruction*) with the Law of March 21, 1948, and the Investment Commission (*Commission des investissements*) with the decree of June 10, 1948, whose secretariat was attached to the Ministry of Finance. He also restructured the financial administration, leading in 1948 to the creation of the General Tax Office (*Direction générale des impôts*). The Law of January 6, 1948, created a commission to audit the accounts of public undertakings (*Commission de vérification des comptes des entreprises publiques*).

During his second term in office, René Mayer created the *École Nationale des Impôts*, a higher education institution responsible for training tax controllers and inspectors in France. As a result, the General Tax Office went on to become one of the most efficient in the world.

As much of René Mayer's time had to be devoted to negotiating the financial contribution of the United States towards France's war effort in Indochina, less time was devoted to combating inflationary dirigisme during his second term of office. Nonetheless, he did oversee the signing of the Treaty of Paris instituting the European Coal and Steel Community (ECSC), a first draft of the law authorizing the treaty's ratification being adopted by the French Lower House on December 13, 1951. He also established a guarantee fund for the victims of motor vehicle accidents (*Fonds de garantie pour les victimes des accidents d'automobiles*) by the Law of December 31, 1951 (*Loi n° 51–1508 du 31 décembre 1951 relative aux comptes spéciaux du Trésor pour l'année 1952*).

Inflationary dirigisme is a chronic illness that plagued the French economy for four decades and now risks resurfacing in the twenty-first century. This way of managing the economy does not correspond to France's republican values, in particular the individual freedoms inherited from the Age of Enlightenment. René Mayer was the first, after the Second World War, to fight inflationary dirigisme, arguing that changes in prices and wages needed to keep pace with productivity and the state of public finances coupled with a monetary policy designed to defend the exchange rate so as to limit imported inflation.

The Poujadist Revolt

The Poujadist revolt was a political movement that emerged in the 1950s around the Union for the Defense of Shopkeepers and Artisans (*Union de défense des commerçants et artisans—UDCA*), which was set up in 1953 and dissolved in 1962.

It was led by Pierre Poujade [1920–2003], a stationer-librarian and wholesaler of stationery and books in Saint-Céré, Lot. The movement was not a product of the traditional political parties. The Lot was one of ten French départements in the throes of depopulation and desertification, at a time when the French population was growing. A declining population does nothing for local business and disseminates a feeling of decline.

By extension, "*poujadisme*" has entered the French language as denoting "a dissenting attitude that focuses on the advancement of narrow socio-professional objectives."[31]

Antoine Pinay [1891–1994], who was appointed President of the Council of Ministers in 1952 by President Vincent Auriol, issued a decree granting a tax amnesty. This measure did not lead to a massive repatriation of funds as had been hoped, but it was instrumental in stirring up the Poujadist movement. With nothing to be gained from controlling the taxes of the country's business leaders and entrepreneurs, tax inspectors turned their attention to shopkeepers and artisans, which resulted in an avalanche of fines and penalties:

> "Until then, tax inspectors had audited the accounts of large companies, foreign contracts and so on. This kept them very busy. Overnight, with the amnesty on tax liabilities, they found themselves idle. Their bitterness was great, and they hunted down and cornered the only category of taxpayers still at their mercy, and came in for the kill."[32]

As Edgar Faure [1908–1988] explained, the noose around the necks of shopkeepers and artisans was all the tighter as a new generation of tax inspectors had been formed who were competent for all taxes (direct and indirect taxes, and registration fees) when before these inspections were carried out by different inspectors at different times. The three controls "fell together like a sledgehammer."[33] The number of tax inspections shot up from 108 thousand in 1952 to 142 thousand in 1953, the number of cases referred to the court rising twofold from 25 thousand in 1952 to 50 thousand in 1954.[34] This created the feeling that the tax system failed to embrace fairness and equality:

> "Shopkeepers were all the more exasperated in that the tax amnesty had convinced them that big-time tax evaders had been given a free pass. Mr. Blot, head of the National Tax Department, had warned me: 'The tax inspectors are going in too hard: it will end badly.'"[35]

The tax burden having risen steadily since 1950, shopkeepers were experiencing hardship. They felt unloved by society, being associated by the population with the black-market profiteers during the war. Published in 1952, the novel by Jean Dutourd, *Au bon beurre*, won the Prix Interallié that year, becoming a best-seller,

---

[31] https://www.larousse.fr/dictionnaires/francais/poujadisme/63072.

[32] Faure, Edgar, October 18, 1965.

[33] Faure, Edgar (1984), *Mémoires,* Volume II, *Si tel doit être mon destin ce soir...*, Paris, Plon, p.120.

[34] Ardant, Gabriel (1972), *Histoire de l'impôt*, Volume II, Paris, Fayard, p. 650.

[35] Faure, Edgar, October 18, 1965.

with 80 thousand copies sold in its first year, revealing the low regard in which the country's shopkeepers were held.

Fervent admirers of Marshal Pétain, going on a pilgrimage to Vichy to offer him black-market eggs, Julie and Charles-Hubert Poissonard, the owners of a dairy store called Au Bon Beurre, build up huge stocks of food in anticipation of the Occupation, and then obtain supplies from black-market farms during the war. They take advantage of the rationing to enrich themselves until ration coupons are abolished in 1948. They mistreat their employees, who do not eat to their fill, collaborate with the Germans, and denounce members of the Resistance. Having denounced to the French Resistance a German soldier who had taken refuge with them during the liberation of Paris, Charles-Hubert Poissonard and his family are hailed as Resistance fighters.

One of the resistance fighters denounced to the Germans by the Poissonards and who escaped from the camp where he was imprisoned goes on to teach the family's son after the Liberation. The Poissonards ask him to give their son good marks, even though he doesn't work in class. When the teacher refuses, Charles-Hubert Poissonard asks his son-in-law to have him transferred from Paris to Algeria.

Was it the behavior of shopkeepers during the Occupation that led the French to start dreaming of big supermarkets like in American movies? Today, with almost 20 million square meters of supermarkets and hypermarkets, France is the European country with the highest concentration of large and medium-sized stores per square meter. Was such growth the consequence of the rationing in the 1940s?

In any case, by the 1950s, French consumers were no longer shopping at their corner stores, just as they preferred mass-produced goods to handicrafts. This was reflected in the declining sales generated by shopkeepers. In the Lot region, where the Poujadist revolt began, a household in which one spouse was a shopkeeper earned a monthly income (including social and family benefits) of 36,500 old francs on average (the equivalent of €876). That was half what a factory worker earned.

Pierre Poujade was adept at channeling animosity towards tax officials. By appealing to the "common sense" of ordinary French citizens, he incited shopkeepers and artisans to revolt against the despised tax bureaucracy.

He attended a Roman Catholic school, was active in Jacques Doriot's fascist movement, the French Popular Party (*Parti Populaire Français—PPF*), and was seduced by Marshal Pétain's so-called National Revolution. In 1952, Pierre Poujade, who now called himself a Gaullist, ran on a radical-socialist list and was elected town councilor in Saint-Céré.

He was married and had four children. In 1952, his business generated sales of 3 million old francs (the equivalent of €72,000), but, as he writes in his book *J'ai choisi le combat*, the month ends are difficult, and the economic status of small business owners is challenging and disheartening, which he bemoans, being of the opinion that small business owners are an elite, "the backbone of the nation, the pivot of all social strata".[36] This new status to which he aspired when an employee turns out to be a social demotion, rather than an elevation: "The more it goes on, the less is left; that's because, now, I'm no longer entitled to an automatic tax allowance as I

[36] Declaration of Pierre Poujade on May 9, 1955, in Marseille.

no longer have my 30% deduction, no longer have 10% off for hospitality expenses, no longer have Social Security, not even family allowances…so am I not the same anymore? Because I want to be independent by working my fingers to the bone, am I to be demoted socially?".[37]

On July 23, 1953, warned by a Communist town councilor of the arrival of tax inspectors who had come to audit some twenty tax records, Pierre Poujade rallied the town's shopkeepers and artisans, who chased them out of Saint-Céré:

> "They were barred from entering the stores, while the gendarmes stood by impassive. On July 29, in the presence of the sub-prefect of Figeac, Poujade had the town council vote unanimously a motion expressing solidarity with shopkeepers and artisans 'persecuted' by the tax administration and a demand addressed to Parliament asking for an immediate vote on a reform the tax system."[38]

This marked the start of a revolt that went down in the annals of French history.

Less than two months after this incident, in September 1953, Henri Ulver added fuel to the fire by deciding to increase penalties by 100% if a taxpayer suspected of fraud could not prove he had acted in good faith.

Henri Ulver [1901–1962] served as Assistant Secretary to the Budget in the governments of Joseph Laniel (July 2, 1953, to June 18, 1954) and Pierre Mendès France (June 19 to September 3, 1954), during which time he pressed ahead with the tax crackdown, stoking the revolt. While Joseph Laniel was forced out of office, Henri Ulver stayed on.

On October 19, 1953, Poujade gathered his first supporters in Gramat, in the Lot département in the south-western part of the country. They adopted a program calling for equality before taxation and social security for all. The Union for the Defense of Shopkeepers and Artisans (*Union de défense des commerçants et artisans—UDCA*) was created on November 29 in Cahors. The membership fee was set at 300 old francs a year (equivalent of €7). In less than a year, the UDCA had four hundred thousand members. The first national congress was held in Algiers in November 1954. The weekly *Fraternité française* was launched that year. The Poujadist movement would go on to spread throughout France.

In August 1954, at Henri Ulver's request, the government and the General Assembly resurrected a law last used by the tax-farmers general during the Ancient Regime to suppress the slightest whiff of dissent. This law provided for prison sentences for any act of rebellion against the tax authorities.

In its issue of January 29, 1955, *Paris Match* sang the praises of Pierre Poujade and gave him a real platform. In the weeks that followed, he organized a revolt to have the law withdrawn. On March 18, 1955, his supporters occupied the public gallery of the National Assembly. At Edgar Faure's request, the General Assembly postponed the vote.

---

[37] Poujade, Pierre (1955), *J'ai choisi le combat*, Société générale des éditeurs et des publications, Saint-Céré, p.19.

[38] Elgey, Georgette (2018), *Histoire de la IVe république, De 1945 à 1957*, éditions Robert Laffont, p. 986.

Though more than two and a half million French people made a living from the trade in wines and spirits, Pierre Mendès France embarked on a crusade against alcoholism in the autumn of 1954. He announced the abolition of alcohol in public and private schools, to be replaced by the distribution of sweetened milk from January 1, 1955. A "patriotic resurrection" rose against the then President of the Council, who dared to drink milk in front of the American press in Washington on November 20, 1954. Pierre Poujade became the mouthpiece for the general indignation:

> "If you [Pierre Mendès France] had a drop of Gallic blood in your veins, you, the representative of France, a global wine- and champagne-producing country, would never have dared to be served a glass of milk at an international reception! It was a slap in the face, Monsieur Mendès France, that every Frenchman received that day, even when not a drunkard."[39]

Pierre Mendès France went a step further with the decree of December 9, 1954, organizing the distribution of one milk ration per day in army barracks. As explained in the December 10, 1954, issue of the French newspaper *Le Figaro*, this measure was intended to kill two birds with one stone: combat alcoholism and find an outlet for the country's surplus milk production.

Behind this revolt was once again the fight against new taxes, as the twelve anti-alcohol decrees of November 13 and 17, 1954, concerned alcohol producers and traffickers. The decrees attacked the distillers' privilege, which dated back to Louis XIII [1601–1643], as well as the parallel network that collected cheap alcohol distilled at farms and sold it on the black market in the big cities. In the 1950s, France numbered 3.5 million home distillers, and the decrees removed the status of home distiller from more than a million small grape harvesters, giving rise to a great deal of discontent. Only farmers could now benefit from the home distiller's privilege. The decrees also regulated activities renting stills and selling alcohol and put an end to the fraudulent transfer of alcohol licenses from one drinking establishment to another. For many, that was the final straw.

Alcohol consumption was a huge problem in France in the 1950s and still is seventy years later. France has the fourth-highest recorded alcohol consumption of all the OECD countries, after Latvia, the Czech Republic, and Austria.[40] The French consume more alcohol than the Poles or Russians. At 11.4 L of alcohol per person per year, France is way above the OECD average of 8.7 L.

Even today, the subject remains taboo. During the first lockdown, the government ordered the closure of bookshops as being non-essential, whereas liquor stores remained open. Had they been closed, this would have reduced domestic violence. Declaring war on age-old alcoholism was heroic on the part of Pierre Mendès France. But it proved to be fatal, his tenure as President of the Council of Ministers lasting only seven months. What this episode shows is that, in those days, politicians were prepared to put the interests of the nation above their careers.

Anti-Semitic, xenophobic, and anti-parliamentary rhetoric was rife at all Poujadist meetings. Jean-Marie Le Pen, who flirted with the Poujadist movement, was one of

---

[39] Rioux, Jean-Pierre (1983), *La France de la IVe République*, Édition Histoire, Points, p. 63.

[40] https://www.oecd-ilibrary.org/sites/5d1643e8-fr/index.html?itemId=/content/component/5d1643e8-fr.

just two Poujadist deputies to win a seat at the 1958 general elections. While the movement fizzled out in 1958, Jean-Marie Le Pen's career was only just getting started.

Chapter 3
European Construction

"In moving towards European unity, we are moving in the direction of history"[1]

Charles de Gaulle

Surprising as it may seem after Brexit, the first to announce the European Union based on a Franco-German partnership was an Englishman, Winston Churchill. The best-known and best-loved man in the Western world at the end of the Second World War lent his credibility to the European project by advocating "a kind of United States of Europe" in his speech at Zurich University on September 16, 1946:

> "But for the fact that the great republic across the Atlantic realised that the ruin or enslavement of Europe would involve her own fate as well, and stretched out hands of succour and guidance, the Dark Ages would have returned in all their cruelty and squalor. They may still return. […] Yet all the while there is a remedy [...]. What is this sovereign remedy? It is to recreate the European fabric, or as much of it as we can, and to provide it with a structure under which it can dwell in peace, safety and freedom. We must build a kind of United States of Europe."[2]

Winston Churchill considered that:

> "Much work has been done upon this task by the exertions of the Pan-European Union which owes much to Count Coudenhove-Kalergi and which commanded the services of the famous French patriot and statesman, Aristide Briand. There is also that immense body which was brought into being amidst high hopes after the First World War — the League of Nations. The League did not fail because of its principles or conceptions. It failed because those principles were deserted by those States which brought it into being, because the governments of those states feared to face the facts and act while time remained."[3]

---

[1] Cohen, William B., *De Gaulle and Europe Prior to 1958*, French Politics and Society, vol. 8, no. 4, 1990, pp. 1–12. JSTOR, http://www.jstor.org/stable/42844577.

[2] https://www.cvce.eu/en/obj/address_given_by_winston_churchill_zurich_19_september_1946-en-7dc5a4cc-4453-4c2a-b130-b534b7d76ebd.html.

[3] Ibid.

C. Peicuti, *A Monetary and Economic History of France since 1944*, Contributions to Economics, https://doi.org/10.1007/978-3-032-17596-0_3

He then urged the construction of the United States of Europe, so a federal union, under the aegis of the United Nations:

> "I now sum up the propositions which are before you. Our constant aim must be to build and fortify the United Nations Organisation. Under and within that world concept we must recreate the European family in a regional structure called, it may be, the United States of Europe, and the first practical step will be to form a Council of Europe. If at first all the States of Europe are not willing or able to join a union, we must nevertheless proceed to assemble and combine those who will and who can."[4]

After the harrowing experience of the Second World War, Winston Churchill cites Gladstone, four times Chancellor of the Exchequer and four times Prime Minister:

> "There must be what Mr Gladstone many years ago called a 'blessed act of oblivion'. We must all turn our backs upon the horrors of the past and look to the future. [...] I am now going to say something that will astonish you. The first step in the re-creation of the European family must be a partnership between France and Germany. In this way only can France recover the moral and cultural leadership of Europe. There can be no revival of Europe without a spiritually great France and a spiritually great Germany."[5]

The speech ends with a few words on his vision of a new Europe, based on the Franco-German couple, defending the right to life and prosperity:

> "The salvation of the common people of every race and every land from war and servitude must be established on solid foundations, and must be created by the readiness of all men and women to die rather than to submit to tyranny. In this urgent work France and Germany must take the lead together. Great Britain, the British Commonwealth of Nations, mighty America—and, I trust, Soviet Russia, for then indeed all would be well—must be the friends and sponsors of the new Europe and must champion its right to live. Therefore I say to you, Let Europe arise!"[6]

Churchill called on Russia to join with other Western peoples in defending the right to life and prosperity. The conditional tense of "for then indeed all would be well" speaks volumes about his judgment on the likelihood of this wish coming true. Moreover, in his speech "The Sinews of Peace" given in Fulton, Missouri, on March 5, 1946, Winston Churchill had already denounced "the Iron Curtain" and spoke of the vital need for a strong France to counter it:

> "An attempt is being made by the Russians in Berlin to build up a quasi-Communist party in their zone of Occupied Germany by showing special favours to groups of left-wing German leaders. At the end of the fighting last June, the American and British Armies withdrew westwards, in accordance with an earlier agreement, to a depth at some points of 150 miles upon a front of nearly four hundred miles, in order to allow our Russian allies to occupy this vast expanse of territory which the Western Democracies had conquered.
>
> If now the Soviet Government tries, by separate action, to build up a pro-Communist Germany in their areas, this will cause new serious difficulties [...] this is certainly not the Liberated Europe we fought to build up. Nor is it one which contains the essentials of permanent peace.

[4] Ibid.

[5] https://www.cvce.eu/en/obj/address_given_by_winston_churchill_zurich_19_september_1946-en-7dc5a4cc-4453-4c2a-b130-b534b7d76ebd.html.

[6] Ibid.

The safety of the world requires a new unity in Europe, from which no nation should be permanently outcast. [...] In front of the iron curtain which lies across Europe are other causes for anxiety. [...] Again one cannot imagine a regenerated Europe without a strong France. All my public life I have worked for a strong France and I never lost faith in her destiny, even in the darkest hours."[7]

The Birth of Post-War European Institutions

"Europe will not be made all at once, or according to a single plan. It will be built through concrete achievements which first create a de facto solidarity"[8]

Robert Schuman, 1950

The Congress of Europe opened its doors on May 7, 1948, in The Hague. Seventeen countries took part. At the end of the Congress, the participants adopted a Political Resolution calling for the unification of Europe. This resolution was implemented on May 5, 1949, in London, when the Foreign Ministers of ten countries signed the Treaty establishing the Council of Europe, laying the foundations for the European Union.

Robert Schuman, born in Luxembourg to parents from Lorraine, part of Germany until 1918, considered that Europe was experiencing a "providential moment" because there were three men, all Christians torn between two European nationalities, motivated to establish a lasting peace and in positions accomplish this: himself, as the French Foreign Minister, Konrad Adenauer, Chancellor of the Federal Republic of Germany since September 15, 1949, and Alcide de Gasperi, President of the Italian Council since December 10, 1945. Added to this was the American demand for a German renaissance, and the presence of Jean Monnet, capable of transforming projects into texts acceptable to all.

The crisis between France and Germany was over the Ruhr and Saar. Konrad Adenauer [1876–1967], as a Catholic Rhinelander who had long chafed under Prussian rule, had campaigned for the autonomy of this province. On May 9, 1950, together with Jean Monnet and with Adenauer's agreement, Robert Schuman put forward a proposal (later known as the Schuman Plan) for the pooling of French and German coal and steel resources in an organization open to other European countries, called the European Coal and Steel Community (ECSC). The Franco-German couple tied the knot, and would be the backbone of today's Europe:

"The pooling of coal and steel production [...] will change the destinies of those regions which have long been devoted to the manufacture of munitions of war, of which they have been the most constant victims. The solidarity in production thus established will make

---

[7] https://winstonchurchill.org/resources/speeches/1946-1963-elder-statesman/the-sinews-of-peace/

[8] https://www.strasbourg-europe.eu/la-construction-europeenne/.

it plain that any war between France and Germany becomes not merely unthinkable, but materially impossible."[9]

René Mayer, the Minister of Justice, and René Pleven, the Minister of Defense, also supported the plan. They were the only members of the government to have been in the know from the outset.

On April 18, 1951, Belgium, France, Germany, Italy, Luxembourg, and the Netherlands signed the Treaty of Paris, establishing the first European Community: the European Coal and Steel Community (ECSC). Decisions are taken by a High Authority, a supranational body comprising nine members designated by the governments of the States party to the treaty. The supranational character of this new European Community troubled the United Kingdom, which consequently refused to join. The treaty establishing the European Coal and Steel Community was signed on April 18, 1951, and ratified in May 1952.

The European Coal and Steel Community was the first of the supranational European institutions that preceded the establishment of the European Union as we know it today. European integration would continue with the founding of the European Economic Community (EEC) and the European Atomic Energy Community (EAEC or EURATOM) with the signing of the Treaties of Rome on March 25, 1957.

The European Atomic Energy Community had for principal aim the joint development of atomic energy in Europe for peaceful purposes.

The goal of the European Economic Community was to create a common market that would permit the free movement of goods and people. One objective was also to implement common policies in all member countries, the first to be implemented being the Common Agricultural Policy (CAP), implying a common approach to agriculture. In the short term, the aim was to feed a war-ravaged Europe; in the medium term, to achieve food sufficiency at the level of the European Union and to put an end to non-harmonized national agricultural policies, which led to varying levels of competitive intensity and hindered access to food. The Common Agricultural Policy was also intended to address the fact that farm incomes were much lower compared with other sectors of the economy.

In 1962, the Common Agricultural Policy was introduced with the following aims:

"- increasing agricultural productivity

- ensuring a fair standard of living for farmers
- guaranteeing the availability of supplies
- stabilising the markets
- establishing a secure supply chain with reasonable prices
- harmonising competition rules across all countries

To achieve these goals, an economic system of price and market support was put in place. This mechanism provided farmers with a guaranteed price for their products, introduced tariffs on external products, and introduced state intervention in case market prices fell. Farmers received support according to their total levels of production."[10]

---

[9] https://european-union.europa.eu/principles-countries-history/history-eu/1945-59/schuman-declaration-may-1950_fr.

[10] https://www.consilium.europa.eu/en/policies/cap-introduction/timeline-history/.

The Common Agricultural Policy has produced excellent results when it comes to the economic performance of the European agriculture and agri-food sectors. While the European framework has liberalized trade in agricultural produce, family farms have been maintained even in less-favored territories thanks to the aids provided under the Common Agricultural Policy. In 2021, the emphasis remained on a redistribution of support to target in priority direct payments to small farms and young farmers. Funding has always been conditional on compliance with EU environmental and climate legislation, with a real emphasis on ecology since 2021 through the adoption of dedicated programs.

Back at the start of 1958, new institutions were established: the European Commission, a Council of Ministers, a Parliamentary Assembly (which later became known as the European Parliament), and a Court of Justice.

In the same spirit of integration, in a speech to the French National Assembly on October 24, 1950, René Pleven put forward a plan for the creation of a European Defense Community (*Communauté européenne de defense—CED*). Although it became known as the Pleven plan, it was in fact drafted mainly by Jean Monnet. General de Gaulle was not in favor of this project, as for him a common army meant the loss of national sovereignty. On February 19, 1952, the French National Assembly supported in principle the creation of a European Defense Community. The Treaty of Paris establishing the European Defense Community would be signed later that year, but its ratification was rejected on August 30, 1954, by the French General Assembly.

Europe's economic integration would make greater strides than its military integration… In time, it would enable France to rid itself of inflationary dirigisme. Upon joining the Single Market, France was obliged to open up its economy, which in turn would lower inflation over the medium term, as successive governments would ultimately have to liberalize prices. This disinflation was amplified by the rise in cheap imports from China after it joined the World Trade Organization in 2001.

Six years after the creation of the European single market, also referred to as the internal market or common market, at the Cabinet meeting held on June 19, 1963, Valéry Giscard d'Estaing, the Minister of the Economy and Finance, and Charles de Gaulle, President, had this to say:

> "Giscard d'Estaing – 'Growth is going well: over 5%. Exports are up 8%. But imports have jumped by 37%; this abnormally rapid growth is favored by the single European market...'
>
> De Gaulle (cutting him off) – 'The Common Market began by stimulating our activity; now it's stimulating imports and inflation!'
>
> Giscard d'Estaing (unperturbed) – 'This trend will inevitably continue.'
>
> De Gaulle – 'For the 1964 budget, there will be some important decisions to be made. In reality, we're not putting the brakes on prices. Between May 1962 and May 1965, they rose by 5.5%.'"[11]

In an exchange with Alain Peyrefitte on December 4, 1963, Charles de Gaulle shared his views on European integration since 1950. He asserted that an integrated

[11] Peyrefitte, Alain (2002), *C'était de Gaulle*, Quarto Gallimard, p. 922.

Europe is "an excuse for all kinds of cowardice," and that those behind the European texts are "a handful of phrase-makers who strut about":

> "What have the European projects since 1950 been all about? Giving Germany back its coal, its army, and its place in Europe. But because we didn't dare do it directly, for fear of braving public opinion, we did it behind a screen, slyly. The same for Italy, which was purged of all the sins committed during the war. It was a way, without seeming too obvious, of turning them back into countries that could look others in the face. I'm not against it; in fact, I am doing just that [...].
>
> And then, an integrated Europe was a way of making the smaller countries - Belgium, Holland, not to mention Luxembourg - the equals of the great powers. In a European Council, Spaak[12] carries the same weight as General de Gaulle, maybe even more."[13]

Charles de Gaulle went on:

> "An integrated Europe was not for France, nor for the French... Except for a few lunatics like Jean Monnet, whose main concern was to serve the United States; or all those lamentable characters of the Fourth Republic. It was a way for them to offload their responsibilities! They couldn't assume them, so they had to pass them on to others. Hold their own in their own world? No way! Let's huddle under the umbrella. Have an army and make them obey? No way! Give it to others! Put the country back on its feet and set an example to the world? Not for them!
>
> Europe was the perfect alibi. The ready-made excuse for all the sidestepping, for all the acts of cowardice: integrated Europe."[14]

Even though we do not see eye to eye with General de Gaulle, it has to be conceded that France has used the European Union to evade its duty to have a cyclically balanced budget by running a surplus at the top of the cycle and a small deficit during cycle downturns. France's accounts have constantly been in deficit, and on the rare occasions when there has been a surplus, it has been referred to as a "nest egg," when in fact it was just reserves built up at the top of the cycle to be employed during economic downturns. It should not be seen as normal for a country to take on debt to tide it through an economic downturn.

This situation led to an exponential increase in France's debt, bearing out the General's dire assessment. The debt-to-GDP ratio rose from 31.8% in 1951 to 110.6% in 2023. It should be noted that France's deficit was 0.8% in 1951, whereas it reached 6.5% in 2021. As de Gaulle said, "It is unfortunate to legalize an additional deficit."[15] Coupon rates on government bonds have remained low thanks to the currency France shares with Germany: France is huddled under the European umbrella, which is currently held over its head by Germany. But France needs to hold its own, not just for its own sake, but also for the betterment of the European Union as a whole.

---

[12] Paul-Henri Spaak [1899–1972] served as Belgium's Prime Minister until August 1949, then as President of the Common Assembly (European Coal and Steel Community) and, finally, as the second Secretary General of NATO.

[13] Comments by Charles de Gaulle in the Salon Doré, Élysée Palace.
Peyrefitte, Alain (2002), *C'était de Gaulle*, Quarto Gallimard, p. 810.

[14] Comments by Charles de Gaulle in the Salon Doré, Élysée Palace.
Peyrefitte, Alain (2002), *C'était de Gaulle*, Quarto Gallimard, p. 810.

[15] Peyrefitte, Alain (2002), *C'était de Gaulle*, Quarto Gallimard, p. 921.

The European Payments Union

The Organization for European Economic Co-operation (OEEC) was established in 1948 to help administer the aid granted by the United States to Western Europe under the Marshall Plan. It was within this framework that the European Payments Union (EPU) was created in 1950. The 15 Members of the Organization for European Economic Co-operation were all members of the European Payments Union. Its first President was Guido Carli [1914–1993], who represented Italy at the Bretton Woods Conference in 1944. He became Executive Director for Italy at the International Monetary Fund in 1947. He would later serve as the Governor of the Bank of Italy from 1960 to 1975.

For the actual execution of the transactions, the European Payments Union relied on the Bank for International Settlements (BIS) in Basle, which had been established in 1930 to administer German war reparation payments. At each month-end, each EPU country's net balances with each other country were reported to the Bank for International Settlements, acting as the European Payments Union's financial agent, which canceled offsetting claims. Remaining balances were consolidated, leaving each country with claims on or liabilities to not individual countries but the union as a whole. The requirement that countries with a net debt eventually settle part of their liability in dollars or gold (the payment in dollars or gold being proportional to the size of the liability in relation to the country's quota) was intended to discourage the governments of the fifteen Member States from running excessively negative balances of payments.

The purpose of the European Payments Union was to provide multilateral clearing for the claims and debts of Western European countries, for as long as currencies were not convertible, thereby enabling international settlements in Western Europe. It was a transitional mechanism for managing European currencies until it became feasible to restore the convertibility of currencies on current account. Each country received a quota based on the size of its trade with the EPU area. The United States provided financial support to enable the European Payments Union to function. The European Payments Union also acted as an intermediary, enabling member countries to open up credit lines to each other automatically.

The European Payments Union was dissolved in 1958 when the convertibility of the Deutsche mark was restored, coming after Britain had indicated it wanted to withdraw sterling from the EPU area and France had totally used up its quota (meaning all deficits by France would have to be settled in gold, with nothing to be gained from remaining in the EPU area).

Chapter 4
The Missed Rendezvous of 1958

The Algerian War of Independence broke out on November 1, 1954. The Algiers military putsch occurred on May 13, 1958.

Two days later, in a press release on May 15, Charles de Gaulle said that he was ready to "assume the powers of the Republic." On June 1, the National Assembly appointed him President of the Council of Ministers, the last of the Fourth Republic.

On September 4, de Gaulle gave a speech at the Place de la République in Paris, presenting his proposal for a new Constitution:

> "It was inevitable that the paralysis of the State would lead to a serious national crisis, and that the Republic would immediately be threatened with collapse... A tearing apart of the nation was narrowly prevented... It was within the law that I and my government have assumed the exceptional mandate of drawing up a draft of a new Constitution and submitting it to the will of the people. […]
>
> If you answer yes, the result will be to make the Republic strong and efficient, provided that those in charge now do want it... The rest will depend on the men."[1]

It was not his first speech setting out his vision for the Fifth Republic. Twelve years earlier after his resignation from the provisional government on June 16, 1946, de Gaulle had already set out his constitutional ideas in the Bagneux speech. Everything was already there. When Alain Peyrefitte asked him why he had not established the Fifth Republic as early as 1945, de Gaulle replied:

> "I wanted to be the man of the nation, not the man of a party. [...] I had announced that a Constituent Assembly would be elected at the end of the war. I wouldn't have succeeded in uniting the Resistance if I hadn't made that commitment publicly. And you can't imagine the extent to which the parties rejected me."[2]

On September 28, a referendum was held in which voters were asked whether they approved the adoption of a Constitution for the Fifth Republic. It was overwhelmingly

[1] Peyrefitte, Alain (2002), *C'était de Gaulle*, Quarto Gallimard, p. 38.

[2] Peyrefitte, Alain (2002), *C'était de Gaulle*, Quarto Gallimard, p. 47–48.

C. Peicuti, *A Monetary and Economic History of France since 1944*, Contributions to Economics, https://doi.org/10.1007/978-3-032-17596-0_4

approved, by 79.25% of votes cast. Overseas, only in Guinea was there a majority against. Guinea would become independent shortly after.

Legislative elections were held on November 23 and 30, 1958. De Gaulle was elected President of the Fifth Republic on January 8, 1959. He resigned on April 28, 1969, after losing a constitutional referendum, with 52.4% of votes cast against the proposed government decentralization and changes to the Senate. This referendum had been intended to shore up de Gaulle's position after the events of 1968.

What was de Gaulle's economic record after ten years? Did he succeed in establishing a strong, economically efficient, and competitive economy? Did he achieve price stability? Napoleon Bonaparte created the Germinal franc in 1803, Raymond Poincaré created the Poincaré franc; did de Gaulle create the de Gaulle franc? Did he put an end to inflationary dirigisme? Was it really a meeting of a great people and a great man, or was it another missed opportunity in economic terms?

The Decolonization of Algeria and the Evian Accords

There was a missed rendezvous between de Gaulle and Algeria because, on his return to office, de Gaulle imagined that it was possible to live with the uprisings in Algeria without decolonizing the country:

> "The most common mistake by all statesmen is to believe that, at every moment, there is a solution for every problem. Yet, during certain periods, some problems have no solution. This is currently the case for Algeria."[3]

These comments made in the summer of 1958 come after those made in May of the same year:

> "Algeria is not a problem you solve: you live with it."[4]

The human, political, and economic toll would be on the scale of this indecision, which is astonishing coming from de Gaulle.

Georgette Elgey's exhaustive, six-volume history of France's Fourth Republic, *Histoire de la IVe République*, a monumental account of the system of government in France between 1946 and 1958, ends with the following question:

> "At this point in the history of the Fourth Republic, a fundamental question remains unanswered, and I fail to see how it could ever be answered: without the Algerian War, would de Gaulle have returned to power, would he have been able to push through the countless measures taken under the last government of the Fourth Republic, which have left a lasting mark on France?"[5]

---

[3] Faure, Edgar (1984), *Mémoires*, Volume II, *Si tel doit être mon destin ce soir...*, Paris, Plon, p. 688.

[4] Comments made to Charles Merveilleux du Vignaux on May 28, 1958.
Elgey, Georgette (2018), *Histoire de la IVe république, De 1945 à 1957*, Éditions Robert Laffont, p. 680.

[5] Elgey, Georgette (2018), *Histoire de la IVe république, De 1945 à 1957*, Éditions Robert Laffont, p. 680.

During the miners' strike of 1963, Prime Minister Georges Pompidou [1911–1974] lamented 1958: "Those were the good old days. All we had to do was say: 'Algeria, Algeria', and any problems with the trade unions would vanish."[6]

In other words, following the referendum that strengthened the powers of the executive, and with the threat of Algeria looming, the field was clear in the four years from 1958 to 1962 to banish inflationary dirigisme forever. Was everything done that was needed?

Evian Accords

It was only on March 18, 1962, after 12 days of "tight negotiations",[7] that the Evian Accords were signed by Louis Joxe [1901–1991] and Krim Belkacem [1922–1970], who headed the two delegations. Negotiations between France and the National Liberation Front (*Front de libération nationale—FLN*)/Provisional Government of the Algerian Republic (*Gouvernement provisoire de la République algérienne—GPRA*) had started about a year before on May 20, 1961. The Evian Accords put an end to more than eight years of war, which took an immense human and moral toll.

The conflict was also a huge burden on France's budget. The government decided to eliminate any direct reference to military operations in Algeria in defense budgets. There are two headings: "the total cost of the war (which includes all defense expenditures caused by the conflict) and its incremental cost (which includes only the additional expenditures caused by the war compared with usual expenditures before 1955, considered as 'normal')."[8]

Concerning 1959:

> "The total cost of the war this year exceeds that of 1958 by some FRF50 billion to FRF100 billion [equivalent of €0.93 billion-€1.85 billion], i.e., comes to between FRF800 billion and FRF950 billion [equivalent of €14.84 billion-€17.62 billion]. These expenditures bring the total cost of military operations since November 1954 to around FRF3100 billion [equivalent of €57.49 billion]. This puts the incremental cost from 1955 to 1959 at around FRF1700 billion [equivalent of €31.53 billion]."[9]

In addition to the burden on the budget, the conflict in Algeria hampered France's modernization, as investment efforts were geared towards the war effort. France's competitiveness and exports suffered as a result. Additionally, as with any war, it exerted a great deal of inflationary pressure on the French economy over the years, which altered France's entire economic dynamic. Of course, the conflict inflicted an even greater toll on Algeria.

---

[6] Lachaise, Bernard, Le Béguec, Gilles, and Turpin, Frédéric (2006), *Georges Pompidou, directeur du général de Gaulle, juin 1958-janvier 1959,* p. 125.

[7] Video, *L'heure de la paix,* source: https://fresques.ina.fr/independances/fiche-media/Indepe00175/les-accords-d-evian-et-le-cessez-le-feu.html.

[8] https://www.lemonde.fr/idees/article/2009/10/31/le-cout-de-la-guerre-d-algerie_1261060_3232.html.

[9] Ibid.

On March 18, 1962, in radio broadcasts from Tunis, Rabat, Tangier, Tripoli, and Cairo, Benyoussef Ben Khedda, Premier of the Algerian Provisional Government, announced a ceasefire. At 8 p.m. in France, de Gaulle addressed the French nation from the Élysée Palace, announcing the signing of the Evian Accords "that the people might decide their own destiny," "opening up the prospect of an independent Algeria, cooperating closely with France," and paid tribute to "the common sense, solidity and confidence of the French people [...] who have allowed a solution to mature, and then to succeed",[10] bringing the war to an end. The ceasefire was to come into effect at 12 noon the following day, March 19, 1962.

The Evian Accords established a Provisional Executive and provided for the French Republic to be represented in Algeria by a High Commissioner (*Haut-Commissaire*) during the period of transition until the referendum on self-determination, the vote to take place within a period of not less than three months and not exceeding six months. The Accords stipulated that a general amnesty shall be proclaimed immediately and that persons interned, whether in France or Algeria, shall be released within a maximum period of twenty days from the date of the ceasefire. The withdrawal of French military personnel is scheduled. The Accords contained provisions regarding the legal situation of persons in Algeria opting to remain French citizens of ordinary civil status.

Under the Accords, Algeria is to belong to the franc area and to have its own currency and foreign exchange assets.

Regarding the exploitation of the Algerian subsoil, the Accords provide as follows:

> "In the existing Departments of the Oases and the Saoura, the wealth of the subsoil will be developed according to the following principles:
>
> (a) Franco-Algerian co-operation will be ensured by a technical body for Saharan co-operation. This body will have a membership representing both sides equally. Its role will be, in particular, to develop the infrastructure necessary for the exploitation of the subsoil, to give advice on Bills and draft regulations concerning mining, and to examine requests for entitlements in regard to mining. The Algerian State will issue entitlements in regard to mining and will enact mining legislation in full sovereignty.
>
> (b) French interests will be assured, in particular, through:
>
> - The exercise, in accordance with the rules of the Saharan petroleum code, as it exists at present, of the rights attaching to mining entitlements issued by France;
>
> - The according of preference, other offers being equal, to French companies in the granting of new mining entitlements, in accordance with the terms and conditions provided for in Algerian mining legislation;
>
> - Payment in French francs for Saharan hydrocarbons up to the amount required for the supply of France and the other countries of the franc area."[11]

During the Cabinet meeting held on May 4, 1962, de Gaulle declared:

---

[10] Video, *L'heure de la paix*.
Source: https://fresques.ina.fr/independances/fiche-media/Indepe00175/les-accords-d-evian-et-le-cessez-le-feu.html.

[11] United Nations—Treaty Series, Exchange of letters and declarations adopted on March 19, 1962, at the close of the Evian talks, constituting an agreement. Paris and Rocher Noir, 3 July 1962. https://treaties.un.org/doc/Publication/UNTS/Volume%20507/v507.pdf.

"'The date from which France will no longer assume any responsibility in Algeria has been set. France's interests are no longer confused with those of the Pieds-noirs.[12] We must not give the impression that France's future in Algeria is theirs.'

Pisani. – 'It could have been theirs!'

De Gaulle. – 'It could still be theirs! But they're not going down that road. There's still the problem of disarmament. Nothing is being done about it. Everyone has weapons in Algiers and Oran. I'm asking for a text to specify what will happen to those found in possession.'"[13]

During this same Cabinet meeting, to a comment by Raymond Triboulet [1906–2006] that "many Europeans have not yet understood this, and are speculating about France remaining in Algeria,"[14] Charles de Gaulle replied:

"The OAS is no longer really looking for a solution in Algeria. It's targeting who you know for what you know. They hope that all this will never end. Well, it will! Independence is independence. Take it, gentlemen, and live with it! And the more you oppose it, the crueler it will be! It won't come without incredible upheavals, especially between Algerians. But we'll be rid of it. Napoleon said that in love, the only victory is escape. In decolonization, too, the only victory is to leave."

The Secret Armed Organization (*Organisation de l'armée secrète - OAS*) was a French dissident paramilitary organization opposed to Algeria's independence. Nineteen days after the Cabinet meeting, on May 23, there was an attempt on de Gaulle's life. There was a second assassination attempt on August 22 in the Paris suburb of Le Petit-Clamart.

European Construction

Like the British, de Gaulle never appreciated what he called the "supranational," but he was always in favor of collaboration between States. In 1950, he had openly mocked the European Coal and Steel Community, which he described as a "mishmash of coal and steel." In 1954, he contributed to the failure of the European Defense Community. On his return to office, however, de Gaulle had to deal with the entry into force on January 1, 1958, of the Common Market, created at France's initiative by the 1957 Treaty of Rome. He considered that a single market "was not a bad thing," that it was good that France was opening up to foreign competition, but he made no secret of the fact that had he been in office, he would have drafted the Treaty of Rome "quite differently." However, as René Mayer would say, he had to "exploit the inevitable," for France was bound by its signature.

The first customs tariff reductions came into effect on January 1, 1959. However, given the state of France's finances, de Gaulle was obliged to invoke the safeguard

[12] The pieds-noirs are people of French and other European descent who were born in Algeria during the period of French rule from 1830 to 1962. Many would depart for Metropolitan France once Algeria gained its independence.

[13] Peyrefitte, Alain (2002), *C'était de Gaulle*, Quarto Gallimard, p. 140.

[14] Ibid.

clause, which allowed the date of application of the tariff cuts to be postponed. France was the only country to invoke this clause. From being a founding member, France became a weak link, the last of the class. France was also the only country to oppose the free-trade area championed by Great Britain.

At de Gaulle's invitation, Konrad Adenauer came to Colombey-les-Deux-Églises on September 14, 1958. For de Gaulle, it was the beginning of the restoration of France's and Europe's independence from the United States. As he summed up in his 1969 Memoirs: "On September 14, 1958, I hoisted the colors."[15] This meeting was held behind closed doors, lasting four hours; the press was not invited.

Both men were convinced of the need for a strong France and Germany to build Europe in tandem. During their meeting, de Gaulle asserted that he expected nothing from the Americans, whom he often referred to as "the others," or from the British, "a secondary problem," and that Europe could only be built on Franco-German friendship: "In Europe, France has a possible, even desirable partner: Germany, the new Germany. It's a historical miracle, but it's no less a fact… And now, for our two countries, there is no other path than the one we must travel together."[16]

Speaking about France, he explained: "The French people have been through a serious affliction. They were a very great people. Especially, they thought they were very great. They thought they were the stars of the world. Indeed, they often were. But they failed to adapt to the real situation. They can't console themselves for the fact that France is no longer the star. That's why we have communism and intellectual anarchy in many circles. France must find a new moral balance that aligns with current realities if the nation is to become a coherent whole once again."[17]

France's Economic Situation in 1958

> "Demand financial order or accept slavery. Financial equilibrium is the necessary consequence of any moral order"[18]
>
> Jacques Rueff

In 1958, there was economic growth and full employment, but inflation reached a 15% peak, there was a balance of payments deficit and the country had been running a budget deficit for years.

Between June 11, 1958, and January 7, 1959, 335 ordinances were signed. Never had a government had recourse to ordinances on such a scale. France's legislative apparatus underwent its biggest overhaul since the Consulate, when Napoleon Bonaparte was First Consul. Although the ordinances concern all ministries, many are of

---

[15] Gaulle, Charles de (1971), *Mémoires d'espoir*, Volume I, *Le Renouveau*, 1958–1962, Plon, p. 214.

[16] Elgey, Georgette (2018), *Histoire de la IVe république, De 1945 à 1957*, Éditions Robert Laffont, p. 836.

[17] Ibid, p. 797.

[18] Communication of Jacques Rueff to the Société française de philosophie in 1946.

an economic or financial nature. The first, the ordinance of June 11, 1958 (*Ordonnance n° 58–529 du 11 juin 1958 autorisant le ministre des finances à émettre un emprunt à capital garanti et bénéficiant d'exemptions fiscales*) concerned the authorization to issue a guaranteed capital loan; the second, the ordinance of June 24, 1958 (*Ordonnance n° 58–544 du 24 juin 1958 portant aménagement des dispositions de l'article 1er de la loi n° 48–178 du 2 février 1948*) concerned French assets abroad, their conversion into francs, the special tax on these assets and exemption therefrom; the third, the ordinance of June 27, 1958 (*Ordonnance n° 58–548 et décret n° 56-5i9 du 27 juin 1958 relatifs au régime fiscal de certains produits ou services d'utilisation courante*) concerned the tax regime for certain everyday products and services, and the list goes on.

The French State's coffers were empty. In January 1958, at the request of the United States, the International Monetary Fund agreed to save France from bankruptcy by granting a new $650 million credit and agreeing to payment deferrals. In June 1958, Antoine Pinay [1891–1994], who had just been appointed Minister of Finance, informed de Gaulle that "We are on the brink of disaster in every respect."[19] In a note dated June 10, 1958, *Éléments pour un programme de rénovation économique et financière*, sent by French economist Jacques Rueff [1896–1978] to Charles de Gaulle via Antoine Pinay, the mission of the new government is described as follows:

> "The present government has been formed not to apply a certain policy, but to re-establish the conditions necessary for the country's very existence. For this reason, its program cannot be that of one group or one party, but only that of all the French people who want their country to continue to exist."[20]

From an economic point of view, the situation was indeed extremely perilous.

Faced with a budget deficit of FRF1200 billion[21] (equivalent of €22.26 billion) and a foreign debt of $3 billion, half of which was due for repayment in a year, Antoine Pinay launched a national loan on June 17, 1958, barely a fortnight after the government was sworn in. It was also a way of testing the public's confidence in the government's capacity to manage the economy.

The loan paid interest at 3.5% which was exempt from income tax and inheritance tax, the main selling point—and the one that would cost the French government the most, leading to the loan's early repayment in 1973. Repayment was to be by lot until 1970 and at the holders' initiative thereafter.

The loan was not indexed to inflation, which reached 15% in 1958, but to the average price of the 20-franc gold coin known as the Napoléon, which traded 10% lower in 1958 than in 1952. Between 1949 and 1958, the price of the Napoleon fell by 18%, while over the same period prices rose by 51% and the US dollar appreciated by 10%. Nevertheless, gold has always been perceived as the ultimate safe haven, a perception reinforced by the two world wars. Some 870 thousand

---

[19] Gaulle, Charles de (1971), *Mémoires d'espoir*, Volume I, *Le Renouveau*, 1958–1962, Plon, p. 145.

[20] Elgey, Georgette (2018), *Histoire de la IVe république, De 1945 à 1957*, Éditions Robert Laffont, 2018, p. 841.

[21] Ibid, p. 836.

subscribers invested an average of FRF350,000 (equivalent of €6,491.28). The loan raised a total of FRF325 billion (equivalent of €6 billion). This is of the same order of magnitude as the so-called Ramadier loan of 1956, but much less than the so-called Pinay loan of 1952, which raised FRF430 billion (equivalent of €8 billion). The Exchange Stabilization Fund (*Fonds de Stabilisation des Changes*) would recoup 150 tons of gold over the term of the loan.

This national loan did provide a breath of fresh air, but it still failed to balance the books. The mandate given by de Gaulle to Antoine Pinay was to prepare a balanced budget. Save for the National Education budget, which benefited from an extra FRF5 billion, all other ministries had to tighten their belts. The increase in civil service pay was postponed.

No stone was left unturned. The ordinance of July 31, 1958 (*Ordonnance n° 52–655 du 31 juillet 1958 relative au prix du blé tendre pour la récolte 1958*) cut the price of soft wheat for the 1958 harvest by FRF100 per hundredweight (equivalent of €1.58). Another ordinance (*Ordonnance n° 52–653 du 31 juillet 1958 relative à diverses mesures d'ordre fiscal*) promulgated the same day contained various tax measures, establishing an extraordinary tax contribution on companies, introducing a wealth tax on second homes, racing horses and yachts, and raising excise duties on gasoline, which in total generated an additional FRF50 billion of tax receipts (equivalent of €0.93 billion).

It was not just the European Economic Community (EEC) created by the Treaty of Rome, but also the Organization for European Economic Co-operation (OEEC), established to allocate and distribute Marshall Plan aid to the countries of Western Europe, that were pushing France to continue lowering customs duties, which were a considerable source of tax receipts for the State. As with the European Economic Community, France tried to win a respite by postponing until December 18, 1958, the next round of trade liberalization with OEEC countries.

Following this raft of reforms, by December 1958, the budget deficit was reduced from FRF1200 billion (equivalent of €22.26 billion) to FRF690 billion (equivalent of €12.80 billion), the balance of trade returned to surplus, and the rise in retail prices was checked.

Rueff Plan

Jacques Rueff, when he worked at the financial section of the League of Nations in 1927 and 1928, was involved in drawing up financial recovery plans for Greece, Bulgaria, and Portugal. He wanted to apply the same recipes to France in 1958. To this end, on June 10, 1958, he presented Antoine Pinay with a note, *Éléments pour un programme de rénovation économique et financière*, setting out measures to combat inflation and the chronic current account balance of payments deficit[22] that, by feeding on each other, were pushing the country to the wall. For Rueff, the keystone of the economy is a stable currency. Moreover, he considered that borrowing on the international capital market was tantamount to "begging abroad." In his note, he called for an end to inflationary dirigisme by ending the practice of money printing and by taking investments out of the State's current budget to finance them on the stock market.

Jacques Rueff had doubts as to whether this note was ever forwarded by Pinay to de Gaulle.

So on November 12, 1958, he presented personally to de Gaulle, Pinay, and Banque de France Governor Wilfrid Baumgartner [1902–1978] a series of measures to address the country's dire fiscal and monetary situation and to boost international trade, and thereby bring inflationary dirigisme to an end. His view was that priority must be given to achieving savings by cutting many of the subsidies and by raising direct and indirect taxes.

The Rueff plan called for trade liberalization, with 90% of French products to be traded freely, without taxation, with all European countries.

For France to regain its competitiveness, he considered it necessary to devalue the franc by 17.5% and introduce a new currency to replace the devalued franc. It seems that Wilfrid Baumgartner, the Governor of the Banque de France, was the one that set the devaluation at 17.5%, on the one hand to boost exports when the French market opened up, and on the other to establish a simple ratio for the franc against gold (200 mg gold at 900/1,000th or 180 mg fine gold) and against the US dollar ($35 per ounce). The dollar went from 420 to 493 francs. The effect of this devaluation was a 6.5% rise in prices, which had been forecast by the *Direction générale des prix et des enquêtes économiques*. The switch from old francs to new francs would take place later in 1960.

On November 25, de Gaulle summoned Rueff to inform him that he would implement his plan. He told Rueff that he was "absolutely sure" that the balance of payments would be in equilibrium within a few weeks. For the rest, de Gaulle was more circumspect. He asked his economic adviser Roger Goetz to confirm that the plan had a two-thirds probability of success since he considered that, in politics, there is always an element of uncertainty accounting for the remaining third, a risk that he was prepared to take. Roger Goetz having done so, the Rueff plan was presented at the Cabinet meeting held on December 26: "That evening was the roughest I'd ever known",[23] said Georges Pompidou, while the General exclaimed: "What a tussle! Of all the political battles I've had to fight in my life, this one can be compared in its

[22] Balance of payments statistics record economic transactions between residents and non-residents. They provide a series of balances between inward and outward transitions and show how these flows of transactions are funded. The balance of payments is an important set of macro-economic statistics for a country, describing its economic and financial relationships with the Rest of the World. Source: https://www.oecd.org/sdd/its/quarterly-balance-of-payments-statistics.htm.

[23] Elgey, Georgette (2018), *Histoire de la IVe république, De 1945 à 1957*, Éditions Robert Laffont, 2018, p. 847.

acrimony to my confrontation with Giraud in Algiers",[24] alluding to the difficulties encountered by de Gaulle in taking over all the powers held by General de Giraud since 1942. As for Jacques Rueff, he would write: "I will never forget the tragic atmosphere of that meeting."[25]

To get the Cabinet's backing, de Gaulle threatened to quit the government, assuming paternity for this plan, which "all said and done, was his own." The problem of Algeria not having yet been resolved, all the members of the government were keen for the General to stay on.

The cover of the January 1959 edition of Time News Magazine carried a portrait of General de Gaulle by Bernard Buffet, for the General had been selected Man of the Year 1958.[26] There was a 10-page cover story about the French leader. The magazine saluted his comprehensive plan, which proposed both fiscal and monetary solutions to remedy the structural difficulties of the French economy. But what were the long-term effects of this plan? How would France's economy have fared without this plan?

It is difficult to discern the full effects of the plan, therefore, what would have been the dynamics of the French economy without it. General de Gaulle's only initial certainty about the plan was confirmed: the balance of payments did improve, but did not reach equilibrium in the next five years. For the first time since the Poincaré franc, there was a stabilization of the franc. In 1959, 1960, and 1961, the budget was back in surplus. On the other hand, as a result of the measures adopted in 1958 and the Rueff plan, GDP growth slowed to 2.4% in 1958 and again in 1959, before jumping to 7.1% in 1960. The money stock continued to expand, by over 13% in 1959, 16% in 1960, 17% in 1961, and 18% in 1962, proving that the government was still cranking up the printing press, not heeding Jacques Rueff's recommendations.

A deceleration in prices did get underway, with inflation subsiding from 15% in 1958 to 6.2% in 1959, 3.7% in 1960, and 3.2% in 1961.

But this relative stabilization of the currency and rebalancing of the accounts would last less than five years. The effects of the plan proved more cyclical than structural. By 1962, France was back in deficit. Price and currency stability would gradually deteriorate.

The new stabilization plan in the autumn of 1963, which focused on locking in prices, demonstrated the inadequacy of the 1958 plan, which was not applied to the letter despite Jacques Rueff's insistence, and which consequently failed to get the French economy back on track. Although de Gaulle held all the cards for reorienting France's post-war economy, he failed to stabilize it in any significant way. Despite 335 ordinances and the Rueff plan, France's economy missed the boat in 1958.

In 1963, de Gaulle went back on the offensive, wanting to further solidify economic stability, as he considered he had already done with the measures taken

[24] Elgey, Georgette (2018), *Histoire de la IVe république, De 1945 à 1957*, Éditions Robert Laffont, 2018, p. 847.

[25] Ibid.

[26] https://content.time.com/time/covers/0,16641,19590105,00.html.

at the end of 1958, which he claimed enabled France "to experience the boom and revival of prestige that we have just lived through."[27]

In June 1963, the General was not dreaming of an American-style French society, living on credit. He wanted to reduce demand to bring down inflation. At the Cabinet meeting the following month, he would add:

> "When it comes to foreign trade and the balance of payments, it's quite simply about rising consumption, not imports of raw materials for industry, which would be healthy. Excuse me for stating the obvious! What are we doing, in practice, about prices and fiscal expenditures? That's where we need to act!"[28]

Alain Peyrefitte has asserted that, on several occasions, de Gaulle used the expression "the opium of inflation," a sign for the confidant that he was "chewing the cud." In May 1963 for instance, he said: "We are at full employment. [..] But the opium of inflation is lurking. We must take energetic measures. For example, we must abolish misleading advertising, which artificially encourages consumption. That's a law that would be easy to pass."[29]

For de Gaulle: "Stabilizing prices and wages and salaries is a policy worthy of a government. Inflation is complacency; it's leaving things to dawdle and drift. The government must realize that the increases in wages and prices are beyond reasonable."[30]

Inflation subsided again, reaching 5%[31] in 1963, 3.2% in 1964, 2.7% in 1965, 2.6% in 1966, and 2.7% in 1967, but price stability could not withstand the 1968 social unrest and 1974 energy shock.

Only the momentum generated by European construction showed lasting power, bringing immediate benefits.

At the Cabinet meeting held on July 10, 1963, Giscard d'Estaing was able to announce:

> "We are ready to repay early all our foreign debts. We have a net surplus of $600 million!'
> De Gaulle (jubilant) – 'What a difference that makes! To think that, after four years, we can pay off all the debts of the Fourth [Republic], which had borrowed to the hilt!'"[32]

Many economists claim that France's public debt is perpetual: it only repays the interest and rolls over the principal or, in other words, issues a new debt for exactly the same amount as the old one when it falls due. That would be to forget there was a time when debt was repaid at maturity.

---

[27] Comment during the Cabinet meeting of June 19, 1963.
Peyrefitte, Alain (2002), *C'était de Gaulle*, Quarto Gallimard, p. 922.

[28] Comments by de Gaulle, Cabinet meeting of June 19, 1963.
Peyrefitte, Alain (2002), *C'était de Gaulle*, Quarto Gallimard, p. 922.

[29] Peyrefitte, Alain (2002), *C'était de Gaulle*, Quarto Gallimard, p. 926.

[30] Comments by Charles de Gaulle in the Salon Doré, Élysée Palace, on August 28, 1963.
Peyrefitte, Alain (2002), *C'était de Gaulle*, Quarto Gallimard, p. 925–926.

[31] https://www.inflation.eu/fr/taux-de-inflation/france/inflation-historique/ipc-inflation-france-1963.aspx.

[32] Peyrefitte, Alain (2002), *C'était de Gaulle*, Quarto Gallimard, p. 924.

De Gaulle measured the ground covered, which it has to be said had been impressive. However, he did not put an end to inflationary dirigisme when he had the power to do so, and inflation would resurface at the first shock.

The Ordinance of August 17, 1967, on employee profit sharing (*Ordonnance n°67–693 du 17 août 1967 relative à la participation des salariés aux fruits de l'expansion des entreprises*) has to be put to the credit of de Gaulle's presidency for, unlike measures to stabilize prices, it did lead to a lasting and structural improvement in employee purchasing power.

May 68

May 68 started as a student revolt caused by dissatisfaction with the quality of teaching at French universities and the lack of job opportunities for graduates. It began at the University of Nanterre, which had been moved to the outskirts of Paris in the middle of a shantytown to alleviate overcrowding at the Sorbonne. The March 22 Movement, led by Daniel Cohn-Bendit [1945-], played a significant role in organizing and directing the revolt. In an attempt to quell the protests, the University of Nanterre was closed on May 2. But all this did was move the revolt to the heart of Paris, fanning the flames and then setting fire to the whole of France.

When reference is made to May 68, very rarely is the term "crisis" employed, though that is very precisely what it was. What kind of crisis was it? Were there any economic reasons that might have contributed to the outbreak of May 68?

The period that began in 1958 with the establishment of the Fifth Republic and ended in 1963 with the launch of the stabilization plan was one of the most extraordinary in French economic history. Growth subsequently slowed due to the restrictive economic and monetary policy and also the effect of declining growth in other Common Market countries.

From 1963 to 1967, the annual rate of increase in industrial production slowed to 4.7%, from 6.4% from 1959 to 1963. This caused the price index for industrial stocks to fall from 100 in 1963 to 70 in 1967. Although the number of registered job seekers doubled from 97 thousand in 1963 to 196 thousand in 1967, unemployment remained moderate. The annual rate of increase in purchasing power slowed from 3.9% between 1959 and 1963 to 3.4% between 1963 and 1967, but it did continue to improve.

What all this suggests was that the economic situation was not responsible for the May 1968 crisis. It was not an economic crisis in the strict sense of the word, although the strikes obviously had an economic impact, but a widespread social crisis that threatened the highest levels of government.

Nevertheless, the less favorable economic climate may have prompted workers to join the students on the evening of May 14, 1968. This followed the night of May 10–11, known as the "Night of the Barricades" (when students and special mobile French police forces clashed in the Latin Quarter) and after trade unions joined the students in protesting police brutality on May 13. Kicking off on May 14 at the site of

Sud-Aviation in the Nantes suburbs before spreading to the Renault plants at Cléon, Sandouville, Flins, and Boulogne-Billancourt, the strike became general from May 22. Trade unions at the national level did not call a general strike, but they followed the movement.

In 1936, there were 2 million strikers in the private sector. In 1968, there were 7 million declared strikers in the public and private sectors, plus all those who could not work because of lack of transport or access to the work site. France came to a standstill. The impact of the strikes, which lasted around five weeks, was an around 3% contraction in annual non-agricultural gross domestic product.

On May 27, at the prompting of Prime Minister Georges Pompidou, Jacques Chirac [1932–2019], the Assistant Secretary for Social Affairs with responsibility for employment, and representatives of the trade unions and the employers' federation concluded the so-called Grenelle Agreements (*Accords de Grenelle*). They provided for a general wage increase of 5% on June 1, 1968, and 3% on October 1, 1968. 1.5 million low-wage workers received a 35% pay rise in June. Certain social benefits were increased: family allowances and small pensions were raised, and the planned reduction in the rate of medical expense reimbursement by the Social Security did not go ahead.

Annual paid leave entitlement was increased to four weeks in 1969. It was May 68 that marked the beginning of a decline in the collective number of working hours, which had increased post-war during France's reconstruction. In 1982, annual paid leave entitlement was increased to 5 weeks, while the hours worked each week were cut to 39 h, then to 35 h in 1998. All in all, the working week for a full-time employee was reduced by around ten hours since the 1950s. Back in 1950, employees worked 1900 h a year on average. In 2024, they worked 1,607 h a year,[33] or around 15% less. There is now a push for a 4-day week, with some businesses making the switch in 2022 to improve their appeal in the job market.

This decline in working hours is not specific to France. It is a general trend in Western countries. According to INSEE, the reasons for this trend are the reduction in collective working hours, the increasing salarization of the self-employed, and the development of part-time work from the 1980s onwards.

This expansionary economic policy and the renewed growth in the other Common Market countries had an immediate beneficial effect: France's industrial production rose by 32% between 1968 and 1972, compared with 18% between 1963 and 1967. The measures taken in response to the strikers' demands did, however, accentuate the two weaknesses that post-war economic policy had constantly tried to combat: inflation and a trade balance deficit.

On the one hand, the lower production reduced supply, causing prices to rise. When this happens, it tends to stifle exports and encourage imports as a replacement for domestic production, all the more so when wages are rising, as was the case

[33] For full-time employees, the legal limit on working hours is 1,607 h per year (which corresponding to 35 h worked each week), adjusted for the five-week statutory holiday, public holidays, and the solidarity day.

Source: dares.travail-emploi.gouv.fr/donnees/la-duree-individuelle-du-travail.

following May 1968. On the other hand, rising wages alone fuel inflation. In addition, higher costs for businesses made French products less competitive, simultaneously encouraging imports and hindering exports. Because the management of the May 68 crisis pushed up inflation and led to a negative trade balance, therefore to capital outflows, there was the risk that the government would have to devalue the franc.

For Charles de Gaulle, devaluing the franc was out of the question for two reasons. First, he did not want a devaluation for fear it might disrupt the mechanisms of the Common Agricultural Market and undermine European integration. Second, he wanted to modify the international monetary system imposed by the United States in 1944 at Bretton Woods, since this system allowed the United States to run a structurally negative balance of payments. It also overvalued the dollar against all other currencies, enabling the United States to conquer the world economically and militarily. Influenced by the theories defended by Jacques Rueff, de Gaulle's ambition was to return to the gold standard, after significantly revaluing the price of gold.

Be that as it may, the government's immediate priority was to get the French economy back up and running after five weeks at a virtual standstill. After the experience during the first lockdown in 2020, one can appreciate the colossal resources required to get an economy moving again at a time when remote working did not yet exist and when being denied access to the place of work meant not working at all.

To get the economy back on its feet and avoid layoffs, the Banque de France pursued an expansionary monetary policy. As a result, between April 30 and November 30, 1968, credits increased by 16%, compared with 9% for the same period in 1967. They significantly exceeded business financing needs. Excess credits granted during this period are estimated at FRF10 billion,[34] which had for effect to reduce France's foreign exchange reserves by FRF20 billion,[35] triggering a flight of capital and driving up inflation.

The government's strategy for fighting inflation was to freeze prices. To offset this and help businesses cope with the compulsory wage increases, measures were taken to relax price controls, reduce the tax burden, and provide state subsidies. The payroll tax paid by businesses was cut by 15%. Small and medium-sized enterprises were granted advances at a 5% interest rate, capped at their sales or three times their average payroll for 1967. Price controls were relaxed in return for a commitment by businesses not to increase their prices by more than 3% between April 30 and December 31, 1968.

Despite the economic woes caused by May 1968, France's integration into the European Economic Community (EEC) went ahead as scheduled. On July 1, 1968, internal tariffs were removed on trade between EEC Member States, which adopted a common set of tariffs on imports from countries outside the EEC. Concurrently, the reduction in tariffs agreed to during the sixth session of the General Agreement

[34] Allowing for the fact that inflation erodes the value of money, the purchasing power of FRF10 billion in 1968 is equivalent to €13.37 billion in 2022.

[35] Allowing for the fact that inflation erodes the value of money, the purchasing power of FRF20 billion in 1968 is equivalent to €26.74 billion in 2022.

on Tariffs and Trade (GATT) multilateral trade negotiations, known as the Kennedy Round, was applied, opening France up even further to world trade.

To preserve the competitiveness of French exporters, the government expanded the economic risk guarantee provided by Compagnie Française d'Assurance pour le Commerce Extérieur (COFACE) to include abnormal cost increases (so-called production cost insurance): allowance equal to 6% of the amount of payroll costs included in the value of exports entering customs between July 1 and October 31, 1968 and 3% between November 1, 1968 and January 31, 1969.

To support the country's exports, the Banque de France set the rediscount rate for bills of exchange representing export credits at 2%.

After May 1968, there was a flight of capital from France, first out of fear that the revolt would turn into a revolution, and then after the June legislative elections, in anticipation of a devaluation of the franc. Many economic agents hurried to sell their francs and avoided exchanging foreign currencies for francs. The anticipated increase in the inheritance tax and the expansionary credit policy also contributed to the transfer of capital abroad. Given the scale of these movements, a system of limited exchange controls was put in place until September 5, 1968. As interest rates on the international capital markets rose, France's central bank had to step in and raise its own rates to keep the franc attractive for foreign investors. As indicated above, special measures were introduced for small and medium-sized enterprises and exporters.

Given the circumstances, the outcome of the economic policy put in place to limit the economic damage of May 1968 could have been worse. The first success was that industrial production quickly picked up again, and by July had surpassed pre-strike levels. The second success was that the labor market improved, with the number of job seekers falling by 14% between August and November.

In the first quarter of 1968, inflation crept higher, at much the same pace in France and West Germany. However, the measures taken in response to the May 1968 crisis fueled French inflation. As a result, inflation continued to rise compared with January 1968, reaching 1.9% in August (whereas in West Germany it was flat), then 2.6% in September (in West Germany it fell to 0.1%), and 3.7% in October and 4% in November in France (in West Germany it rose to just 0.3% and 0.4%, respectively). The inflation gap between France and Germany was widening, to the detriment of the Common Market.

Inflation would continue in the following years, as the Grenelle Agreements became the reference rather than the exception for wage negotiations. The change in wage determination mechanisms was a direct consequence of May 1968, even though it came about at the end of 1969. In particular, wages were fully indexed to prices. Wage agreements included clauses guaranteeing increases in purchasing power. There followed that wages came to account for an increasing proportion of business margins. Insofar as wage increases were not entirely justified by improvements in productivity, this would increasingly feed the inflationary spiral from 1968 onwards.

The overall tax burden remained stable from 1967 to 1968 at 22.6% of GDP, but the taxation of households rose by 23.6% in 1968, whereas corporate income tax increased by only 2%. Tax policy "corrected" the Grenelle Agreements by shifting the tax burden onto households.

If one adds to the capital outflows the current account deficit, there followed that France lost a quarter of its gold reserves and half of its foreign currency reserves.

Despite the measures taken, May 68 led to a flight of capital in the short and medium term and an imbalance in the balance of trade from September 1968 onwards. The decision to abolish exchange controls proved to be a mistake. Stricter controls were reintroduced on November 25, 1968.

At the end of 1968, monetary policy became restrictive and fiscal policy was tightened up. Credit was restricted, while reserve requirements and interest rates were raised. However, the policy adjustments were not sufficient, as the external imbalance was partly the result of excessive domestic demand. Thus, despite this reorientation, the index measuring France's market share of world demand fell from 93.4 in the second quarter of 1968 to 90.4 in the second quarter of 1969. The rise in imports accelerated. Government action failed to halt expectations that the franc would be devalued. Yet de Gaulle categorically refused to devalue. How could French products become competitive again on the world market? What would de Gaulle's successor do to restore their competitiveness?

Industrial Policy Under Pompidou

> "It is a fact that each problem solved gives rise to others, usually more difficult"[36]
>
> Georges Pompidou

After serving as Managing Director of Banque Rothschild from 1956 to 1962, Georges Pompidou [1911–1974] would be the longest-serving prime minister under the Fifth Republic, staying in office from 1962 to 1968. As President of the Republic from 1969 to 1974, he had to deal with two major global economic upheavals: the first oil crisis and the end of the Bretton Woods international monetary system of fixed parities established in 1944. Like de Gaulle, in addressing the monetary and economic issues of the moment, Georges Pompidou pursued a long-term vision. He will go down in French and European history for his industrial policy.

Georges Pompidou came to power at almost the same time as Richard Nixon, who was President of the United States from 1969 to 1975. Georges Pompidou's unlikely friendship with Nixon was of great benefit to France's industrial policy, particularly in the aeronautical and nuclear sectors. While in Paris on a state visit, Richard Nixon presented French President Georges Pompidou with a fragment of lunar rock brought back by Neil Armstrong. In return, the French President gifted the last thorn retrieved from the Crown of Thorns relic, to the displeasure of the Catholic Church, which

[36] Speech given by Georges Pompidou on February 28, 1970, at the Alliance Française dinner held in Chicago.
https://newcorpconseil.com/en/2016/01/06/pompidou-1970-discours-visionnaire-de-chicago/.

had not been informed. Since its purchase from a Venetian merchant by Louis IX (commonly known as Saint Louis) in 1239, the relic has been the property of the French State and the Catholic Church. Over the centuries, the Crown of Thorns has been used to seal alliances.

General de Gaulle's successor was a man of letters, a humanist. Without going so far as to conceive of a "green" industrial policy, Pompidou nevertheless considered that "man's hold on nature has become such that it carries the risk of destroying nature itself"[37] and that, just as with the competition policy and economic information, the importance of the country's environmental policy had not been fully appreciated, as indicated in the foreword to the Sixth Plan. In this plan, the focus is mainly on the three major types of pollution: air, water (including oceans), and land (notably waste disposal), as well as noise pollution. Georges Pompidou accelerated France's modernization to reposition it in the global economic race, for May 68 had seen it lose a few places in the pecking order, coming when other countries had begun to grow faster.

To partially offset the wage increases agreed to following May 1968, and restore the competitiveness of French exports, the franc was devalued in August 1969. The government's main economic policy objectives would be defined in the Sixth Social and Economic Development Plan (*VIe Plan de développement économique et social*) covering the period 1971 to 1975.

As it happened in August, the foreign exchange markets were taken by surprise since just about everyone was on vacation. The effect of the announcement of the franc's devaluation was therefore positive. If de Gaulle had devalued the franc in November 1968, when the economy was in the doldrums and everyone was expecting a devaluation, the effect would have been attenuated. This positive effect was compounded by the tightening of credit controls that followed the devaluation and by a management of public finances designed for the Treasury to achieve monetary and financial neutrality. The Minister of Economy and Finance between 1969 and 1974 was Valéry Giscard d'Estaing [1926–2020]. France had a negative current account balance in 1969 (-1.1%), which would move back into positive territory in 1970 (+0.1%) and 1971 (+0.6%).

During the first year of Georges Pompidou's presidency, twenty-five Cabinet meetings devoted to economic and industrial policy were held at the Elysée Palace. They dealt with French investment abroad and foreign investment in France in the fields of steel, automobiles, information technology, aeronautics, energy, oil, and commodities, also the development of applied research in industry and in the pursuit of socio-economic goals.

In the field of nuclear energy, efforts were stepped up in early 1971 to increase and diversify the sourcing of uranium ore, while a decision was made to assimilate and master American reprocessing and fuel fabrication techniques as much as possible. A program was launched to increase nuclear capacity by 8000 MW between 1971 and 1976. Following the 1974 oil crisis, the program was expanded with the launch of six additional 1000 MW units and the construction of the Tricastin nuclear power plant.

---

[37] Ibid.

This plant, which is still in operation, has four reactors with a production capacity of 900 MW each, equivalent to the consumption of around 3.5 million inhabitants.

Westinghouse would grant a license to France in 1974, but in the interval, the decision was reached to "Frenchify" the reactor components as much as possible, with the long-term objective of becoming altogether independent of the Westinghouse license. As a result, 54 of EDF's 56 nuclear reactors (and half of the world's reactors) would be built with this technology. The Westinghouse Electric Corporation was an American manufacturing company founded in Pittsburgh in 1886 by George Westinghouse. The nuclear power division, Westinghouse Electric Company, was spun off from the Westinghouse Electric Corporation in 1999. It passed first under British control (British Nuclear Fuels Limited) and then under Japanese control (Toshiba). In 2017, Westinghouse Electric Company filed under Chapter 11 of the United States Bankruptcy Code. Faced with similar difficulties in the wake of the Fukushima nuclear accident, and plagued by project delays and poor risk assessments, Areva was bailed out, whereas Westinghouse went under.

In July 1971, the French government decided to step up its oil exploration and production program. A study was launched into the possibility of storing an additional 10 million tons of oil over and above existing safety stocks.

Raw materials were a major concern for the government. At the defense council meeting held in November 1971, plans were drawn up to create stocks of non-energy raw materials.

In the Sixth Social and Economic Development Plan (*VIe Plan de développement économique et social*), it was proposed to aim for:

> "Annual growth in gross domestic product [...] of between 5.8% and 6.0%, which represents an increase of one-third over the period 1971 to 1975. [...]
>
> The proposed rate of growth is consistent with an average growth in industrial production of 7.5% per year, equivalent to an around doubling in the next ten years or so [...]. This rate of growth must be accompanied by a very substantial job creation effort in the industrial sector: at least 250 thousand jobs will have to be created in industry if it is to deliver this growth, impose itself on external markets and guarantee full employment.
>
> This development of industry will lead to the development of all other productive sectors, in particular transport, commerce and ancillary services. [...]
>
> As already mentioned, the prerequisite for growth is to have a balanced current account. [...]
>
> The objective set for the Sixth Plan is an average annual growth rate of around 7% for all productive investment. In the case of industry in particular, continued efforts should enable the investment rate to rise from 14.7% in 1965 to around 16.7% in 1975. To achieve this ambitious objective, far in excess of what has been achieved in the past - apart from the exceptional rates of increase recorded in 1969 and 1970 - the State will use its financial policy to ensure that industry has access to abundant long-term resources, and use its economic policy to ensure investment proceeds at a steady pace and, if necessary, to provide support as a matter of priority."[38]

The Sixth plan identified three priority sectors:

[38] https://www.strategie.gouv.fr/sites/strategie.gouv.fr/files/atoms/files/sixieme-plan-1971-1975.pdf, p. 21–22.

"- Chemicals, this sector nowadays being one of the driving forces behind the development of an industrial nation. [...]

- The electronics, computing and telecoms sector, which is forecast to grow by around 15% a year over the period covered by the Sixth Plan. [...]

- A special place must be given to the agricultural and food industries, which are of vital importance as they control a proportion of the outlets for agriculture, particularly in the case of exports. Despite the progress already made, a major effort in terms of restructuring is required from businesses in the sector. Compared to other industries, these businesses benefit from substantial State support.

For the Sixth Plan, the aim will be, on the one hand, to implement a policy of penetrating foreign markets for agri-food products, with priority given to supporting the efforts of the most export-oriented businesses in setting up operations abroad, and on the other hand, to create, within the next ten years, a small number of groups whose size and activities abroad should enable them to occupy leading positions in the European food market."[39]

Investments in telecommunications increased by 20% from 1968. Following the new industrial policy adopted in 1969, they would increase by 40% in 1970. The Sixth Plan provided a five-year envelope of FRF28.4 billion (equivalent of €34 billion) to fund the government's telecommunications policy.[40]

The Sixth Plan called for the development of Orly airport and the construction of a new airport at Roissy, with the first terminal scheduled to come into service in time for the first tourist season of 1974.

"For the three leading airlines, continued efforts to improve their profitability and competitiveness will mean renewing and expanding their fleets, which are set to undergo a major overhaul in view of [...] the gradual introduction of the Concorde supersonic aircraft and the new Airbus and Mercure aircraft."[41]

Concorde 001 made its first test flight from Toulouse on March 2, 1969. The development of the twin-engine narrow-body Mercure was launched in 1969. On May 29, 1969, French Transport Minister Jean Chamant and German Economics Minister Karl Schiller launched the Airbus A300 program at the Paris Air Show. The goal of gaining market share by building a smaller, lighter, and more economical twin-engine aircraft than its American three-engine rivals would be achieved.

In 1970, Airbus Industrie was officially created as an economic interest grouping (EIG) between France's Aerospatiale (formed by merging SEREB, Sud Aviation, and Nord Aviation) and Germany's Deutsche Airbus.

The A300, the first twin-engine wide-body aircraft in the world, took off for its maiden flight on October 28, 1972, from Toulouse.

Concurrently with the development of commercial aviation, the Ariane satellite launch vehicle project was launched at the end of 1973 after one year of negotiations with other European countries.

---

39 Ibid, pp. 54–55.

40 Ibid, p. 239.

41 https://www.strategie.gouv.fr/sites/strategie.gouv.fr/files/atoms/files/sixieme-plan-1971-1975.pdf, p. 234.

The Plan also called for "the start of construction of the new Paris-Lyon TGV line",[42] which would be the country's first high-speed rail line. The oil crisis that would follow heightened interest in high-speed rail lines.

Conclusion

From 1968 to 1973, France increased its production by a third, recording the strongest growth in Europe. Exports doubled. France overtook Great Britain in world trade rankings, in third place after the United States and Germany, and on a par with Japan.

The French population saw living standards improve by 25% during this period. Only Japan did better.

The initiatives taken during Georges Pompidou's presidency structured a high-tech Europe with the success that we know in the 1990s. What would aeronautics be without Airbus, which now shares the world market with Boeing, rail without the TGV, aerospace without Ariane, telecommunications and nuclear energy without the industrial strategy pursued under his presidency? What would France be without the Pompidou presidency, and what would it have been had he not died unexpectedly before the end of his first term?

Factors Behind France's Economic Growth During the Glorious Thirty

After 1945, France experienced economic growth unparalleled in its entire economic history, what became known as the Glorious Thirty. This era can be broken down into four periods:

- Restart and reconstruction from 1945 to 1951;
- First post-war cycle from 1951 to 1957;
- Second post-war cycle from 1957 to 1963;
- Third post-war cycle from 1963 to 1969.

In terms of productivity, there were troughs, with low points set towards the end of 1952 and 1958, and then at the start of 1965.

All three post-war cycles experienced the same inflationary dynamics, followed by a deflationary intervention on the part of the government, which attempted to stabilize prices by causing a slowdown in growth for a year or two before the growth and inflation dynamics kicked in again.

The 1973 oil crisis put an end to this exponential growth, which will go down in history as the most prosperous period in the French economy and the most beneficial

42 Ibid, p. 238.

for the population as a whole. What were the causes of this exceptional growth? Was it French demographics? Was it investment, or perhaps capital or innovation? Was it global demand or foreign trade? What is the explanation? Can the French economy one day return to the growth trajectory of the Glorious Thirty?

In the article published in 1911, *Les trois notions de la productivité et ses revenus*, Albert Aftalion [1874–1956] defined productivity as "the ratio between total production over a specific period of time and the total number of agents engaged in this production."[43]

The work of French economists on productivity was interrupted by the two world wars. During the interwar period, economic research focused on the economic issues of the time. Single-factor productivity measuring output to labor input was of great interest to entrepreneurs, but only really established itself as a macroeconomic criterion in France at the start of the Glorious Thirty.

In 1952, Jean Fourastié wrote a text simply entitled *Productivité* as part of the *Que sais-je?* editorial collection, which became a classic of French economic literature, reprinted by Presses Universitaires de France until 1980.

Thanks to the remarkable work of Jean Fourastié in providing the layman with an accessible introduction to economic concepts and for whom productivity is synonymous with output, and to the modernity of the team assembled to work on France's First Plan, productivity became a central measure of France's overall efficiency from 1944 onwards.

Productivity became a synonym for measuring growth at the macroeconomic level, while at the same time being a measure of performance at the microeconomic level. The more this economic concept was used by the Fourth Republic, the more it was transformed thanks to the refinement of labor and production measurements to take into account new production factors and use conversion coefficients enabling comparisons over two centuries.

Given the circumstances, the team working on France's First Plan, in majority financed by the Marshall Plan, had to liaise with the Economic Cooperation Administration (ECA), which administered the Marshall Plan, and the Bureau of Labor Statistics (BLS). As early as the end of the nineteenth century, the Bureau of Labor Statistics began conducting systematic surveys of gross labor productivity to study the threat posed by possible technological unemployment. To implement the Marshall Plan and modernize a France in ruins, Jean Monnet's team had to take an interest in productivity. Given Jean Monnet's entrepreneurial background, this came naturally to him.

When working on France's First Plan, Jean Fourastié would meet British economist and statistician Colin Clark [1905–1989] thanks to Robert Marjolin, before traveling to the United States on assignment, where he met James Silberman, Chief, Branch of Productivity and Technological Developments, Bureau of Labor Statistics at the US Department of Labor. On his return from the United States, Fourastié was

[43] Aftalion, Albert (1911), *Les trois notions de la productivité et ses revenus*, Revue d'économie politique, Vol. 25, No. 2, p. 145-184, Editions Dalloz, 1911.
https://www.jstor.org/stable/24681961.

involved in the work of the Labor Productivity sub-commission, chaired by Noël Pouderoux, a convinced Taylorist, and made up of representatives drawn from the ranks of the trade unions and employers' federations, civil servants, and two experts in the persons of René Magron and Jean Dayre. Their task was to study the general, technical, and human causes of France's low productivity, and to propose ways of increasing it. However, faced with the slow progress of the commission's work, Jean Monnet took matters into his own hands and drew up an American-inspired national productivity enhancement program that would meet the criteria of the Marshall Plan.

Demographics, Capital Accumulation, and Productivity Gains During the Glorious Thirty

Immediately after the Second World War, the central statistical information system was modified. The pre-war organization, known as Statistique Générale de France, was located solely in Paris and had a staff of around 100 employees, including a dozen executives. It became the Service National de Statistique during the war, and the Institut National de la Statistique et des Études Économiques (INSEE) after the war. Created by the Finance Act of April 27, 1946, INSEE was provided from the onset with resources far in excess of those of Statistique Générale de France. At the end of the Glorious Thirty, INSEE employed 4 thousand people, including 400 senior executives in 18 regional divisions attached to the Paris headquarters. In 2019, INSEE employed 5,295 people, including 1,580 executives. Since 1962, INSEE has been responsible for drawing up retrospective national accounts and technical work on global economic forecasting for the short, medium, and long term.

INSEE defines productivity as follows:

> "In economics, productivity is defined as the ratio, in volume, between production and the resources used to obtain that production.
>
> Production means goods and/or services produced. The resources used, also called production factors, mean labor, technical means (installations, machines, tooling, etc.), the capital invested, intermediate consumption (raw materials, power, transport, etc.) as well as factors less easy to grasp but extremely important, such as the accumulation of know-how.
>
> Productivity can also be calculated in relation to a single type of resources such as labor or capital. Then we speak about apparent productivity.
>
> The apparent productivity of labor is a widely used measurement. The apparent productivity of capital can also be calculated."[44]

Productivity needs to be considered in light of population trends and the structuring of the workforce.

> "The study of population trends is based on the calculation of a certain number of standard indicators which make it possible, in particular, to apprehend the probabilities of the occurrence of demographic events (birth, death, marriage) and the average ages of occurrence of these events: fertility rate, marriage rate, average age at marriage, life expectancy, etc.

[44] https://www.insee.fr/en/metadonnees/definition/c1452.

Demographic indicators are calculated from vital statistics and population estimates."[45]

The French national office for statistics started to publish demographic series in 1901. At the time, the statistics concerned Metropolitan France alone. Until June 28, 1919, when the Treaty of Versailles was signed, Alsace and Moselle were not part of the national territory, and this was the case again during the Second World War. As a rule, the data produced during the two world wars was not comprehensive. Since 1946, Metropolitan France's borders have not changed. There follows that demographic trends during the Glorious Thirty and right up to present days are comparable and reliable. In 1946, France had a population of 40,503,000, with a density of around 73 inhabitants per square kilometer, the lowest in Western Europe after Spain. Until 1960, France's crude mortality rate[46] was slightly higher than in other Western countries. From 24% between 1851 and 1860, the rate dropped to 20% at the beginning of the twentieth century, then to 16‰ between the two wars, 12% in 1960, 9% from the 1980s onwards, and 8% since the turn of this century. The COVID-19 pandemic pushed the crude mortality rate up to 9.9% in 2020.[47]

France's population was smaller in 1946 than in 1901, as the two world wars had taken a heavy toll: 1.4 million dead between 1914 and 1918, or 3.5% of the population at the time; 0.6 million dead between 1939 and 1945. What's more, older age groups were in the majority, as it was the young who died in the wars. Also, unlike COVID-19, the so-called Spanish flu killed those in their prime and spared the elderly. At the end of the First World War, the number of births picked up for a very short time. The same trend was expected after the Second World War, but between the 1946 and 1968 censuses, the French population jumped from 40.5 to 49.8 million. The birth rate averaged 20% between 1946 and 1954, 18% between 1954 and 1962, and 17.5% between 1962 and 1968. In addition to the spectacular rise in the birth rate, there was a fall in mortality, so that the natural growth rate settled at 0.7% after the Second World War, whereas there had been negative growth of 0.1% per year between 1936 and 1946. In 22 years, therefore, population growth was higher than in the previous hundred years, thanks to peace and the prosperity brought about by productivity gains—considered by Fourastié to be the "fuel" of economic growth—leading to higher living standards.

During the Glorious Thirty, population growth was also due to immigration. Decolonization led to an extraordinary rise in net immigration, from 40 thousand a year between 1946 and 1954 to 155 thousand a year between 1955 and 1961. At the end of the Algerian War in 1962, 700 thousand people were repatriated and settled in France. From 1963 to 1969, net immigration continued at a rate of 150 thousand a year, even though the labor market had not been tight since 1964.[48]

---

[45] https://www.insee.fr/fr/metadonnees/source/indicateur/p1667/description.

[46] The crude mortality rate or crude death rate is defined as the ratio of the number of deaths during the year to the average population of the territory concerned in that year; the value is expressed per 1000 inhabitants.

[47] https://www.insee.fr/fr/statistiques/2383440#tableau-figure1.

[48] Carré, Jean-Jacques, Dubois, Paul, and Malivaud, Edmond (1972), *La croissance française*, Éditions du Seuil, p. 58.

After peaking in 1964 at 203,089, net immigration fell steadily until 1992, bottoming at 740.[49] It then picked up, reaching 155,943 in 2005, before declining and then stabilizing at around 20 thousand in 2020. It is interesting to note that there is no correlation between the increase in votes cast for the far right, which has been restrictive in terms of immigration policy, and reality as measured by immigration statistics. In 2016 and 2021, the year before the presidential election that saw the far-right reach the second round, net immigration reached 14,729 and 20,614, respectively. This proves that populism is all about demagogy, not reality.

The post-war increase in France's population was unprecedented in the last hundred years. The population increased by 1% a year on average between 1946 and 1965 in France, compared with 0.7% in Italy and 0.6% in Britain. In Germany and the United States, the population increased by 1% and 1.7% a year on average, respectively, over the same period.[50]

The structure of the economically active population by sector of activity changed over the course of the Glorious Thirty, laying the foundations for the economy as we know it today. There was a dramatic fall in the economically active population in the agricultural sector, from 43.4% in 1896 to 31.4% in 1938 and 14.6% in 1968. This decline was offset by the 6.4% growth in production per man-hour in this sector between 1949 and 1963. The proportion of the economically active population employed in industry increased steadily from 31.3% in 1896 to 32.3% in 1938 and then to 38.9% in 1968. There was a spectacular increase in the proportion of the economically active population employed in services, from 25.3% in 1896 to 36.3% in 1938 and then 46.5% in 1968.[51]

Intuitively, one would expect a rising labor participation rate among women to have made a substantial contribution to economic growth. Not so, the overall participation rate falling from 36% in 1901 to 32% in 1946 and then to 28% in 1968.[52]

Despite the rural exodus, there was but a slight increase in France's economically active population. It was flat between 1950 and 1962. The total number of hours worked fell by 30% between 1896 and 1963, after the Popular Front reduced the legal workweek to 40 h in 1936. However, the effect of the reduction in working hours "was offset by an increase of the same order in the quality of the working population. It would appear therefore that, apart from the last few years, the increase in French output [...] has been attributable solely to an improvement in labor productivity."[53] The increase in output was not therefore due to an increase in the labor force, as the economically active population between 1945 and 1969 was smaller than at the beginning of the century, and especially had come off its peak in 1929.

---

49 https://donnees.banquemondiale.org/indicateur/SM.POP.NETM?end=2021&locations=FR&start=1960&view=chart.

50 Carré, Jean-Jacques, Dubois, Paul, and Malivaud, Edmond (1972), *La croissance française*, Éditions du Seuil, p. 60.

51 Ibid, p. 126.

52 Ibid, p. 69.

53 Ibid, p.105.

Productivity growth during the Glorious Thirty was faster than in previous periods. Between 1949 and 1969, overall output per man-hour rose by 5.2%, more than double the strong growth recorded between 1913 and 1929. This increase was also due to the continuing effort to educate the French population. "In 1896, half of all working people had not attended school or had interrupted their studies before the age of 13, and only 13% had continued their studies until the age of 15 or over. In 1931, the corresponding proportions were 15% and 21%. In 1946, they were 6% and 27%. This better-educated population was poorly employed at the end of the war. But, once oriented towards modern activities, and after a few years' experience, productivity would be far superior to that achieved twenty years earlier."[54]

The accumulation of productive capital during the Glorious Thirty took place in two stages. The first, from 1946 to 1951, corresponded to an extraordinary public investment drive, aided by the Marshall Plan. These investments made it possible to rebuild and modernize the country's infrastructure, which was vital to have a highly performing economy. The second phase, from 1955 to 1969, saw an increasingly rapid increase in gross capital formation in a climate of optimism, with France's entry into the Common Market and competition being perceived as opportunities by business managers. Businesses invested to take advantage of this. The high level of investment and the high birth rate reflect the same confidence in the future, which in turn led to higher growth.

The unprecedented accumulation of capital, reflecting the reconstruction effort, fueled productivity growth. One contributing factor was that, from 1900 onwards, French industry expanded into those sectors that would thrive in the future, notably the capital goods industry. The capital goods industry refers to businesses that manufacture and distribute machinery and tools used primarily to manufacture other goods, notably mechanical, electrical, and electronic equipment. The share of foreign equipment in capital spending on plant and equipment was 38% in 1899 and 1900 and 40% from 1911 to 1913, but would fall to 15% in 1949 and 20% in 1963, despite trade liberalization.

Analyzing this decline in the share of foreign equipment, what will be observed is how France, for example, is currently lagging in the production of semiconductors, which are essential to the whole industrial sector. The country is therefore entirely dependent on foreign suppliers for many components, hence vulnerable. This is a serious error of economic policy in a strategic sector of activity. France is a world leader in luxury goods because it was the French kings and queens (Marie-Antoinette being the first, as previously it was only the king's mistresses who were fashion leaders) who put French luxury on the world stage. Today's entrepreneurs have capitalized on this cultural heritage. De Gaulle launched France's nuclear industry. Jean-Luc Lagardère created Airbus with the financial backing of the French and German governments. Who will make France the world's high-tech leader? In the past, the French State has intervened massively to enable businesses to expand into

[54] Carré, Jean-Jacques, Dubois, Paul, and Malivaud, Edmond (1972), *La croissance française*, Éditions du Seuil, p. 617.

new sectors of activity and go on to be world leaders. Timing was of the essence, as was choosing the right people. Time for France to do it again…

Strong Pent-Up Demand and Priority to Work

The two World Wars and the Great Depression led to the postponement of capital goods purchases by individuals and businesses. The penetration rate for home and household appliances in France was initially much lower than abroad, and the housing stock was largely destroyed during the Second World War, while the population was growing rapidly. Also, productive equipment had to be renewed, as most dated back to the 1920s. As a result, demand for goods from households and businesses was extremely high during the Glorious Thirty, especially from 1958 onwards. For example, the proportion of household heads aged 40 owning their own home rose from 23% in 1955 to 48% in 1967, reflecting a considerable savings effort. In addition, high inflation virtually wiped out old debts, encouraging borrowers to take on new ones.

American cooperation and the Marshall Plan led to the modernization of the production apparatus and a ramping up of the French economy. With half of Europe expanding strongly with the support of the United States, French industrialists found many ideas for improving productivity in neighboring countries and through exchanges with their American interlocutors. French business managers perceived access to the Common Market as a positive step and prepared for the competition by rushing to equip and modernize their businesses. The investment effort during the Glorious Thirty was significantly higher than in the preceding and following periods. This is not specific to France, but a trend common to most industrialized countries.

During the Glorious Thirty, work was the central preoccupation of the French. This is demonstrated by the fact that, despite housing difficulties, geographic mobility was considerable compared with earlier periods. Of course, it remained low compared with the United States, whose population has always been exceptionally mobile. During the Glorious Thirty, many French people moved to a different region, often for professional reasons, to find better jobs in the same or a different sector of activity.

Until May 1968, the population was not clamoring for a reduction in working hours, which meant that the unions, which had pressed for shorter working hours at the end of the war, did not pursue this issue further with employers. In the post-war period, annual working hours were in fact at the same level as in 1929, as the introduction and extension of paid leave was offset by an increase in hours worked each week. In 1965, France was one of the countries with the highest working hours. Why was this? Was it patriotism? Was it confidence in the future? The desire to spend on the house and niceties of life after years of shortages and deprivation? Was it to maintain one's standing? To be flush with money to spend on the latest gadget? Was it because the high birth rate led to large families that had to be clothed and fed? Was it a belief in meritocracy? That recognition at work and promotions would reward personal qualities?

Conclusion

Work centrality in French society, the high birth rate, educational efforts, capital accumulation, and high overall demand do not entirely explain the economic growth. Moreover, there is no single predominant cause. Residual factors such as the better manpower allocation, improved internal organization, a better division of labor between businesses, technical progress, and economies of scale linked to constantly rising production volumes in a favorable international environment, all contributed to growth during the Glorious Thirty. Barring a major economic policy error, post-war growth was bound to be high. But without the unrelenting efforts of the French population, it would not have lasted three decades.

Chapter 5
Oil Shock, European Monetary System, and Creative Destruction

In 1973, the confluence of an internal shock and an external shock brought the Glorious Thirty to an end. The internal shock came from the international monetary system, specifically the US dollar, while the external shock came from the oil industry. The transmission mechanism between the two was that oil prices were denominated in US dollars, as they still are. The sharp fall in the price of the dollar in the foreign exchange market led to a substantial shortfall in income for oil-exporting countries.

The Pact with the Devil

Having earlier been appointed to the Privy Council of the Duchy of Weimar, Johann Wolfgang von Goethe [1749–1832] took on the War Commission in 1779, in addition to the Mines and Highways commissions, and in 1782 became Chancellor of the Exchequer. Goethe thus came to be in charge of the duchy's economy, finances, mines, highways, and waterways. His final work, *Faust II: Der Tragödie zweiter Teil in fünf Akten,*[1] opens with the pact between Mephistopheles and the Holy Roman Emperor of the German Nation for the creation of magic money *ex nihilo*, designed to solve all the cash flow problems of the country. This paper money is in fact more than a banknote; it is magical money that ultimately refers only to itself and, not being backed by gold, depends only on the infinite trust that men place in it. Mephistopheles issues paper money with as counterparty hypothetical riches and treasures hidden in 'deep earth,' which under Roman law were the Emperor's property. The magical money is in fact based on as-yet-undiscovered treasures:

"Faust:

'The wealth of treasure that solidifies,

That in your land, in deep earth lies,

[1] *Faust: the Second Part of the Tragedy.*

C. Peicuti, *A Monetary and Economic History of France since 1944*, Contributions to Economics, https://doi.org/10.1007/978-3-032-17596-0_5

Is all unused. In our boldest thought,
Such riches are only feebly caught:
Imagination, in its highest flight,
Strives to, but can't reach that height.'"

Magical money benefits from limitless confidence:

"Faust:
But grasping Spirits, worthy to look deeply,
Trust in things without limit, limitlessly."[2]

This creation takes place during a carnival, a celebration of the overthrow of the established order and its replacement by a new order, which magical money would later overthrow in its turn:

"The Steward (Entering hastily.):
Your Supreme Highness, I never thought
To announce such luck, the finest wrought,
As this is, for me the greatest blessing,
Which I've revealed in your presence:
For debt after debt I've accounted,
The usurer's claws now are blunted,
I'm free of Hell's pain, and then,
It can't be any brighter in Heaven.
The Commander in Chief (Follows hastily.):
Something's paid of what we owe,
The Army's all renewed their vow,
The Cavalry's fresh blood is up,
And girls and landlords can sup.
The Chancellor (Coming forward slowly.)
I'm happy enough to do so, in my old age. –
See and hear the scroll, heavy with destiny,
That's changed to happiness, our misery.
To whom it concerns, may you all know,
This paper's worth a thousand crowns, or so.
As a secure pledge, it will underwrite,
All buried treasure, our Emperor's right.
Now, as soon as the treasure's excavated,
It's taken care of, and well compensated.
The Emperor:
I smell a fraud, a monstrous imposture!
Who forged the Emperor's signature?

[2] Source: https://antilogicalism.com/wp-content/uploads/2017/07/faust.pdf.

Have they gone unpunished for their crime?
The Treasurer:
Remember! You yourself it was that signed:
Last night. You acted as great Pan
Here's how the Chancellor's speech began:
'Grant yourself this great festive pleasure,
The People's Good: a few strokes of the feather.'
You wrote it here, and while night ruled the land,
A thousand artists created another thousand,
So all might benefit from your good deed,
We stamped the whole series with your screed,
Tens, Thirties, Fifties, Hundreds, all are done.
You can't think how well the folk get on.
See your city once half-dead with decay,
Now all's alive, enjoying its new day!
Though your name's long filled the world with glee,
They've never gazed at it so happily.
The Emperor:
And my people value it as gold, you say?
The Court and Army treat it as real pay?
Then I must yield, though it's wonderful to me."[3]

It is significant that the emperor should represent the great Pan during the carnival. According to Greek mythology, Pan caused people to lose their minds through the collective panic fright (Greek: *panikon deima*, panikon meaning pertaining to Pan) he inspired. The modern economy is thus placed under the sign of fear. It generates fear, the fear of losing one's job, the fear of not having enough, the fear of not owning everything, the fear that even when surrounded by wealth something is missing. As Faust says: "To feel in the midst of this wealth, what we lack, is to undergo the cruellest of tortures."[4]

A visionary, Goethe described what was to happen a century and a half later. On August 15, 1971, President Richard Nixon [1913–1994] temporarily suspended the direct international convertibility of the dollar into gold, the gold reserves of the United States, which had represented 66% of world reserves at the end of the Second World War, having fallen to just 24% in 1971. As is often the case, what was presented as a temporary measure lasted, the withdrawal from Vietnam and the Watergate affair diverting attention from the monetary problem, allowing a regime based on freely floating exchange rates to take hold.

In 1972, when addressing a group of European Finance Ministers concerned about the fluctuations of the US dollar following the suspension of its convertibility into gold, John Bowden Connally (who served as Treasury Secretary during Richard

[3] Source: https://antilogicalism.com/wp-content/uploads/2017/07/faust.pdf.

[4] Source: https://antilogicalism.com/wp-content/uploads/2017/07/faust.pdf.

Nixon's presidency) said: "The dollar is our currency, but it's your problem." This does sum up rather well the new global economic order, unprecedented in the history of mankind over the last two millennia: the link has been severed between gold and money, which ultimately refers only to itself.

Meeting in Kingston, Jamaica, on January 7 and 8, 1976, the Interim Committee of the Board of Governors of the International Monetary Fund chaired by Willy De Clercq, the Minister of Finance of Belgium, and attended by the Finance Ministers of the member countries decided to adopt a monetary system of freely floating exchange rates. Gold ceased to have an official status within the IMF and in relations between its members.

Croesus, who ruled Lydia from 561 to 546 BC, has gone down in history for issuing the Croeseid, the first true gold coins with a standardized purity intended for general circulation, Richard Nixon for suspending the convertibility of the reference currency into gold. Thus ended gold's monetary era, replaced by the US dollar, which became "as good as gold," literally. However, in contrast to gold which is finite in nature, printing US dollars is not…

The First Oil Shock

The fluctuations and sharp devaluation of the dollar due to the suspension of its gold convertibility had a direct impact on oil prices, which were denominated in dollars. The Arab members of the Organisation of the Petroleum Exporting Countries (OPEC) used the Yom Kippur[5] War between Israel and its neighbors, which broke out on October 6, 1973, as a pretext to drive up oil prices, also taking advantage of the fact the United States could no longer play referee to drive down the price of oil, as the country's crude production had reached a peak.

The conflict ended officially when a ceasefire agreement, brokered by the United States and the Soviet Union and proposed by the UN Security Council, entered into force on October 25, 1973. The definitive Six-Point Agreement for the stabilization of the ceasefire was signed at Kilometer 101 on the Cairo-Suez road on November 11, 1973. This armed conflict, short as it was, had a major international consequence, triggering the 1973 oil shock. In solidarity, Arab members of OPEC imposed a total oil embargo against countries that had supported Israel at any point during the war. The embargo was accompanied by production cuts. By December 1973, production had been slashed by 25% compared with September. As a result, the price of oil surged from $3/bbl to $10/bbl in December 1973, bringing the Glorious Thirty to an end.

The report published by the Organisation for Economic Co-operation and Development (OECD) in December 1973 begins by taking stock: "The economic situation in the OECD countries is a very troubled one. Inflation is continuing at an extremely high rate and the current restrictions on the supply of oil threaten to check economic

[5] Yom Kippur, the Day of Atonement and the holiest day on the Jewish calendar.

growth in many countries and cause considerable dislocation of ordinary life. The sharp rise in oil prices by the producing nations will not only make anti-inflationary policies more difficult but will create awkward problems of adjustment of the balance of payments of a good many Member countries."[6]

The OECD considers that: "The total increase in prices might be of the order of 1 percent. Although this may seem small in relation to the prevailing rate of inflation, it comes at a time when earlier increases in commodity prices had initiated a wage/price spiral which will now prove that much more difficult to control."[7]

To deal with what it calls "the oil crisis," the OECD indicated that it is generally thought that most OECD countries could economize between 5 and 15% of their oil consumption. With regard to France, the OECD states: "But given the large share of oil in energy resources (approximately 65 percent) and the pattern of energy consumption, in which households account for only roughly 30 percent as against for industrial uses, the scope for savings in non-productive activities is somewhat limited."[8] In other words, France is expected to feel the full force of the oil crisis.

To check the fall in purchasing power caused by rising energy costs, the OECD recommended that its members stimulate the economy through budget deficits. As OPEC members buy the sovereign debt issued by oil-importing countries, this would allow petrodollars to be recycled. The OECD believed that countries such as Germany and Japan should become locomotives of growth for the global economy because they were running a current account surplus when the oil crisis erupted. The OECD therefore argued that these countries needed to do more than others to stimulate activity and pull other countries along in their wake.

Although not one of the locomotives identified by the OECD, France followed the OECD's recommendations, its Prime Minister Jacques Chirac embarking in 1975 on a Keynesian-style recovery with a FRF38.2 billion (€29.29 billion) plan to support growth. Part of the resources was earmarked for infrastructure, with FRF15 billion for major works, in particular the TGV high-speed rail line (a literal application of what had been dubbed the 'locomotive strategy' by its creators at the OECD). The plan also included measures to bolster purchasing power, with a FRF5 billion increase in social benefits, FRF18 billion in tax cuts and rises in the minimum wage of 8.4% in 1974, 6.6% in 1975, and a further 4.7% in 1976. By 1976, the country's GDP growth rate had recovered to 4.3%, its level in 1974, but at the cost of a substantial current account deficit and without addressing the unemployment problem, the number of unemployed climbing above the one million mark. It was at the end of the Glorious Thirty that the OECD began to describe unemployment as structural. This was borne out by the high levels of unemployment in the following decades.

[6] OECD, OECD Economic Outlook, Volume 1973 Issue 2, https://read.oecd-ilibrary.org/economics/oecd-economic-outlook-volume-1973-issue-2_eco_outlook-v1973-2-en#page6.

[7] OECD, OECD Economic Outlook, Volume 1973 Issue 2, https://read.oecd-ilibrary.org/economics/oecd-economic-outlook-volume-1973-issue-2_eco_outlook-v1973-2-en#page7.

[8] OECD, OECD Economic Outlook, Volume 1973 Issue 2, https://read.oecd-ilibrary.org/economics/oecd-economic-outlook-volume-1973-issue-2_eco_outlook-v1973-2-en#page77.

In 1958, the New Zealand economist Alban Phillips [1914–1975], whose work had focused on British data, highlighted a consistent inverse relationship between the unemployment level and the growth in nominal wages. Robert Lipsey [1926–2011], an economist at the National Bureau of Economic Research, then Paul Samuelson [1915–2009] and Robert Solow [1924–2023], two future Nobel Prize winners, interpreted this statistical relationship as offering a trade-off between the inflation rate (positively correlated to wage growth) and the unemployment rate. The implication is that an expansionary fiscal policy will reduce unemployment but risks driving up inflation, whereas a contractionary fiscal policy coupled with a monetary policy aimed at curbing inflation leads to an increase in unemployment.

After the first oil shock, inflation became a major concern for governments. Valéry Giscard d'Estaing, President of the French Republic from May 1974 to May 1981, was aware of the deleterious effect of inflation on the economy as a whole, but put less faith in the Phillips curve than his predecessor Georges Pompidou. Rightly so, the stagflation experienced in the 1970s demonstrating that higher unemployment did contain inflation by putting pressure on wages, but that the reverse was not always true.

Jean Serisé, a senior government official and advisor of Giscard d'Estaing, was a Keynesian. He interpreted inflation as being cost-push inflation, which prompted him to advise Giscard d'Estaing to adopt a very aggressive fiscal policy against companies that increased wages way more than desired by the government. The employers opposed this tax reform. Jacques Chirac, the then Prime Minister, proposed exempting small businesses. Little by little, the reform was unpicked, with taxation abandoned as a tool for fighting inflation in favor of monetary policy. The introduction of the European Monetary System (EMS) in 1978 reinforced this trend, with France aligning itself with Germany, which was already using monetary policy to stabilize prices. And so the Banque de France tightened monetary policy to combat inflation. The Minister for the Economy set as target that the money supply should grow at a slower rate than nominal GDP, which is why money supply growth was limited to 11% in 1979.

Fairly quickly, OECD members realized that the stimulus was not worth the effort, having cost more than it had brought in. In 1976, the OECD abandoned its so-called locomotive strategy and asked the commission chaired by Paul McCracken, Professor of Economics at the University of Michigan and Chairman of the Council of Economic Advisers to the President of the United States between 1969 and 1971, to look at policies for a resumption of non-inflationary growth. The other members of the International Committee of Economists (or McCracken Group) included Raymond Barre (replaced once he became a minister by Robert Marjolin), Guido Carli, former Governor of the Bank of Italy and former Governor of the World Bank, Robin Matthews, Master of Clare College, Cambridge, Assar Lindbeck, Director of the Institute for International Economic Studies and Professor at Stockholm University, and Ryutaro Komiya, Professor at the University of Tokyo.

As explained by Paul McCracken: "Amidst the sense of unease about economic developments in the OECD countries, there is also emerging a new mood of realism about the management of economic policy. The old conventional wisdom that, by accepting a higher rate of inflation, we could, on a sustained basis, have more rapid gains in employment and real incomes has not worked out. There is now a disposition to take a harder look at what needs to be done. This new mood of realism offers hope that the route to a more enduring expansion of employment, real incomes and import markets can yet be found."[9]

The Commission chaired by Paul McCracken identified the causes of the prevailing economic and social imbalances, of which inflation was one of the main symptoms, as the US budget deficit due to the Vietnam War and the explosion of wages in Europe. As solutions, it recommended making the labor market more flexible to combat unemployment and improving the efficiency of public programs, ensuring that, in each country, government, trade unions, and employers reach a consensus on the need to increase profits and investment. In other words, the Commission recalled how the market economy works, in which "the profits of today are the investments of tomorrow and the investments of tomorrow make the employment of the day after tomorrow."[10] There is no such thing as wealth created ex nihilo. Only labor efficiency (as measured by its productivity) and competition can guarantee the prosperity of a nation.

Raymond Barre, who replaced Jacques Chirac at the end of August 1976, adopted an austerity policy aimed at returning to a balanced budget. He was Prime Minister until May 1981, the year François Mitterrand was elected, when his successor Pierre Mauroy [1928–2013]reverted to Keynesian-style stimulus before switching back to an austerity policy in 1983. For France's economic policy, it was a roller-coaster ride that put businesses to the test and that the country's European partners struggled to comprehend.

To balance public finances, Raymond Barre increased taxes. The total tax burden rose from 33.6% in 1974 to 39.4% in 1980 (by way of comparison, in 2022, the total tax burden was 45.4%[11]). Of this increase, 4.4 percentage points were due to contributions to balance the social security accounts. Raymond Barre felt that the intergenerational transfer (from the current generation to future generations) of part of the cost of the healthcare system in the form of debt could not be countenanced and that the aging of the population should be anticipated by having pension schemes generate surpluses. His efforts were undone by the next government, which lowered the retirement age from 65 to 60 from April 1, 1983.

[9] OECD, The OECD Observer no 87, July 1977, *What has Gone Wrong with Economic Performance? An Analysis by the McCracken Group and Recommendations for the Future*, p. 7.

[10] Schmidt Helmut, speech delivered on November 3, 1974.

[11] INSEE, *Poids des prélèvements obligatoires, Données annuelles de 1959 à 2022*, source: https://www.insee.fr/fr/statistiques/2381412#graphique-figure1.

The Consequences of the Management of the First Oil Shock

While the monetary shock would prove beneficial in the medium to long term for the United States, which consolidated its global hegemony, and for the European Union, laying the foundations for the single currency, the oil shock failed to encourage Europe or the United States to innovate and turn to alternative sources of energy. Economies remained dependent on oil, the share of oil in energy resources reaching 23% in 2023 in the case of France. What would be the state of the planet had we set about changing the paradigm of the Industrial Revolution?

Climate Disruption

Everything happens as Goethe metaphorically predicted in *Faust II: Der Tragödie zweiter Teil in fünf Akten*[12]: nature is ultimately destroyed by human activity.

Goethe saw the dawn of modern times, bringing with it the Industrial Revolution, characterized by incessant activity. In his final work, Goethe replaced "In the beginning was the verb" by "In the beginning was the act."

In *Faust II*, Mephistopheles and Faust thus decide together to put fire to the haven of the old world, which is like a thorn in Faust's eye:

> "Faust
> 'My realm's laid out there, endlessly,
> But, at my back, this vexes so,
> Proclaiming, with its jealous sound:
> My great estate is less than fine,
> The old hut, all the trees around,
> The crumbling chapel, are not mine.
> And even if I wished to rest there,
> A strange shadow makes me shudder,
> It's a thorn in my eye, and deeper:
> Oh! Would I were somewhere other!
> What used to please my eyes, below,
> Has vanished with the centuries.'"[13]
>
> On the charred remains of his great estate, Faust plans to build a belvedere "to gaze into the infinite."

In *Faust II*, Goethe describes the destruction of Creation, of what has been bequeathed to us and, subsequently, the emergence of a new world that radically turns its back on Creation. This obsession with the infinite, with the limitless, is the

[12] *Faust: the Second Part of the Tragedy.*

[13] Source: https://antilogicalism.com/wp-content/uploads/2017/07/faust.pdf.

hallmark of our century. In the face of climate change, it is time for us to modify our paradigm and start thinking about our lives and the world differently.

In terms of the energy transition, which is vital to tackle climate change, more and more oil and coal are being consumed even now. When the day comes when there truly is a determination to change consumption patterns, it may be too late. Humanity is behaving like the mouse in Franz Kafka's short story, *Kleine Fabel*[14]:

> "'Alas,' said the mouse, 'the whole world is growing smaller every day. At the beginning it was so big that I was afraid, I kept running and running, and I was glad when I saw walls far away to the right and left, but these long walls have narrowed so quickly that I am in the last chamber already, and there in the corner stands the trap that I must run into.'
>
> 'You only need to change your direction,' said the cat, and ate it up."[15]

The Birth of the European Monetary System

One of the positive consequences of the oil crisis was the birth of the European Monetary System (EMS). This breakthrough came at the initiative of Germany, which proposed to its partners the creation of a European system of fixed exchange rates. Meeting in Basel on April 10, 1972, the Committee of Governors of the Central Banks of the Member States of the European Economic Community decided to create a mechanism called the Snake in the Tunnel to narrow exchange rate fluctuations. This mechanism did not deliver the expected stability, proving unsustainable. The French franc left then rejoined the Snake, before leaving for good in 1976. On July 6, 1978, in Bremen, the European Monetary System (EMS) was created under the German Presidency of the EEC to establish "closer monetary co-operation." The monetary agreement stipulated that the differences in value between European currencies would be limited to 2.5% and that if this were overstepped, the effort to be made would be shared between the stronger currency and the weaker currency. It also stipulated that each currency would be expressed in terms of a reference unit. At the suggestion of President Giscard d'Estaing, this new European monetary unit, in which the value of the national currencies would be expressed, was given the name ECU (European Currency Unit).

The "closer monetary co-operation" was not without wider implications given the monetary trilemma (or impossible trinity), a concept developed by Robert Mundell in 1963, whereby a country or monetary union cannot have, at the same time, the free movement of capital, fixed exchange rates, and an independent monetary policy.[16] The EMS is based on a system of fixed exchange rates requiring countries to pursue a common monetary policy, whose objective is to have a low level of inflation.

---

[14] *A Little Fable.*

[15] Source: East of the Web, http://www.eastoftheweb.com/cgi-bin/version_printable.pl?story_id=LittFabl.shtml.

[16] Mundell, Robert (1963), *Capital Mobility and Stabilization Policy under Fixed and Flexible Exchange Rates*, Canadian Journal of Economics and Political Science, Vol. 29,475–85.

Point 5 of the agreement emphasized that: "A system of closer monetary cooperation will only be successful if participating countries pursue policies conducive to greater stability at home and abroad; this applies to deficit and surplus countries alike."[17] France was among the countries running a negative balance of payments, stoking inflation.

The entry into force of the European Monetary System in March 1979 meant the establishment of a liberal-monetarist framework that France sidestepped to some extent by not aligning its fiscal policy with the cycle and by accumulating public spending financed on credit. If there is indeed continuity in France's economic policy, it is unfortunately this one.

The Creation of the G7

Another positive consequence of the oil crisis was the creation of the G7. To find solutions to address the effects of the oil crisis and for industrialized democracies to project a united front in the face of the pressures exerted by OPEC countries, Giscard d'Estaing wanted to host a summit of the "principal economic powers," which he considered to be five in number: the United States, Britain, France, Germany, and Japan. As Henry Kissinger [1923–2023] explained in *Years of Renewal*,[18] it was President Ford, with the backing of British Prime Minister Harold Wilson, who managed to persuade Giscard d'Estaing to include Italy from the outset in 1975, and Canada in 1976. The President of the European Commission has also attended since first invited in 1977. When it was established in 1975 at the unofficial forum held in Rambouillet, it was agreed that an annual meeting would be organized in turn by the member countries.

The report of the commission chaired by Paul McCracken was on the agenda of the G7 meeting in Bonn in 1978, prompting a policy shift by countries with the adoption of a liberal and monetarist stance. By way of example, this led Jimmy Carter [1924-], who was at the White House from 1977 to 1981, to liberalize air transport and nominate Paul Volcker [1927–2019] at the head of the Federal Reserve to combat inflation. During his tenure from 1979 to 1987, the Chairman of the Federal Reserve pursued a restrictive monetary policy. In France, Prime Minister Raymond Barre also set himself the goal of reducing inflation. As in the United States, over the medium term, this decline came not from balancing public finances, which was one of Raymond Barre's topmost objectives, but from greater competition as a result of European integration.

[17] The European Council, Bremen 6–7 July 1978, *The European Council Progresses Towards Monetary Union*, European Community Background Information No. 14/1978.

[18] Kissinger, Henry (2020), *Years of Renewal*, Touchstone/Simon & Schuster.

The Second Oil Shock and Creative Destruction

Just as the economy was picking up after the first oil shock, and demand for oil—then the main source of energy for almost all production in industrialized countries—was rising, a second oil shock rocked the economies of oil-importing countries. It was the political upheaval in Iran that caused this shock. First it was the Iranian revolution, which began with riots on September 8, 1978, and ended with the flight of the Shah on January 16, 1979. It was followed by the Iran-Iraq war, which broke out on September 22, 1980.

The European Monetary System came into being in March 1979. Its existence (credibility) was conditioned on there being low inflation. Yet, oil prices increased by a factor of 2.7 between June 1978 and the end of 1981. This fueled an inflationary spiral: in France, prices rose by 13.6% in 1980, coming after increases of 10.8% in 1979 and 9.1% in 1978. To combat inflation, the Banque de France tightened its monetary policy, raising the 3-month rate to 12.2% in 1979, when this rate reached 9% in Germany.

While industrialized countries enjoyed a situation close to full employment during the Glorious Thirty, unemployment reared its head between 1968 and 1972. In the five years to 1980, the unemployment rate rose from 3.8% in 1976 to 4.3% in 1977, 4.5% in 1978, 5% in 1979, and 5.3% in 1980. Raymond Barre was the first post-war minister who had to find solutions to address youth unemployment. He launched his first employment pact (*pacte pour l'emploi*) in 1977, aimed at young people aged between 16 and 25. The pacts in 1978 and 1979 were aimed not only at young people but also at single mothers. The pacts emphasized apprenticeships, proposed exemptions from social security contributions, and introduced six-month fixed-term employment contracts (*contrats à durée determinée—CDD*).

This economic policy failed to realize that unemployment was due to the deterioration in the profitability of French companies since 1969. On July 21, 1969, Neil Armstrong and Buzz Aldrin, two of the three astronauts on the Apollo 11 mission, made history by becoming the first men to land and walk on the Moon. This marked the beginning of a technological revolution that would be a new source of growth.

Significantly, the term 'Silicon Valley' was coined in 1971 in a series of articles by American journalist Donald C. Hoefler [1922–1986] in reference to the high concentration of semiconductor manufacturers in an area corresponding roughly to the geographical area of the Santa Clara Valley. Silicon is the material of choice for electronic chips that would be the basis of the economy of the future. But instead of supporting the electronics industry and the development of alternative sources of energy, Raymond Barre supported the steel industry, even to the point of having the State buy into the capital of steel companies. Coal and textile were two other industries that floundered.

Faced with this change of economic paradigm, and having experienced, for the first time since the Glorious Thirty, an erosion in their purchasing power due to imported inflation and an inexorable rise in unemployment that left them bewildered, the French electorate voted for the Socialist candidate François Mitterrand.

Part II
Maastricht or No Maastricht?

Dirigisme reached its zenith with the election of François Mitterrand. Between 1981 and 1983, 240 thousand jobs were created in the public sector. Thirty-nine French banks and five major industrial groups were nationalized by the Law of February 11, 1982. Realizing the limits of dirigisme and wishing to avoid following in the footsteps of the British Labour government, forced to go cap in hand to the International Monetary Fund (IMF) in 1976, François Mitterrand did an about-turn just before France faced the prospect of crashing into the wall of dirigisme. He realized the impossibility and absurdity of his initial political project. To preserve his legacy, the French President headed for Maastricht and opened up France to the market economy by integrating it into the single market. The Ordinance of December 1, 1986, on the freedom of pricing and competition chipped away at French dirigisme and represented a major step towards greater competition. European integration did the rest. Inflation disappeared as dirigisme was unpicked. The transition to the euro put price stability on a firmer footing.

Churchill's wish for a strong Europe based on the Franco-German partnership came about. The Iron Curtain he had denounced in 1946 came crashing down. To symbolize the new European harmony, the Ninth Symphony, composed in 1823 by Ludwig van Beethoven to set to music the *Ode to Joy*, a poem written in 1785 by Friedrich von Schiller, became the official anthem of the European Union in 1985. There are no words to this anthem. It uses the universal language of music to evoke the ideals of freedom, peace, and solidarity embodied by Europe.

Chapter 6
The 1981 Election of François Mitterrand and the Radical Reversal of Economic Policy

"Mitterrand is adored today, but he was once the most reviled man in France. So there may be hope yet for many of us."
Laurent Fabius, 2011

President François Mitterrand (1916–1996) was elected on May 10, 1981, having campaigned on a four-part manifesto, *110 propositions pour la France*.[1] The second part, with its evocative title "Employment: social growth through control of the economy. The economic recovery," dealt with the economy. It contains proposals 14 to 43 under the following headings: "Economic recovery," "New growth," "Social justice," "Energy," "Agriculture," and "Fisheries."

The recovery envisaged by François Mitterrand is Keynesian with Soviet structural overtones: "Social growth will be based on the dynamism of the public sector".[2] The section entitled "Economic recovery" provides for a program of major public works, the construction of social housing and public facilities, and the creation of 150 thousand jobs in the public and social services sectors and 60 thousand jobs in the associative and local government sectors. In addition, "research will be stimulated for it to reach 2.5% of GNP by 1985."[3]

As regards public sector employment, the government's economic policy would go beyond the manifesto pledge, as between 1981 and 1983 some 240 thousand additional jobs were created in the public sector.

For energy, what is proposed is a break with France's nuclear tradition in favor of coal: "The country's energy supply will be diversified. The nuclear program will be limited to the power stations currently under construction until the country is properly informed and can vote in a referendum. Credits for new energies or new technologies for exploiting traditional energies (coal) will be considerably increased."[4]

[1] https://www.mitterrand.org/110-propositions-pour-la-france.html.

[2] Proposition 19, https://www.mitterrand.org/110-propositions-pour-la-france.html.

[3] Proposition 17, https://www.mitterrand.org/110-propositions-pour-la-france.html.

[4] Proposition 38, https://www.mitterrand.org/110-propositions-pour-la-france.html.

C. Peicuti, *A Monetary and Economic History of France since 1944*, Contributions to Economics, https://doi.org/10.1007/978-3-032-17596-0_6

Based on the propositions contained in the manifesto, Pierre Mauroy, the incoming Prime Minister, pursued a three-pronged economic policy aimed at: stimulating the economy to improve income redistribution; combating unemployment through a reduction in legal working hours and an increase in public sector employment; and expanding State control through nationalizations.

The 1982 budget called for a 27.5% increase in spending compared with Raymond Barre's last budget, even though the then Prime Minister had already warned that "France is living beyond its means." To finance the stimulus measures aimed at improving income redistribution, a wealth tax (*impôt sur les grandes fortunes—IGF*) was created, which would be repealed, but brought back later in a modified form as a solidarity tax on wealth (*impôt de solidarité sur la fortune—ISF*), then scaled down to a real estate tax (*impôt sur le patrimoine immobilier—IPI*). When introduced, the wealth tax concerned 1% of households. It was one of the propositions contained in the election manifesto: "A wealth tax, based on a progressive scale, will be introduced. Inheritance tax will be reformed to relieve the tax levied on modest inheritances (lineal or not) and to overtax large inheritances."[5]

The tax hikes targeting the wealthiest raised FRF9 billion (€3.31 billion) in tax receipts, while FRF30 billion (€11.03 billion) was distributed to the most modest households through a 5.2% increase in the minimum wage and, above all, two increases in housing benefits (25% in July 1981, then 20% in December). Again, these measures featured in the propositions contained in the election manifesto: "Disablement benefits and minimum old-age pension benefits will be raised to two-thirds of average income. Family benefits will be increased by 50% in two stages. Unemployment benefits will be substantially increased."[6]

With regard to the second aspect of the government's economic policy, legal working hours were reduced from 40 to 39 h a week without any reduction in salary. This stopped short of the proposition in the manifesto: "Working hours will be gradually reduced to thirty-five hours after negotiations between the social partners. […] The fifth week of paid holidays will be generalized." When Pierre Mauroy meet Yvon Gataz, the Chairman of the National Council of French Employers (*Conseil national du patronat français*, the forerunner of the *Mouvement des entreprises de France*) on April 16, 1982, the Prime Minister gave assurances that the reduction in legal working hours would stop at 39 h. Two decades would pass before legal working hours were cut to 35 h a week, this measure coming into force on January 1, 2002.[7] On the other hand, the commitment to have a fifth week of paid holidays was honored. Also, the ordinance of March 25, 1982, lowered the retirement age from 65 to 60.

---

[5] Proposition 34, https://www.mitterrand.org/110-propositions-pour-la-france.html.

[6] Proposition 31, https://www.mitterrand.org/110-propositions-pour-la-france.html.

[7] *Loi no 98-461 du 13 juin 1998 d'orientation et d'incitation relative à la réduction du temps de travail*, https://www.legifrance.gouv.fr/jorf/id/JORFTEXT000000558109.

The four so-called Auroux laws[8] passed in 1982, named after Jean Auroux [1942-], the Minister for Labor from 1981 to 1982, amended one-third of the Labor Code, with the aim of promoting the social dialogue at the workplace. Many provisions remain in force to this day, notably:

"- The creation of the right for employees to express their views on their working conditions;

- The prohibition of any form of discrimination on the grounds of political opinion, trade union activity […];

- The introduction of a requirement to set aside a minimum amount (0.2% of gross payroll) for the functioning of the works council;

- The obligation each year to hold negotiations on pay, working hours and work organization;

- The creation of hygiene, safety and working conditions committees, replacing the hygiene and safety committee and the committee for the improvement of working conditions;

- The introduction of the right for the employee to withhold labor when there is a situation of serious and imminent danger."[9]

Despite these measures, unemployment continued to rise inexorably, from 7.4% the year François Mitterrand was elected to 8.1% in 1982, 8.3% in 1983 and 9.7% in 1984, going on to peak at 10.3% in 1985.

Concerning the third aspect of the government's economic policy, which is to expand State control through nationalizations, this is dealt with under the section entitled "New growth": "The public sector will be enlarged by the nationalization of the nine industrial groups further to the Common Program for Government and the Socialist Program, of the steel industry and the arms and space industries financed from public funds […]. The nationalization of insurance and credit institutions will be completed."[10] The Socialist Party's program was implemented through the nationalization of five major industrial groups and thirty-nine banks in the first year of François Mitterrand's presidency.

Nationalization of Five Major Industrial Groups

"Colin was one day minding his father's cows and not being in love, felt quite dull in his solitude. The gamekeeper emerging from the forest, addressed him, saying: "Ever since day break have I been chasing an old buck, which has twice escaped me, and has quite put me out of breath. He has just passed yonder."

---

[8] *Loi n° 82–689 du 4 août 1982 relative aux libertés des travailleurs dans l'entreprise, Loi n° 82–915 du 28 octobre 1982 relative au développement des institutions représentatives du personnel, Loi n° 82–597 du 13 novembre 1982 relative à la négociation collective et au règlement des conflits collectifs du travail, Loi n° 82–1097 du 23 décembre 1982 relative aux comités d'hygiène, de sécurité et des conditions de travail.*

[9] *Les lois Auroux font entrer la démocratie dans les entreprises*, source: https://www.gouvernement.fr/partage/12414-les-lois-auroux-font-entrer-la-democratie-dans-les-entreprises.

[10] Proposition 21, https://www.mitterrand.org/110-propositions-pour-la-france.html.

"If you are tired," said Colin, "you had better rest yourself, take care of the cows, and I will pursue your game. I'll answer for the buck."

"By Jove! An excellent idea! Here, take my gun and dog, and make sure of him." Colin willingly arms himself, calls Sultan, who though with regret, sets off with him for the forest. The dog beats the bushes, sniffs here and there, and suddenly makes a dead halt.

He has espied the buck. The impatient Colin fires immediately; misses the beast and wounds poor Sultan, who runs back to the meadow followed by the cow-herd. He finds the gamekeeper snoring. But what has become of the cows? They are all stolen. The wretched Colin, tearing his hair, runs distractedly over hill and dale, but finds nothing. Covered with shame, he returns at night to his father, without the cows, and tremblingly related the whole affair. The latter catching up a stout cudgel, teaches his son to be less aspiring; saying to him: "Every one to his trade; if you had adhered to yours, I should now have my cows, and you would be minus a sound thrashing."

The Cow-Heard and the Gamekeeper[11]

Jean-Pierre Claris de Florian [1755–1794]

The Law of February 11, 1982, on nationalization (*Loi n° 82–155 du 11 février 1982 de nationalisation*) stated, in its very first article, that are nationalized the following five companies: Compagnie de Saint-Gobain, Compagnie générale d'électricité, Pechiney-Ugine-Kuhlmann, Rhône-Poulenc S.A., and Thomson-Brandt. These were at the head of major industrial groups, national champions whose century-long histories gave no reason to believe they would one day pass under complete state control.

Nationalization of Compagnie De Saint-Gobain

The letters patent (*lettres patentes*) signed by Louis XIV in 1665 granted a monopoly for mirror glass to Manufacture royale des glaces à miroirs (it would later change its name to Compagnie de Saint-Gobain), initially for a period of twenty years, renewable. The term manufacture came from the Medieval Latin manufactura "a making by hand," and by the early seventeenth century had the sense of making goods or wares of any kind, the production of articles of use from raw or prepared materials by hand labor or machinery. At the time, mirrors were objects of great luxury. The aim was to protect French mirrors from the formidable competition of Venice, notably the manufactories on the island of Murano, which was home to the best glassmakers in Europe.

The venture was started with capital provided by Nicolas Dunoyer, the receiver of taxes for Orléans, and his partners. Colbert commissioned several Venetian glassworkers he had enticed to Paris to work for the manufactory, but as they were unwilling to impart the secrets of glassmaking, they were let go in March 1667. A gentleman glassmaker, Richard Lucas de Nehou, contributed his Tourlaville glassworks in Normandy to the Manufacture, along with his expertise in producing quality

[11] Bussey, G. Moir (1842), *Fables, Original and Selected by the Most Esteemed European and Oriental Authors*, London: Willoughby and Co.

glass mirrors in the Venetian style. In 1684, three hundred and fifty-seven of these mirrors were installed in the famous Hall of Mirrors of the Palace of Versailles facing the windows. Their large size and impressive number were a testament to France's prosperity and know-how, which now rivaled that of Venice. France's perseverance was rewarded in the long run: more than three centuries later, the Hall of Mirrors is better known worldwide than the glassmakers of the island of Murano.

After being rescued from bankruptcy by Genevan bankers who took control in 1702, the Manufacture enjoyed a period of prosperity until the French Revolution. The abolition of privileges on the night of August 4, 1789, marked the de jure end of the Manufacture's monopoly of glass mirrors. To add to its woes, the Paris and Saint-Gobain workshops were caught up in the revolutionary turmoil. The Manufacture ceased trading in 1797. It was not revived until the Consulate in 1801. But competition meant that the Manufacture lost market share and needed to become more competitive. It gave itself the means by becoming a limited company in 1830, changing its name to Compagnie de Saint-Gobain. In 1858, Saint-Gobain expanded by merging with Saint-Quirin and setting up operations in Germany. The now international group accounted for approximately a quarter of European glass mirror production.

The free-trade treaty signed by Napoleon III with Britain heaped pressure on France's chemical industry, as it was lagging far behind its British competitors in terms of technology. This led Saint-Gobain to acquire Perret-Olivier, the leading French producer of sulfuric acid, in 1872 to develop its chemical business.

The two world wars were hugely challenging for Saint-Gobain, as it had operations in both France and Germany. In 1918, Saint-Gobain benefited from the transfer of American hollow glass technologies and began to manufacture the furnaces and machinery needed by French makers of bottles, jars, tableware, and domestic glassware. From 1952, research and development became the group's DNA.

The first oil shock in 1973 dealt a rude blow to Saint-Gobain's activities. To preserve its leadership, the company diversified into information technology, public works, water treatment and distribution, and optical glass with Essilor. It consolidated its traditional activities in fiberglass and fiber cement piping with the acquisition of American company CertainTeed Corporation.

Whereas Louis XIV did not conceive of Manufacture royale des glaces à miroirs being under state control, President François Mitterrand nationalized it in 1982. This company, which had successfully reinvented itself over the centuries in the face of social and industrial change and war, suddenly found itself under state ownership. From now on, it was the French state that would direct its strategy, the view being that civil servants knew better than entrepreneurs what course to chart. France's economic policy was supposed to reduce unemployment and bring prosperity.

After the Left lost the 1986 general elections, François Mitterrand nominated Jacques Chirac as Prime Minister, for what would be the first cohabitation of the Fifth Republic. Fortunately, Compagnie Saint-Gobain did not remain nationalized for forty-five years like the companies in the communist countries of Central and Eastern Europe, but was privatized four years after being nationalized by the center-right coalition led by Jacques Chirac, in the first year of the cohabitation. Its listing on the Paris stock exchange on December 24, 1986, was a resounding success: 10%

of the shares were subscribed by Saint-Gobain employees and 20% by individuals, most first-time investors.

Founded in 1898, Compagnie Générale d'Électricité (CGE) was one of France's five largest companies in terms of consolidated assets at the beginning of the 1980s. As regards technical accomplishments, it ranked third in the world for the construction of high-power turbo alternators, and second for line insulators and telecommunications and energy cables. Thanks to the Alsthom group, which it absorbed in 1970, it ranked third in the world in railway construction and was also the main contractor for France's high-speed train (*Train à Grande Vitesse—TGV*). A world leader in time-division communications, CGE had also established itself as one of the few designers of global telecommunications networks.[12] In 1976, Alsthom absorbed Chantiers de l'Atlantique, which became Alsthom-Atlantique. In 1981, the TGV broke the world rail speed record at 380 km/h. In 1982, CGE was nationalized. The Socialist government thought it could run it better than entrepreneurs. Like Compagnie Saint-Gobain, CGE was returned to the private sector, in 1987.

Pechiney-Ugine-Kuhlmann (aluminum, electrometallurgy, packaging, chemicals, and nuclear fuel), Rhône-Poulenc (chemicals and pharmaceuticals), and Thomson-Brandt (electronics) experienced the same fate, nationalized in 1982. Brandt was not privatized until 1992, Rhône-Poulenc one year later in 1993, followed by Pechiney in 1995, and Thomson in 1996. Saint-Gobain was under state control for four years but managed to restore its fortunes. In 2022, it had sales of €51.2 billion, 168 thousand employees and a presence in 75 countries. Committed to achieving carbon neutrality by 2050, it has addressed the energy transition just as it has many other challenges in its long history. The three other major industrial groups that spent a decade or more under state ownership did not enjoy the same fortunes. They would fall by the wayside, disappearing forever from the French corporate landscape.

Nationalization of Thirty-Nine French Banks

Article 12 of the Law of February 11, 1982, on nationalization (*Loi n° 82–155 du 11 février 1982 de nationalisation*) provided for the nationalization of banks "whose registered office is located in France, if on January 2, 1981, they held one billion francs[13] or more in sight deposits or liquid or short-term investments in franxcs and foreign currencies in the name of residents [...].

However, were not nationalized:

> "- Banks with the status of a real estate leasing company for commerce and industry (*Société immobilière pour le commerce et l'industrie - SICOMI*) [...] or with the status of a discount house (*maison de réescompte*) [...];

---

[12] Rapp, Jule (1985), *Aux origines de la Compagnie générale d'électricité, Bulletin d'histoire de l'électricité*, https://www.persee.fr/doc/helec_0758-7171_1985_num_6_1_949.

[13] Given the monetary erosion due to inflation, the purchasing power of FRF1 billion in 1982 is equivalent to €367,617,102.71 in 2022.

- Banks in which the majority of the share capital is owned directly or indirectly by natural persons not resident in France or by legal persons not having their registered office in France."[14]

Banks are to be nationalized in accordance with the provision of Article 13, which states that: "The nationalization of the banks [...] shall be accomplished by the transfer to the State of full ownership of the shares representing their capital [...]. However, legal entities already belonging to the public sector or which are destined to belong to the public sector as a result of this law may retain the shares they hold in the banks [...]. These shares may only be transferred to other legal entities also belonging to the public sector; they may also be exchanged within one year of the publication of this law for bonds [...]."

Thirty-nine French banks are nationalized:

"a) Listed banks:

Banque de Bretagne;

Banque Hervet;

Banque Rothschild;

Banque Scalbert Dupont;

Banque Worms.

Crédit commercial de France;

Crédit du Nord;

Crédit industriel d'Alsace et de Lorraine (CIAL);

Crédit industriel de l'Ouest;

Crédit industriel de Normandie;

Crédit industriel et commercial (CIC);

Société bordelaise de crédit industriel et commercial;

Société centrale de banque;

Société générale alsacienne de banque (Sogénal);

Société lyonnaise de dépôts et de crédit industriel;

Société marseillaise de crédit;

Société nancéienne de crédit industriel et Varin-Bernier;

Société séquanaise de banque;

b) Unlisted banks:

Banque centrale des coopératives et des mutuelles;

Banque Chaix;

Banque corporative du bâtiment et des travaux publics;

Banque de l'Indochine et de Suez;

Banque de l'union européenne;

Banque de La Hénin;

Banque de Paris et des Pays-Bas;

---

[14] *Loi n° 82–155 du 11 février 1982 de nationalisation*, source: https://www.legifrance.gouv.fr/loda/id/JORFTEXT000000503960.

Banque fédérative du crédit mutuel;

Banque française de crédit coopératif;

Banque industrielle et mobilière privée (BIMP);

Banque Laydernier;

Banque Odier Bungener Courvoisier;

Banque parisienne de crédit au commerce et à l'industrie;

Banque régionale de l'Ain;

Banque régionale de l'Ouest;

Banque Tarneaud;

Banque Vernes et commerciale de Paris;

Crédit chimique;

Monod-Française de banque;

Sofinco La Hénin;

Union de banques à Paris.

III - Shares in Banque Nationale de Paris, Crédit Lyonnais and Société Générale held by shareholders other than the State or public sector entities on the date of publication of this law are also transferred to the State under the conditions set out in Article 13."[15]

Nationalization of Banque Rothschild

"A Jew under Petain, a pariah under Mitterrand — for me it's enough. To rebuild on ruins twice in a lifetime is too much."[16]

Guy de Rothschild [1909–2007]

As the threshold for nationalization was very low, most of the small banks in France passed under State control. These included the famous Banque Rothschild. As Guy de Rothschild explained in 1981: "During a discussion of the bank nationalizations, a minister recently stated that the case of the Rothschilds differed from the rest in that they were a symbol."[17] By way of compensation, the Rothschilds received FRF500 million (equivalent of around €205 million). Guy de Rothschild made the following points in 1981: "Clearly, the nationalization of the banks isn't specifically aimed at the Rothschilds. We may not be the target, but we've been hit—as in a shooting accident, caused by those to whom the French have for a period carelessly entrusted guns. To those who are thinking, "But you're decently compensated," I reply (is it for me to say this): "Money isn't everything. Besides, we've never been for sale."[18]

[15] *Loi n° 82–155 du 11 février 1982 de nationalisation*, https://www.legifrance.gouv.fr/loda/id/JORFTEXT000000503960.

[16] Rothschild, Guy de (1985), *Whims of Fortune: The Memoirs of Guy de Rothschild*, New York: Random House.

[17] Ibid.

[18] Ibid.

When he stepped down as the Chairman of the Supervisory Board of Rothschild & Co in September 2022, replaced by his son Alexandre [1980-], David Rothschild [1942-], the son of Guy de Rothschild, shed light on the chain of events some four decades earlier: "I had been warned of the nationalization not by the President of the Republic, but by Jacques Attali, his adviser at the time. So it came as no surprise. I have since learned that the threshold for nationalization was lowered compared with the initial plan to ensure that the small Rothschild bank fell within the scope of the law! Nevertheless, we were stunned by a decision that seemed to us to be completely absurd. But there was no escaping this decision."[19]

David de Rothschild also refers to the fact that after the nationalization of their bank, the Rothschild name became the property of the French state! As David de Rothschild explained, four years later "when the government changed in 1986, we took advantage of Jacques Chirac's arrival at Matignon to speed things up by regaining the right to use the Rothschild name."[20]

On October 30, 1981, Guy de Rothschild penned an opinion piece in the French daily Le Monde in which he explained: "The Socialist-Communist coalition decreed the nationalization of the banks, thereby evicting them from the family building on rue Laffitte that had been theirs for 170 years—the very street which had become synonymous with the Rothschilds themselves. At the same time, the family lost control of the other businesses it had traditionally managed, such as the mining group based on Pennaroya and Le Nickel, and those inherited from the private holdings of the former railroad companies."[21]

In this opinion piece, the author recalled all the people with whom he had collaborated in giving a new life to an institution, "developing a bank and an industrial complex worthy of the French economy",[22] in the process creating one thousand two hundred jobs. He also dwelled on the Rothschilds' intense philanthropic activities: "Some people appreciate the number of hospitals, schools, homes for children, for convalescents, for the elderly, the number of dispensaries, sanatoriums, public buildings of all kinds that the Rothschild family has built, furnished, and maintained; the number of works of art it has donated to museums; the number of artists, scientists, doctors, writers the family has been fortunate in being able to aid at one time or another."[23] He contrasted France's treatment with the quite different experience of the family's British branch at the time: "In England, their proven professional ability, their celebrity, are recognized and encouraged as a national financial asset."[24]

He concluded the opinion piece thus:

---

[19] Drif, Anne, Barré, Nicolas, and Counis, Alexandre (2022), *La nationalisation de la banque m'a contraint à repartir d'une page blanche*, Les Echos, https://www.lesechos.fr/finance-marches/banque-assurances/la-nationalisation-de-la-banque-ma-contraint-a-repartir-dune-page-blanche-1787995.

[20] Ibid.

[21] Rothschild, Guy de (1985), *Whims of Fortune: the Memoirs of Guy de Rothschild*, New York: Random House.

[22] Ibid.

[23] Ibid.

[24] Ibid.

> "The French Rothschilds made the mistake of believing that they could develop and grow with their time and in their own country; they were wrong.
>
> The Socialist radicals have excluded them from the economic community. Of the House of Rothschild there will remain a few odd pieces, perhaps nothing.
>
> A Jew under Petain, a pariah under Mitterrand — for me it's enough. To rebuild on ruins twice in a lifetime is too much.
>
> Forced into retirement, I have decided to strike."[25]

Unlike most other small banks that ceased to exist independently after the nationalizations, Banque Rothschild rose from the ashes. When asked about the strategy he pursued, David de Rothschild answered: "I've spent my life looking for people more competent than me."[26]

Even though French banks were privatized years later, by weeding out the small banks François Mitterrand contributed to the consolidation of the banking sector, creating banks that, being too big to fail, could afford to take reckless risks because the government would be obliged to rescue them. The French banking landscape and systemic risk would never be the same again.

---

[25] Ibid.

[26] Vidal, François, Barré, Nicolas, and Maujeanm Guillaume (2018), *Rothschild, les secrets d'une renaissance*, https://www.lesechos.fr/2018/04/rothschild-les-secrets-dune-renaissance-988893.

Chapter 7
Rigor, the New Paradigm

With dirigisme driving France to rack and ruin, an about-turn became a pressing financial necessity. This would see France return to the market economy. No longer would it tread in the footsteps of the USSR, but reintegrate the European fold.

The Limits of Mitterrand's Mass Consumption-Driven Stimulus

On October 7, 1981, the French Government submitted to its partners and to the Community institutions proposals in a document entitled *Mémorandum français sur la relance européenne,*[1] hoping to convince Germany and Britain to follow the same economic policy as France, therefore increase wages and public spending. At the G7 Summit held from June 4 to June 6, 1982, France once again urged its partners to join it in pursuing an expansionary fiscal policy. But with the locomotive strategy advocated by the OECD not having delivered non-inflationary growth without a negative trade balance, France did not get its way and there would be no repeat.

The economic revitalization wanted by François Mitterrand, driven by what he termed, symbolically, "popular consumption," stimulated household demand at a time when France was already running a trade deficit equivalent to 2.1% of GDP. It would deteriorate to 4% of GDP in 1982. The monetary tightening by Paul Volcker having led to a strong dollar, France's energy bill climbed to FRF131.5 billion (€48.34 billion) in 1981 and FRF130 billion (€47.79 billion) in 1982. It did subside to FRF121 billion (€44.48 billion) in 1983, but essentially because of

[1] *French Government memorandum on revitalization of the Community,* https://www.cvce.eu/en/obj/french_government_memorandum_on_revitalization_of_the_community_13_october_1981-en-a8377c45-380f-4679-8d17-62d42f4734d5.html.

C. Peicuti, *A Monetary and Economic History of France since 1944*, Contributions to Economics, https://doi.org/10.1007/978-3-032-17596-0_7

a massive destocking by companies (7 million tons, around FRF12 billion) at the public authorities' urging.[2]

On 9 June 1982, three days after the G7 Summit, François Mitterrand held a press conference during which he explained: 'Consumption alone is not enough. It can be dangerous. Inflationary factors are in play without any counterweights. Investment is there to complete a policy."[3] This came when inflation reached 13.4% in 1981 and would reach 11.8% in 1982, putting pressure on the European Monetary System. To offset this, François Mitterrand thought he could initially substitute public investment for private investment, in effect priming the pump for private investment to follow suit: "While private investment was not picking up, public sector companies were investing:

- 1979: FRF10 billion,
- 1980: FRF11.7 billion,
- 1981: FRF12.8 billion, thanks to the interim budget amendment,
- 1982: FRF16.3 billion,
- 1983: FRF24 billion, that is the target, because this is a priority."[4]

Like Giscard d'Estaing, François Mitterrand does not put much faith in the Phillips curve trade-off, which contends that economic policy must choose between unemployment and inflation: "There is one rule, ladies and gentlemen, which will relegate to the sidelines the eternal debate: should we give priority to inflation in the fight against inflation, or to freedom, or priority to the fight against unemployment? Nothing is more inflationary than an unemployed person, and if, to reduce unemployment, we have to control inflation, this means that these terms are inseparable; we cannot cure one of these evils without purporting to cure the other, and as we move, as is still our case, towards curbing the growth of unemployment, with a smaller number of unemployed, even if it is significant, for unemployment may be tending to stagnate, it is not yet diminishing. What then of the countries whose success I am told about, where every point of inflation is paid for by hundreds of thousands of new unemployed, as is the case in the United States of Amcrica, as is the case in West Germany?".[5]

And the French President concluded: "Well, this needs to take on a new dimension. In tackling inflation and unemployment, I say: not one against the other, but one with

[2] *La « facture» pétrolière de la France a diminué en 1983*, Le Monde, 11 February 1984, source: https://www.lemonde.fr/archives/article/1984/02/11/la-facture-petroliere-de-la-france-a-diminue-en-1983_3004964_1819218.html.

[3] *Press conference by François Mitterrand, President of the Republic, on the accomplishments of the government action (growth, solidarity, external relations), the economic situation, and government objectives, Paris, Palais de l'Elysée, 9 June 1982*, https://www.vie-publique.fr/discours/136237-conference-de-presse-de-m-francois-mitterrand-president-de-la-republique.

[4] Ibid.

[5] *Press conference by François Mitterrand, President of the Republic, on the accomplishments of the government action (growth, solidarity, external relations), the economic situation, and government objectives, Paris, Palais de l'Elysée, 9 June 1982*, https://www.vie-publique.fr/discours/136237-conference-de-presse-de-m-francois-mitterrand-president-de-la-republique.

the other. I say we will only respond to both through our creative capacity. We must be capable of creating new wealth and therefore of producing, and this government has given itself the means to invest, which was not available to its predecessors that turned to private investment, which did not respond any more than it did in neighboring countries. Public investment, I stress again, as the point needs to be driven home, will have a knock-on effect."[6]

Since the European Monetary System came into force in 1979, the Deutschmark had been worth 2.30 francs. The franc's depreciation began as soon as pollsters predicted the election of François Mitterrand. On May 10, 1981, the Deutschmark was worth 2.37 francs. The Banque de France raised interest rates by up to 20% to halt the currency's downturn. It also tried to stem the flight of capital by buying up francs to the tune of $5 billion between February 1 and May 10, 1981, and $3 billion between May 11 and 15, 1981. Though against devaluation, Mitterrand was forced to devalue the franc by 3% on October 4, 1981, driving up the exchange rate for the Deutschmark to 2.50 francs. Six days after the end of the G7 Summit in Versailles, the franc was devalued by a further 5.75%. Also, prices and wages were frozen until November, in what was the first of many austerity measures. But as soon as this restriction was lifted, prices and wages began to rise again. But devaluations and price freezes cannot go on indefinitely. Under Mitterrand, France forged ahead blindly with its economic policy but ran out of road. To remain in the European Monetary System, France had to show its commitment to a market economy resolute in combating inflation with a restrictive monetary policy and tightly controlled public spending.

The necessity for an economic about-turn—to avoid following in the footsteps of the Labour government in Britain, forced to go cap in hand to the IMF in 1976 - became obvious. François Mitterrand put a positive spin on this, bowing to the dictate of European integration. On 9 June 1982, he declared: "We want to make a success of Europe".[7] This implied alignment with the economic and monetary policies of other European countries. European integration was thus an excellent pretext for radically changing the course of an economic policy that was leading France straight into the wall. François Mitterrand remained committed to European integration until the end of his tenure in May 1995. Eager to go down in the annals of history, he realized that helping European construction was a safer legacy than advancing social progress on credit.

---

[6] Ibid.

[7] Ibid.

France's Return to a Market Economy

On March 23, 1983, on his return from the European Council in Brussels, François Mitterrand gave a televised address,[8] in which he stated that after "achieving more reforms and more social progress in a few months than France had seen in half a century," it was now necessary "to clinch victory on three fronts: unemployment, inflation and foreign trade." He explained the objectives he had set for the third Mauroy government: to curb inflation, restore foreign trade within two years, support businesses, boost savings, and contain the budget.

Pierre Mauroy used the term "rigor" to describe the new economic policy, going on to define this term as "austerity plus hope." The intention was to differentiate left-wing austerity from right-wing austerity, the latter being austerity without hope.

On March 25, 1983, appearing on the 8 o'clock news, and decidedly ill at ease, the Minister of the Economy Jacques Delors, who had been promoted to number two in the government in the March reshuffle from number seventeen in the order of precedence under the previous government, explained the austerity policy. France could not consume more than it produced, he said, adding that the government had decided on a number of measures, which would come into force immediately, and that while this effort on the part of the French population would be temporary, it had to be massive. As so it was: the tax take on households in the name of austerity amounted to FRF33 billion (€11.07 billion), which is more than they received in the name of the economy's revitalization. Spending was cut by FRF24 billion (€8.05 billion). These measures addressed the first objective, which was to reduce the budget deficit. Another objective is to slow credit. The growth in the money supply was capped at 9%. As a result, demand would fall by FRF60 billion (€20.12 billion).

Encouraging savings by choice, if not then by compulsion, was one of the government's priorities. The remuneration of home saving schemes (*plans d'épargne-logement—PEL*) was raised from 9 to 10%. Taxpayers whose 1981 tax assessment exceeded FRF5,000 (€1676.73) were required to subscribe to a government loan for an amount equivalent to 10% of their income tax liability, a measure which raised FRF14 billion for the French State.

Jacques Delors was behind the Law of January 4, 1984, on the activity and control of credit institutions (*Loi n° 84–46 du 24 janvier 1984 relative à l'activité et au contrôle des établissements de crédit*[9]), which gave birth to the universal bank by authorizing French deposit banks to engage in corporate and investment banking. This became the prevailing banking model, geared as much towards small depositors as towards businesses and financial markets. This law sounded the death knell for the doctrine formalized in 1904 by Henri Germain [1824–1905], the founder of Crédit Lyonnais in 1863. This doctrine called for a strict separation between commercial

[8] *Televised address given by François Mitterrand, President of the Republic,* Paris, Palais de l'Elysée, 23 March 1983, https://www.ina.fr/ina-eclaire-actu/video/cab83005000/allocution-du-president-de-la-republique-francois-mitterrand.

[9] *Loi du 4 janvier 1984 relative à l'activité et au contrôle des établissements de crédit*, source: https://www.legifrance.gouv.fr/download/securePrint?token=nTw5WM7iGS!Of7yC7ren&pagePdf=2.

banking and investment banking to prevent the short-term savings of household from being tied up and therefore unavailable in the event of banking panics. This doctrine was developed in response to the failure of Union Générale, which triggered a stock market crash in 1882 that plunged France into recession until the late 1880s. This bankruptcy was masterfully described by Émile Zola [1840–1902] in his novel *L'Argent*, published in 1891, even though the novel was set earlier during the Second Empire. This doctrine would inspire Roosevelt, leading to the passing in the Glass-Steagall Act of 1933, and de Gaulle, leading to the passing of the law of December 2, 1945 (*Loi n° 45–15 du 2 décembre 1945 relative à la nationalisation de la Banque de France et des grandes banques et à l'organisation du credit*).

It was under Jacques Delors that the indexation of wages to inflation was suspended in 1983.

Also, Jacques Delors urged his compatriots to buy French. The so-called *carnet de change*, used to record foreign currency purchases by individuals, was reintroduced. The foreign exchange allowance for an adult going on holiday abroad was reduced by FRF2,000 (€670) for 1983, a measure that was supposed to improve France's balance of payments by FRF5 billion (€1.68 billion).[10] But while one in four French people did give up travelling abroad following the introduction of the *carnet de change*, French people did not substitute holidays abroad with holidays in France. The tourism sector was hard hit. The government had underestimated the psychological effect, coming as it did with a "massive" tax effort. This measure, whose aim was purely economic, was reminiscent of the measures taken by the communist regimes in Central Europe to curtain the freedom of movement. This was yet another first in French history.

In reality, although François Mitterrand and his ministers often referred to this period as a *parenthèse*, meaning a temporary digression, in order to push through these exceptional tax takes, France reverted to a market economy, pursuing the same policy as Raymond Barre in 1979. There never would be a return to the economic policy pursued in 1981. If there was a temporary digression in the country's economic policy, it was from May 1981 to March 1983, not from 1983.

Pierre Mauroy stepped down as Prime Minister on July 17, 1984. He was replaced by Laurent Fabius [1946-], the Minister for Industry and Research from 1983 to 1984, whose economic policy would be inspired by market reality. During his tenure as Prime Minister from 1984 to 1986, Laurent Fabius sought to modernize France by boosting research, training, and investment. His view was that this modernization should be spearheaded by the private sector. In other words, the economy took a liberal turn in all but name, diametrically opposed to the policy in François Mitterrand's election manifesto.

Whereas one of the propositions in this manifesto, as indicated above, was to "increase considerably" credits in favor of new technologies for the exploitation of coal resources and that in 1981 it was all about "re-launching the coal industry,"

---

[10] Faujas, Alain, *La suppresion du carnet de change à contrecoeur*, source: https://www.lemonde.fr/archives/article/1983/06/18/la-suppression-du-carnet-de-change-a-contrec-ur_3076877_1819218.html.

Laurent Fabius announced that the objective now was to reduce the production of Charbonnages de France (CdF) from 18 million tons in 1983 to 11 million tons, while reducing the 57 thousand headcount by 6 thousand each year. The steel industry, which had passed under State control, was directed to reduce the headcount by 25 thousand out of a total of 90 thousand over three years.

On January 6, 1985, the then Minister of the Economy and Finance Jacques Delors was appointed at the head of the European Commission and would serve as its President for the next decade.[11] He was replaced by Pierre Bérégovoy [1925–1993] on July 19, 1984. Before taking up this office, Pierre Bérégovoy served as the Minister of Social Affairs and National Solidarity. The social security and unemployment schemes presented a surplus of FRF20 billion (€6.71 billion) in 1980 on account of Raymond Barre's sound management but were in deficit to the tune of just shy of FRF5 billion (€1.68 billion) the very next year. There was a structural deterioration in this deficit in 1982 when the retirement age was lowered from 65 to 60 years. To balance the accounts, Pierre Bérégovoy increased contributions and introduced a solidarity contribution for unemployment to be paid by civil servants, as a result of which these schemes were practically in balance at the end of 1983.[12]

As regards financial markets, Pierre Bérégovoy worked to transform Paris into a major financial center capable of rivaling London, New York, and Chicago. On February 20, 1986, a financial futures market (*Marché à terme des instruments financiers—MATIF*) was established. One of its aims was to make French government bonds (*obligations assimilables du Trésor—OAT*) sufficiently liquid for the Treasury to have access to new categories of investors seeking hedging instruments. The MATIF also enabled banks to trade these long-term securities directly. Success was immediate, with 2 thousand contracts exchanged during the maiden session. The threshold of one million contracts was passed in November of the same year. The listing of derivatives put Paris on par with other major financial markets.

As mentioned above, François Mitterrand set two objectives in 1983, which were to overcome unemployment and inflation. Inflation declined from 13.6% in 1980 to 13.4% in 1981, then to 11.8% in 1982 and 9.6% in 1983. Under the Fabius government, inflation fell from 7.4% in 1984 to 5.8% in 1985. Disinflation would gather momentum, inflation slowing spectacularly in 1986, falling to 2.7%, where it remained for the next three years. The European Monetary System was saved. As indicated above, unemployment acts as a dampener on inflation. Given the rise in unemployment over the same period, one may well wonder whether it was not a major cause of this disinflation. Despite the creation of public sector jobs and the lowering of the retirement age from 65 to 60, unemployment rose from 5.3% in 1980 to 7.4% in 1981, then to 8.1% in 1982 and 8.3% in 1983. The rise continued under the

[11] Jacques Delors stepped down as President of the European Commission the same year as François Mitterrand stepped down as President of the French Republic.

[12] Statement by Pierre Bérégovoy, Minister of Social Affairs and National Solidarity, concerning the cash situation of the Social Security Funds in 1983, Paris, 5 January 1984, https://www.vie-publique.fr/discours/213078-declaration-de-m-pierre-beregovoy-ministre-des-affaires-sociales-et-de.

Fabius government, to 9.7% in 1984 and 10.3% in 1985. This was the unemployment rate that would be inherited by the next government led by Jacques Chirac.

The Socialist government also left a profuse legacy in terms of jurisprudence dealing with early retirement, vocational integration, and community services. It provided incentives to extend studies by increasing the number of baccalaureate holders and so reduce the number of registered unemployed. In 1984, for example, the Minister of Education Jean-Pierre Chevènement reported that "250 thousand candidates passed the exam, i.e., 2.2% more than in 1983, representing a success rate of 63%." In the same press release, the Minister "emphasized" the improvement in results for the technical baccalaureate, "with a success rate of 59.7%, higher than in 1983 (57.9%)."[13]

The European Council of June 25 to 26, 1984, was a grandiose affair, held at the Château de Fontainebleau. The very first conclusion of the session was that: "Expenditure policy is ultimately the essential means of resolving the question of budgetary imbalances."[14] Was it a nod to France?

While Germany did not waiver from its view that the federal budget should be balanced, François Mitterrand directed Laurent Fabius to ensure that the budget deficit did not exceed 3% of GDP. In 1985, the Prime Minister achieved the feat of reducing the deficit to just under 3%, and in 1986, the deficit reached 3.2%.

In exchange for the appointment of Jacques Delors as President of the European Commission, a post that was to have gone to a German, François Mitterrand agreed to Britain's longstanding demand, as put by the country's Prime Minister from 1979 to 1990 Margaret Thatcher [1925–2013]: "What we are asking is for a very large amount of our own money back."[15] The arrangement adopted was "for 1984, a lump sum of ECU1,000 million is fixed," recalculated every year thereafter. Of course, there is also an economic justification for this rebate on both the expenditure and receipts sides. Regarding the former, customs duties collected by Britain were paid into the European budget, when the country was the biggest exporter to the United States. On the other hand, since the value added generated by the agricultural sector relative to GDP is three times less than in France,[16] Britain benefited little from the Common Agricultural Policy (CAP), which accounts for the bulk of expenditure in the Community budget. This arrangement was facilitated by Helmut Kohl [1930–2017], the German Chancellor for sixteen years, from 1982 to 1998.

Three months later, on September 22, 1984, the partnership between France and Germany as the basis for the re-creation of the European family called for by Winston

---

[13] Bolloch, Serge, *La proportion de reçus est en baisse dans les séries générales et en hausse dans les séries techniques*, Le Monde, 11 August 1984, source: https://www.lemonde.fr/archives/article/1984/08/11/la-proportion-de-recus-est-en-baisse-dans-les-series-generales-et-en-hausse-dans-les-series-techniques_3009007_1819218.html.

[14] The European Council, Fontainebleau, 25–26 June 1984, Conclusions, source: https://aei.pitt.edu/1448/1/Fountainebleau_june_1994.pdf.

[15] Margaret Thatcher, Press Conference after Dublin European Council, November 30, 1979, sometimes misquoted as "We want our money back".

[16] Agriculture, forestry, and fishing, value added (% of GDP), World Bank, https://data.worldbank.org/indicator/NV.AGR.TOTL.ZS.

Churchill in his speech of September 19, 1946[17] was sealed at the Verdun ceremony. The photo of Mitterrand and Kohl hand in hand in front of the Douaumont ossuary seventy years after the start of the Great War has remained in Europe's collective memory. This was a powerful image that made history. François Mitterrand was still a politician who was determined to go down in history. Thirty years on, one wonders whether this type of politician still exists in Europe. Right up to the end, François Mitterrand was a politician determined to go into the annals of history. Forty years on, does Europe still have politicians like that?

The policy of austerity pursued by the government paid off as early as 1986 when the current account was once again in balance, while inflation had been lowered to 2.7%, and the unemployment rate to 8.6%.

Thanks to the sound management of public finances under Raymond Barre, France's debt-to-GDP ratio reached 20.83% in 1980. Although the GDP ratio was 'only' 33.3% when the government swung from left to right in 1986, the break with the market economy in the first three years of Mitterand's presidency, and the economic policy's roller-coaster ride over five years had complex economic and financial consequences that would prove damaging over the medium to long term. The nationalizations and then the privatizations came at a huge cost to the French taxpayer. This shuffling of the deck had nothing to do with economics but with the political will of the moment. Intervening brutally and artificially in the conduct of several major companies by nationalizing them upset the natural course of business and market equilibriums, triggering chain reactions. At the end of 1994, shortly before François Mitterrand stepped down as President on May 17, 1995, the debt-to-GDP ratio had risen to 49.89%.

---

[17] See . Chapter 2

Chapter 8
Towards Maastricht?

No democratic country forcibly nationalized so many financial and nonfinancial corporations in the 1980s. How would these banks and firms have fared without this Soviet-style interlude, which interrupted their natural development in a market economy? Nationalizations and then re-privatizations are not without consequences. Small French banks disappeared, making way for too-big-to-fail banks that the French taxpayers would have to rescue, whatever the cost. As for firms that passed under State control, some never recovered. The French taxpayer is still footing the bill for these two Soviet-inspired years.

The opposition won the 1986 general elections. Jacques Chirac [1932–2019] moved into Hôtel Matignon and would serve as Prime Minister until May 1988, while François Mitterrand stayed on at the Élysée Palace. France would gradually abandon State dirigisme as it participated in the European construction.

Jacques Chirac at Matignon and the Fight Against French State Dirigisme

In his General Policy Statement (*Déclaration de politique générale*) to the country's National Assembly on April 9, 1986, Jacques Chirac delivered a critical analysis of French state dirigisme:

> "For decades - some would even say centuries - the French temptation par excellence has been to succumb to State dirigisme. Whether it be the economy or education, culture or research, new technologies or environmental protection, it's always been the State that citizens have turned to for ideas and subsidies. In this way, little by little, an administered, even collectivized society was built, with power concentrated in the hands of experts trained in the management of large organizations. This system of government, which is at the same time a social model, is not without its qualities: it flatters our national taste for equality; it ensures the continuity and stability of the social body; it is perfectly reconciled with the need for security embodied in the welfare state.

C. Peicuti, *A Monetary and Economic History of France since 1944*, Contributions to Economics, https://doi.org/10.1007/978-3-032-17596-0_8

But it has two fatal defects: it's self-destructive, through being oversized; and above all, it threatens to erode individual freedoms."[1]

Jacques Chirac considers that the vote for the return of a right-wing government meant that:

"The French have understood the dangers of state dirigisme and no longer want it. In one of those paradoxes of which history has the secret, it is precisely at a time when socialization seemed triumphant that the need for personal autonomy, nurtured by rising levels of culture and education, is expressing itself most forcefully. [...] It's high time to turn our backs on closed ideologies, on systems designed to replace failing individual autonomy with some form of collective empowerment.

It is to the values that look to the future while harking back to the long lineage of Western humanism that we need to aspire. These values are freedom, creation, responsibility, and the dignity of the human being."[2]

That President François Mitterrand should be re-elected in 1988 with 54.02% of votes cast, compared with 51.76% in 1981, and after the Socialist Party lost the 1986 general elections, would show Jacques Chirac that the French had not really understood the dangers of dirigisme. Fortunately for France, Mitterrand in 1988 was not same as in 1981.

War is declared on state dirigisme by Jacques Chirac: "The French economy needs additional freedom if it is to regain its dynamism and create new jobs. Three freedoms fundamental to the smooth running of businesses will be rapidly guaranteed: freedom to set prices, freedom to trade with foreign countries without controls, and greater freedom in human resource management to eliminate obstacles hindering employment."[3]

The lifting of price controls was accomplished through an ordinance, which is examined in the next chapter. The greater freedom in human resource management led to the suspension of the requirement for the administrative approval of redundancies by Philippe Seguin [1943–2010], the Social Affairs Minister from 1986 to 1988, this being pushed through at the request of Jacques Chirac (a measure that, paradoxically, had been introduced by him in 1975). The liberalization of the labor market would go no further.

The attack on state dirigisme continued with the announcement of privatizations: "The list of companies that may be denationalized over the next five years will be clearly set out. It will include all companies in the competitive sector, whatever—it goes without saying - the date of their nationalization."[4]

Privatizations were carried out under the authority of Edouard Balladur [1929-], who was number two in the order of precedence as the Minister of the Economy, Finance, and Privatization from 1986 to 1988. The reference to the date of their

[1] *Déclaration de politique générale de M. Jacques Chirac, Premier ministre, sur le programme du gouvernement*, à l'Assemblée nationale le 9 avril 1986, source: https://www.vie-publique.fr/discours/130093-declaration-de-politique-generale-de-m-jacques-chirac-premier-ministre.

[2] Ibid.

[3] Ibid.

[4] Ibid.

nationalization was no slip of the pen, for the privatization program would concern companies such as Société Générale and Havas, nationalized in 1945, as well as those nationalized in 1981, such as Saint-Gobain mentioned above. The television channel TF1, which had always been state-owned, would also be privatized. As a result of these privatizations, employment in the public sector would be cut by half a million.

There was to be no let-up in the fight against inflation, a consequence French state dirigisme:

> "Policy choices for the economic recovery are clear: on the one hand, major equilibria must be established, to consolidate the results achieved in the fight against inflation; to this end, monetary policy will be rigorous, there will be significant curbs in public spending and deficits and the policy of wage de-indexation will continue."[5]

Jacques Chirac defined "the twin objectives of the government's economic and social policy: fiscal consolidation and economic liberalization." But added: "Let's not lose sight of what's essential: the people."[6]

In the fashion of his predecessors, who never shied away even from a roller-coaster ride, Jacque Chirac's tenure kicked off with a competitive devaluation, though contrary to the spirit of the European Monetary System:

> "First and foremost, we had to wipe clean the slate of the past and draw the consequences of the ground lost by France to some of its European partners, especially Germany, since 1983. French products have been suffering from a lack of competitiveness that penalized our businesses, while interest rates could not be cut sufficiently. This is the reasoning behind last Sunday's parity readjustment within the framework of the European Monetary System. Its purpose was to establish the true value of our currency, once appearances have been dispelled. With a return to a sound situation, the French economy can now be put on a sound footing for a fresh start."[7]

To the great dismay of France's European partners, on April 6, 1986, the franc was devalued by 3%, even though the country's external accounts were in balance and it had pledged in 1983 not to devalue again. The result was not what had been hoped for: initially, the devaluation drove up the cost of imports, but without stimulating exports, leading to a foreign trade deficit. It was only in the second phase that lower export prices, by making exports more competitive, contributed to an increase in their volume and, consequently, to a rebalancing of the external accounts. As a result, France's external balance swung into the red in 1987 and would remain there until 1992.

It was not just that there was a trade deficit. There was also a government deficit that reached 3.2% of GDP in 1986, 2% in 1987, and 2.6% in 1988. The reason for this was the massive reduction in tax receipts due to the abolition of the wealth tax on January 1, 1987, compounded by a tax cut on the income of the most modest households, intended to make the handout to the rich palatable. A tax policy not unlike

[5] Ibid.
[6] Ibid.
[7] Ibid.

the one President Macron would pursue thirty years later, with the same results in terms of deepening the deficit.

The Single European Act

The enlargement of the then European Community took place in successive waves: in 1973, Denmark, Ireland, and the United Kingdom joined, followed in 1981 by Greece and in 1986 by Spain and Portugal. When it came to competition within the European Community, it was not a level playing field. Some countries put up barriers to entry against products from other European countries. Roy Jenkins [1920–2003], the only British president of the European Commission, played his part in bringing about fair competition.

Before serving as President of the European Commission from January 1977 to January 1981, Lord Jenkins of Hillhead was Chancellor of the Exchequer from 1967 to 1970. As Home Secretary from 1965 to 1967 and again from 1974 to 1976, Jenkins advanced individual freedoms for what he called "a civilized society," overseeing measures such as the effective abolition of capital punishment and theater censorship, the partial decriminalization of homosexuality, the relaxation of divorce law, the liberalization of abortion law, and the suspension of birching to punish violent breaches of prison discipline.

It is hardly surprising that the Single European Act should have been a British initiative originally, as Britain has historically been ahead of other European countries in advocating free competition.

On the other hand, what is surprising from a British politician is that from the onset Roy Jenkins was an ardent defender of the European Monetary system. On November 6, 1978, Roy Jenkins, as the President of the European Commission, gave a speech to the Belgian Royal Society for Political Economy (*Société royale d'économie politique de Belgique*) on the key events in the development of European monctary affairs, welcoming the recent establishment of the European Monetary System:

> "I am convinced that we can construct a monetary system which avoids failures of the past. For I believe we have at long last recognised the real fragility that exists both in the international monetary system and in our internal Community arrangements. There is never a perfect moment to launch any new scheme. The arguments for procrastination are always persuasive."[8]

The President of the European Commission felt that the time was ripe:

> "Nevertheless the arguments to move now on 1st January are, to my mind, overwhelming. The rhythm of inflation is declining in all our countries, while the convergence of our economies is greater than in the past. [...] The imminent enlargement of the Community forces us to act now and not delay. [...]

[8] Conference given by Roy Jenkins in Brussels, November 6, 1978, http://www.cvce.eu/obj/conference_given_by_roy_jenkins_bruxelles_6_november_1978-en-dff92cfb-0bb3-42ad-8300-ac39691d88ba.html.

As Shakespeare made Caesar say:
'There is a tide in the affairs of men
Which, taken at the flood, leads on to fortune.'
I believe that tide is now at the flood. We must not miss it."[9]

The European Monetary System came into force on March 13, 1979. For Roy Jenkins, it was a means of preventing competitive devaluations, but Jacques Chirac went ahead regardless, for no reason and without any positive outcomes for the French economy.

Nevertheless, the Ordinance of December 1, 1986, on the freedom of pricing and competition (*Ordonnance n°86–1243 du 1 décembre 1986 relative a la liberte des prix et de la concurrence*[10]) chipped away at French dirigisme and represented a major step towards greater competition. Only the single book price mechanism adopted in 1981 remained on the statute book. Other price controls established in 1914 or by the Front Populaire were abolished. It has to be said that these controls had been totally ineffective in the fight against inflation. Inflation in France was higher than in the United States or the Federal Republic of Germany. Prices in 1986 were 1,500 times their level in 1914! Indirectly, the State still controlled prices set by public companies, but plans were to privatize a large proportion of these companies. The ordinance created a national competition authority (*Conseil de la Concurrence*, which would change its name to *Autorité de la Concurrence* in 2008), an independent body serving competitiveness and the consumer, tasked with regulating competition in France.

It was some time in the making, but the Single European Act was finally adopted on February 28, 1986, under the presidency of Jacques Delors, and came into force on July 1, 1987. It marked the transition to a more collaborative legislative process, later known as the cooperation and assent procedures. Once the Single European Act (SEA) entered into force, the title 'European Parliament' (which the Assembly had used since 1962) was made official.

Article 13 of the Single European Act is one of the pillars of the European Union as we know it, and it reads: "The internal market shall comprise an area without internal frontiers in which the free movement of goods, persons, services and capital is ensured in accordance with the provisions of this Treaty."[11]

[9] Ibid.

[10] https://www.legifrance.gouv.fr/download/securePrint?token=aU2B7R9bBOO40xU$ceXn&pagePdf=9

[11] Single European Act, https://eur-lex.europa.eu/legal-content/EN/TXT/PDF/?uri=CELEX:11986U/TXT.

Louvre Accord

Paul Volcker [1927–2019] was Chairman of the Federal Reserve from August 1979 to August 1987. Immediately upon taking office, he tightened US monetary policy to combat inflation, which led to a sharp rise in the value of the dollar. The US currency climbed 44% against other leading currencies between 1979 and 1984. With prices no longer competitive and a strong dollar, there was a deterioration in the US trade balance, leading to a record deficit of $122 billion in 1985.

The G5 Summit held at New York's Plaza Hotel on September 22, 1985, bringing together the finance ministers and central bank governors of the United States, France, Germany, Japan, and Great Britain, was aimed at reversing the upward trend having led to the overvaluation of the US dollar. As part of the Plaza Accord, the G5 agreed to an "orderly appreciation of the main non-dollar currencies against the dollar"[12] through market interventions, selling US dollars in exchange for other currencies on the foreign exchange market. The United States agreed to reduce the fiscal deficit, while Germany and Japan pledged to implement policies with the explicit intention of stimulating domestic demand.

The Plaza Accord is held up as a high-water mark for coordinated interventions in the foreign exchange market, something that would be anathema nowadays. Even when G7 countries expressed concerns about "currency manipulation" as they did in 2013, they specifically agreed to refrain from unilateral foreign exchange interventions in a "ministers' agreement that we could call an "anti-Plaza" accord."[13]

In the two years from 1985 to 1987, the US dollar lost 40% of its value. After the exchange rate pulled back, the trade balance swung around and the US Congress refrained from erecting protectionist trade barriers. The dollar's depreciation did, however, propel the Deutschmark and Japanese yen on high. This prompted France to host a new meeting at the Ministry of the Economy and Finances, which at the time was located in the Louvre, rue de Rivoli. Under the Louvre Accord signed on February 22, 1987, G6 Finance Ministers and Central Bank Governors agreed to "cooperate closely to foster stability of exchange rates around current levels",[14] with the US dollar then trading at 1.9 to the Deutschmark and at 145 to the Japanese yen. For the switch to a system of flexible fixed exchange rates, Germany impressed on the United States the need to run a balanced budget and curb inflation. Paul Volcker fully supported the Louvre Accord, but American investors, fearing a rise in long rates, demanded higher and higher long rates from the moment the accord was signed, even though they already towered at 7% at the time.

---

[12] Announcement of the Ministers of Finance and Central Bank Governors of France, Germany, Japan, the United Kingdom, and the United States (Plaza Accord), September 22, 1985, http://www.g8.utoronto.ca/finance/fm850922.htm.

[13] Frankel, Jeffrey (2015), *The Plaza Accord, 30 years later*, National Bureau of Economic Research, Working Paper 21813, source: http://www.nber.org/papers/w21813.

[14] Statement of the G6 Finance Ministers and Central Bank Governors (Louvre Accord), Paris, France, February 22, 1987, http://www.g8.utoronto.ca/finance/fm870222.htm.

Not long after, Ronald Reagan [1911–2004], who served as the 40th President of the United States from 1981 to 1989, decided on a change of strategy. In August 1987, he nominated Alan Greenspan [1926-] at the head of the Federal Reserve. In contrast to his predecessor, Alan Greenspan doubted the pain of balancing the budget was worth the benefit and was prepared to go to any lengths not to have to raise interest rates. The Louvre Accord ended up being kicked into the long grass. The rise in US interest rates culminated in the stock market crash of October 19, 1987, which came to be known as Black Monday.

As Chairman of the Federal Reserve, Alan Greenspan stood out for his unwillingness to fight speculative bubbles, since doing so would have meant raising interest rates. He presided over the birth of the dot-com and subprime bubbles without taking the slightest action. Yet among its five general functions, the Federal Reserve "promotes the stability of the financial system and seeks to minimize and contain systemic risks."[15] To avoid taking action, Greenspan coined formulas that have gone down in history, such as what he termed the markets' "irrational exuberance."[16]

One might ask when precisely it dawned on the Federal Reserve that the dot-com bubble was forming and why it failed to respond.

The answer to the first part of the question can probably be found in the speech, *The Challenge of Central Banking in a Democratic Society,* given by Alan Greenspan in Washington on December 5, 1996, on the occasion of the annual dinner of the American Enterprise Institute for Public Policy Research: "Clearly, sustained low inflation implies less uncertainty about the future, and lower risk premiums imply higher prices of stocks and other earning assets. We can see that in the inverse relationship exhibited by price/earnings ratios and the rate of inflation in the past. But how do we know when irrational exuberance has unduly escalated asset values, which then become subject to unexpected and prolonged contractions as they have in Japan over the past decade? And how do we factor that assessment into monetary policy? We as central bankers need not be concerned if a collapsing financial asset bubble does not threaten to impair the real economy, its production, jobs, and price stability. Indeed, the sharp stock market break of 1987 had few negative consequences for the economy. But we should not underestimate or become complacent about the complexity of the interactions of asset markets and the economy."[17]

Alan Greenspan's reference to an eventual asset bubble triggered a knee-jerk reaction by the markets: the next day, the New York, Sydney, Hong Kong, Tokyo, and London stock exchanges fell by around 2%. But the rate hike widely expected by investors did not occur, nor were there further comments of the same ilk. The stock market continued to rise steadily over the next four years. On January 14, 2000, the Dow Jones set a record high of 11,722.98 points. In five years, it had tripled in value, while the Nasdaq was up sixfold. And then the inevitable happened: the bubble burst.

---

[15] Source: https://www.federalreserve.gov/aboutthefed.htm.

[16] Remarks by Chairman Alan Greenspan at the Annual Dinner and Francis Boyer Lecture of The American Enterprise Institute for Public Policy Research, Washington, D.C., December 5, 1996, source: http://www.federalreserve.gov/boarddocs/speeches/19961205.htm.

[17] Ibid.

Even so, Alan Greenspan stayed on as Chairman until January 2006.

With the United States reverting to an accommodating fiscal and monetary policy, this prompted Germany, which took over the presidency of the European Community in January 1988, to propose the creation of a monetary union and a European central bank, proof that every cloud has a silver lining.

Chapter 9
Towards the Euro

In 1988, during its ninth presidency of the European Council, Germany championed the idea of a European Central Bank modeled on the Bundesbank, and of a single currency, as early as the inaugural address to the European Parliament by Hans-Dietrich Genscher [1927–2016], who served as Foreign Minister of the Federal Republic of Germany from 1974 to 1982 under Chancellor Helmut Schmidt. The governors of the central banks of the European Community formed the Committee for the Study of Economic and Monetary Union, tasked with examining and proposing concrete stages leading to European economic and monetary union. To this end, EMS Member States would have to remove foreign exchange controls, establish independent central banks, and have structurally balanced public finances.

Édouard Balladur, the Minister for the Economy, Finance, and Privatization, tended to have reservations about a common European monetary policy, even though implicitly required by virtue of the European Monetary System. To Germany's demand to balance public finances, Édouard Balladur countered by accusing Germany of being a source of imbalance, also because of the current account surplus generated by the country's savings. This fit of pique would recur from time to time in the discourse of French politicians. As for Édouard Balladur, his tenure ended with the May 1988 elections.

The Birth of the Euro

François Mitterrand, Michel Rocard [1930–2016], France's Prime Minister from May 1988 to May 1991, and Pierre Bérégovoy [1925–1993], the country's Minister of the Economy, Finance, and Budget from May 1988 to April 1992, then its Prime Minister until March 1993, pressed on with European integration. This time, no reverting by Mitterrand to the agenda at the start of his first presidency. His overarching objective henceforth was to bring about a European monetary union. Whereas

C. Peicuti, *A Monetary and Economic History of France since 1944*, Contributions to Economics, https://doi.org/10.1007/978-3-032-17596-0_9

in 1983 he introduced the carnet de change, on January 1, 1990, he abolished the exchange controls established in 1936 by Léon Blum.

During the joint conference held on June 2, 1988, in Evian following the meeting between the French President and German Chancellor Helmut Kohl, François Mitterrand had this to say about their discussion concerning a European central bank: "As you know this is an objective about which we are agreed, for having proposed it ourselves."[1] The euro was born.

On the other hand, the independence of the European Central Bank, a prerequisite for monetary union and self-evident for Germany, is repugnant to France, as it implies an automatic hike in key interest rates whenever inflation rears its head, and would force governments to limit deficits as they can no longer print money. And therein lays the rub. In this respect, during the Evian press conference, Mitterrand stated that France would: "Submit to its partners at the Summit of the Group of Seven, in reality, eight with the European Community, some proposals on the problem of indebtedness."[2]

In his General Policy Statement (*Déclaration de politique générale*) to the country's National Assembly on June 29, 1988, Prime Minister Michel Rocard stressed there were "1,646 days" left until January 1993 to prepare France for the single market: "That's tomorrow for all intents and purposes."[3]

He drew attention to the fact that women generally had difficulties making themselves heard in France:

> "Just consider the situation in which women have been placed by our country! Thanks to the work accomplished, in particular by Yvette Roudy, the urgency is no longer for legislative reforms. She pushed through those that were indispensable.
>
> But no law will ever abolish the fact that women, more than their husbands, worry every day about their children's future, that women, more than their husbands, suffer from cramped or poorly designed housing, and that women, more than men, are victims of delinquency. And do not be mistaken, I am talking about all women, not just the unemployed.
>
> Yet women remain excluded from what we call social dialogue. Where are the two million single, widowed or divorced female heads of household heard, listened to?"[4]

Yvette Roudy [1929-], whose work was recognized by Michel Rocard in his speech, is best known for the Law of July 13, 1984 on gender equality in the workplace (*Loi n° 83–635 du 13 juillet 1983 portant modification du code du travail et du code*

---

[1] Joint press conference by François Mitterrand, President of France, Helmut Kohl, Chancellor of Germany, in Evian on June 2, 1988, concerning the preparation of the European Council meeting in Hanover and the G7 Summit in Toronto, European construction, and the meeting between Ronald Reagan and Mikhail Gorbachev—source: https://www.vie-publique.fr/discours/139561-conference-de-presse-conjointe-de-m-francois-mitterrand-president-de-l.

[2] Joint press conference by François Mitterrand, President of France, Helmut Kohl, Chancellor of Germany, in Evian on June 2, 1988.

[3] *Déclaration de politique générale de M. Michel Rocard, Premier ministre, sur le programme du gouvernement* to the National Assembly on June 29, 1988, source: https://www.vie-publique.fr/discours/146230-declaration-de-politique-generale-de-m-michel-rocard-29061988.

[4] Ibid.

pénal en ce qui concerne l'égalité professionnelle entre les femmes et les hommes[5]). Hers has been a lifelong fight to impose parity in the public domain. As she explained: "As women represent over half the population, democracy imposes parity in the representation and administration of nations."[6]

In his General Policy Statement, Michel Rocard announced the creation of the minimum integration income (*Revenu Minimum d'Insertion—RMI*) funded by the wealth tax:

> "Hope also means giving those hardest hit, whom our society has allowed to be cast adrift, leaving them at risk of being marginalized, the right to a second chance. This is the profound meaning of the minimum integration income. [...]
>
> Oh, of course, the amount of aid will be insufficient in light of what would be desirable. But it will offer all those who receive it a new chance, a new hope. A chance to escape poverty. A chance to find one's place in the world of the others. That's why minimum integration income must be closely linked to efforts to support recipients along the path to integration."[7]

Michel Rocard explained: "The minimum integration income will be partly financed by the re-introduction of a wealth tax. Let there be no misunderstanding: the wealth tax is a solidarity contribution, not a revenge on the rich."[8]

Tax rates for this new version of the wealth tax rates were lower than under the previous version introduced in 1981 and abolished by Raymond Balladur and Jacques Chirac in 1986. The new wealth tax concerned 110 thousand taxpayers whose net wealth exceeded FRF4 million (€1,138,292). Tax rates were 0.5% for net assets between FRF4 million and FRF6.5 million, 0.7% between FRF6.5 million and FRF12.9 million, and 0.9% above that. A tax shield was introduced, capping the total tax take in respect of the income tax and wealth tax at 80% of income.

For public finances to be in balance structurally, the French government was, as usual, more inclined to raise taxes than cut spending. Michel Rocard created a new tax (*contribution sociale généralisée—CSG*) to finance social protection, which proved highly effective for while the rate was initially low it was applied to a broad base:

- Employment income (wages, bonuses, and various allowances, etc.);
- Replacement income (pension benefits, unemployment benefits, per diem sickness benefits, etc.);
- Property income (rents, life annuities, etc.);
- Investment income (income from securities, capital gains on real estate, etc.);

---

[5] *Loi n° 83–635 du 13 juillet 1983 portant modification du code du travail et du code pénal en ce qui concerne l'égalité professionnelle entre les femmes et les hommes*, source: https://www.legifrance.gouv.fr/jorf/id/JORFTEXT000000504474.

[6] Roudy, Yvette, *Les femmes sont une force*, Interview given to Delphine Gardey and Jacqueline Laufer, published in Travail, genre et sociétés 2002/1, vol. 7, pp. 5-38, source: https://www.cairn.info/revue-travail-genre-et-societes-2002-1-page-5.htm.

[7] *Déclaration de politique générale de M. Michel Rocard, Premier ministre, sur le programme du gouvernement* to the National Assembly on June 29, 1988, source: https://www.vie-publique.fr/discours/146230-declaration-de-politique-generale-de-m-michel-rocard-29061988.

[8] Ibid.

- Wagers by gamblers and their winnings.[9]

But this tax would gradually becoming confiscatory, its rate rising from 1.1% when it was first introduced to 9.2% in 2024.

Even so, far from balancing public finances, the policies pursued by the government led to a deterioration.

The Fall of the Berlin Wall

During the press conference in Evian, François Mitterrand mentioned the meeting between the President of the United States and the General Secretary of the Communist Party of the Soviet Union, saying: "In Moscow, talks on disarmament continued between the two countries, which have considerable nuclear arsenals and which, for the moment, are only discussing their own disarmament."[10] His view was that France, and Europe in general, had no business being at the negotiating table between the Americans and the Russians, but said that he would "probably" be meeting Gorbachev "soon."

Mikhaïl Gorbachev [1931–2022]—the General Secretary of the Communist Party of the Soviet Union from May 1985 to August 1991, Chairman of the Presidium of the Supreme Soviet from October 1988 to May 1989, Chairman of the Supreme Soviet from May 1989 to March 1990 and the only President of the Soviet Union until December 1991—had to manage the Chernobyl (or Chornobyl) disaster on April 26, 1986. This was starkly different to the accident at the Fukushima Daiichi nuclear power plant in 2011 in terms notably of their cause, the government's response, and health effects. News of the explosion at the Chernobyl nuclear power plant took a day to reach Gorbachev, such were dysfunctions of the state apparatus at the time. Shaken by this event, Gorbachev realized that the Eastern Bloc was not viable. He allowed the political and economic emancipation of the countries in what the Russians called Eastern Europe. This began with the peaceful fall of the Berlin Wall on the night of November 9, 1989. One by one, the Communist regimes of Central Europe fell like dominoes, with no reprisals from Russia. East Berliners were reunited with their other halves, Western Europe with Eastern Europe.

On September 12, 1990, on the occasion of the signing of the Two Plus Four Treaty (the two Germanys and the four Allied Powers signatories to the 1945 Potsdam Agreement), Hans-Dietrich Genscher expressed his delight at seeing Germany finally reunited and sovereign:

> "This is a historic moment for the whole of Europe and a happy one for the Germans. Together we have come a long way in a short time.

---

[9] *Qu'est-ce que la CSG ?*, https://www.vie-publique.fr/fiches/21973-quest-ce-que-la-csg-contribution-sociale-generalisee.

[10] Joint press conference by François Mitterrand, President of France, Helmut Kohl, Chancellor of Germany, in Evian on June 2, 1988.

> The goal we set ourselves in Ottawa has been achieved: the external aspects of German unification have been settled. Today we are signing the Treaty on the Final Settlement with Respect to Germany."[11]

Though Communism claimed far more victims than Nazism, there would be no equivalent of the Nuremberg trials for those having committed heinous crimes in Eastern Europe. Time was of the essence, lest Russia have a change of heart. The European Union's enlargement continued at a brisk pace, with Austria, Finland, and Sweden joining in 1995, Cyprus, the Czech Republic, Estonia, Hungary, Latvia, Lithuania, Malta, Poland, Slovakia, and Slovenia in 2004, Bulgaria and Romania in 2007, and Croatia in 2013.

This enlargement often saw countries having joined the European Union going on to join the North Atlantic Treaty Organization (NATO). In 1999, Hungary, Poland, and the Czech Republic were the first former Warsaw Pact members to join NATO. Bulgaria, Estonia, Latvia, Lithuania, Romania, Slovakia, and Slovenia became NATO members in 2004.

Following the Russian invasion of Ukraine in February 2022, Finland and Sweden submitted official letters of application to NATO on May 18. In April 2023, Finland became a NATO Ally.

[11] Statement by Foreign Minister Hans-Dietrich Genscher on the occasion of the signing of the Two Plus Four Treaty in Moscow, September 12, 1990, source: https://www.cvce.eu/en/obj/address_given_by_hans_dietrich_genscher_at_the_signing_of_the_two_plus_four_treaty_moscow_12_september_1990-en-e14baf8d-c613-4c0d-9816-8830a7f233e6.html.

Chapter 10
The Euro Settles in, France's Economy Undergoes a Modernization

Gender Parity from Olympe De Gouges to Édith Cresson

In France, the land of equality, it was not until April 21, 1944, that women won the right to vote and stand for election. It was not until May 15, 1991, that a woman was appointed Prime Minister. When will a woman ascend to the highest office in France? By contrast, the state of California gave women the right to vote as early as 1911, followed in 1912 by the states of Kansas, Oregon, and Arizona. On June 4, 1919, the Nineteenth Amendment was passed by both chambers of Congress with the requisite two-thirds majority, giving women the right to vote.

Under the Ancien Régime, widows possessing a fiefdom and mother abbesses were allowed to vote in the Estates General. On July 3, 1790, Nicolas de Condorcet [1743–1794], the great mathematician and philosopher of the Enlightenment, spoke out in favor of women's suffrage in an article that appeared in the *Journal de la société de 1789*.

In *Les droits de la femme. À la reine*, a pamphlet published in 1791, Olympe de Gouges asked:

> "Man, are you capable of being fair? A woman is asking: at least you will allow her that right. Tell me? What gave you the sovereign right to oppress my sex? Your strength? Your talents? Observe the creator in his wisdom, examine nature in all its grandeur for you seem to wish to get closer to it, and give me, if you dare, a pattern for this tyrannical power."
>
> And she goes on:
>
> "Reconsider animals, consult the elements, study plants, finally, cast an eye over all the variations of all living organisms; yield to the evidence that I have given you: search, excavate and discover, if you can, sexual characteristics in the workings of nature: everywhere you will find them intermingled, everywhere cooperating harmoniously within this immortal masterpiece."[1]

[1] Gouges, Olympe (de) (1791), *Les droits de la femme. À la Reine*, source: https://gallica.bnf.fr/ark:/12148/bpt6k64848397/f5.item.

C. Peicuti, *A Monetary and Economic History of France since 1944*, Contributions to Economics, https://doi.org/10.1007/978-3-032-17596-0_10

In this pamphlet, one section entitled *Déclaration des droits de la femme et de la citoyenne* deals with the rights of a woman as such and as a citizen, Article 10 stating that: "None must be disquieted for their opinions however fundamental: woman is entitled to mount the scaffold; she must be equally entitled to mount the rostrum so long as her manifestos do not disturb the public order according to the law."[2] In 1793, aged forty-five, her only right was to be taken to the scaffold. In France, women would have to wait almost a century and a half before being entitled to "mount the rostrum."

France was one of the last European countries to grant women the right to vote, after Finland, Norway, Denmark, Poland, Germany, Austria, Estonia, Hungary, Latvia, Lithuania, Luxembourg, the Netherlands, Sweden, the then Czech Republic, Slovakia, the United Kingdom, Ireland, and Spain.

Édith Cresson [1934-] is appointed Prime Minister just as the downturn in the cycle is getting underway, with growth slowing to 1% and the structural deficit deteriorating to 3.8%. The number of unemployed persons registered at the National Employment Agency (*Agence Nationale Pour l'Emploi - ANPE*) increased to 2,832,800 at the end of 1991, up 11.7% year-on-year. There was a rise in long-term unemployment, with 893 thousand people out of work for a year or more at the end of 1991.[3]

In her General Policy Statement (*Déclaration de politique générale*) to the country's National Assembly on May 22, 1991, Édith Cresson stated:

> "The economic situation is difficult. The downturn in the global economy, the effects of which were highlighted by the Gulf War, has led to a marked slowdown in growth, limiting our capacity to create jobs. It has been the case that the French economy creates fewer jobs than its main partners at like-for-like growth. Fortunately, this trend seems to have corrected itself over the past three years. But to see unemployment fall, at least 300 thousand jobs need to be created every year, which is impossible if the slowdown in activity continues."[4]

Edith Cresson went on:

> "In addition, our structural weaknesses are illustrated by the trade imbalance in industrial goods. Obviously, income redistribution is more difficult when a large part of our growth is used to pay for our external deficit. [...] Unemployment explains a large part of our society's ills. It is the primary cause of inequality. It is at the root of the sense of ill-being experienced by many of our fellow citizens, even if our society as a whole is prosperous: the outbursts of anger in our suburbs and racism are the consequence."[5]

And concluded:

> "We can be proud of our balanced economic record, hailed by our partners as the fruit of a virtuous policy. These successes are a strong franc, inflation that has been reined back,

---

[2] Ibid.

[3] First estimate of employment and unemployment in 1991, published May 11, 1992, Directorate of Research, Economic Studies and Statistics (DARES), vol 17, source: https://dares.travail-emploi.gouv.fr/publication/premier-bilan-de-lemploi-et-du-chomage-en-1991.

[4] *Déclaration de politique générale de Mme Cresson, Premier ministre, sur le programme du gouvernement* to the National Assembly on May 22, 1991, source: https://www.vie-publique.fr/discours/181620-declaration-de-politique-generale-de-mme-cresson-premier-ministre-sur.

[5] Ibid.

public spending that is tightly controlled and a total tax burden that has been stabilized. These achievements are our strengths, which I intend to consolidate."[6]

But the French took little pride in these accomplishments. Distraught, they wanted a change. The defeat suffered by the parliamentary Left in the cantonal and regional elections of March 1992 provided a good pretext for replacing Édith Cresson with Pierre Bérégovoy. Also in 1992, but on the other side of the Atlantic, the Americans, who were also suffering from an economic downturn, blamed George Bush and elected Bill Clinton on November 3, 1992. Convinced that the cyclical downturn would be the undoing of George Bush, James Carville, an adviser to Bill Clinton, confidently told campaign workers to focus on one slogan: "It's the economy, stupid."

After her term of office ended, Édith Cresson took up Olympe de Gouges' fight for gender equality. There is still a long way to go.

This may not have been a glorious period for the economy, but it was for European construction.

Maastricht Treaty

The Treaty on European Union, commonly known as the Maastricht Treaty, was signed on February 7, 1992, in the Dutch city of Maastricht by the twelve foreign and finance ministers of the Member States. It came into force on November 1, 1993. It was the culmination of the process that started with the communiqué released after the European Council held in 1978 in Bremen, but whereas Germany was the driving force at the time, for the Maastricht Treaty it was France. Germany was in the midst of reunification, which brought huge social and economic challenges.

The Treaty marked the formal establishment of a European Union. The European Parliament's legislative and supervisory powers were strengthened by the introduction of the co-decision procedure and the extension of the cooperation procedure.

"A European System of Central Banks (hereinafter referred to as "ESCB") and a European Central Bank (hereinafter referred to as "ECB") shall be established in accordance with the procedures laid down in this Treaty."[7]

Title VI of the Treaty, Economic and Monetary Policy, states that:

"1. Member States shall avoid excessive government deficits.

2. The Commission shall monitor the development of the budgetary situation and of the stock of government debt in the Member States with a view to identifying gross errors. In particular it shall examine compliance with budgetary discipline [...]."[8]

---

[6] Ibid.

[7] Treaty on European Union, source: https://eur-lex.europa.eu/legal-content/EN/TXT/?uri=celex%3A11992M%2FTXT.

[8] Ibid.

The introduction of the euro drew nearer: "1. The ECB shall have the exclusive right to authorize the issue of bank notes within the Community. The ECB and the national central banks may issue such notes. The bank notes issued by the ECB and the national central banks shall be the only such notes to have the status of legal tender within the Community."[9] The third and ultimate stage for the adoption of the euro was set to start on January 1, 1999.

The ECB being modeled on the Bundesbank and Federal Reserve, it is to be independent:

> "In accordance with Article 107 of this Treaty, when exercising the powers and carrying out the tasks and duties conferred upon them by this Treaty and this Statute, neither the ECB, nor a national central bank, nor any member of their decision-making bodies shall seek or take instructions from Community institutions or bodies, from any government of a Member State or from any other body. The Community institutions and bodies and the governments of the Member States undertake to respect this principle and not to seek to influence the members of the decision-making bodies of the ECB or of the national central banks in the performance of their tasks."[10]

The ECB cannot lend directly to Member States, only to commercial banks, but the latter may pledge debt instruments issued by Member States as collateral for amounts owed to the ECB.

> "1. The ESCB shall be composed of the ECB and of the national central banks. [...] The primary objective of the ESCB shall be to maintain price stability. [...] The basic tasks to be carried out through the ESCB shall [include] to promote the smooth operation of payment systems."[11]

François Mitterrand decided to ratify the treaty by referendum. To everyone's great surprise, the Danes, consulted by referendum on June 2, 1992, voted 'no' by just under 51% of the votes cast. On September 3, 1992, ahead of the referendum in France, scheduled on September 20, 1992, François Mitterrand, gnawed by cancer, defended the treaty on television, answering journalists' questions and debating with right-wing politician Philippe Séguin in the Sorbonne's Grand Amphitheatre.

François Mitterrand's gamble paid off: the French voted in favor of ratification by a short majority, 51% of votes cast, with a 71% turnout.

The man, whose 1981 program almost led France down an impasse, straight into the wall, changed direction and gave meaning to his presidency by laying the cornerstone for the European edifice. As Kafka had the cat say to the mouse in his short story: "You only need to change your direction."[12]

---

[9] Ibid.

[10] Ibid.

[11] Ibid.

[12] Kafka, Franz, *A Little Fable*, source: East of the Web, http://www.eastoftheweb.com/cgi-bin/version_printable.pl?story_id=LittFabl.shtml.

EMS Crises

Sterling Forced Out of the EMS

While everyone will have in mind the 2010 sovereign debt crisis, the EMS crisis, which posed an existential threat to monetary integration and could have nipped the euro's very creation in the bud, has largely faded from the collective memory. European monetary integration did not escape unscathed from this episode, as sterling was forced out of the European Monetary System (EMS) by the Bundesbank, much to the chagrin of John Major [1943-], who first as Chancellor of the Exchequer from October 1989 to November 1990 then as Prime Minister since November 1990 (until he stepped down in 1997), did much to move forward relations between the United Kingdom and the Community, which saw the country join the EMS on 6 October 1990, despite Margaret Thatcher's opposition.

Because of the EMS crisis, when the euro was created it was without sterling, considerably reducing the single currency's clout. Even though in 2024 the euro will be the second most traded currency on the foreign exchange market, just behind the US dollar, it might well have been on an equal footing if the United Kingdom had adopted the euro as its currency! Would the public debt crisis have occurred if the United Kingdom had been in the European Monetary Union? If so, would speculators have bet on Greece's bankruptcy and the end of the euro? Would Brexit have happened if France and Germany had supported the United Kingdom during the EMS crisis?

And what if the perfidious Albion was not, in this instance, the United Kingdom? In any case, betrayals always come at a high price: the European Union is weaker without the United Kingdom, and the euro without sterling, which is highly detrimental in the fierce global competition with the United States and China. Faced with these two superpowers, a united Europe in its true borders would be a force to be reckoned with.

The starting point for the EMS crisis was the European leaders' decision to have the Maastricht Treaty ratified by referendum. But Denmark voted against, and it was uncertain which way the vote would go in France. Between the Danish 'no' in June 1992 and the French 'yes' a few months later in September, speculators jumped at the opportunity. Then there was the fact that, on June 30, 1990—even before the signing of the Unification Treaty on August 31, 1990, and the signing of the Treaty on the Final Settlement with Respect to Germany (so-called Two Plus Four Treaty mentioned above) on September 12, 1990—the German government decided to introduce the Deutsche mark as the official currency of East Germany in preparation for its reunification with West Germany. East German marks were exchanged for Deutsche marks on a 1:1 basis, but applying a less favorable exchange rate above certain limits and depending on personal conditions (age, country of residence). The exchange reality was totally disconnected from economic reality, the Deutsche mark being far stronger than the East German mark. Inflation climbed to 5.2% in 1992 in Germany, when it was just 2.4% in France. Under Mundell's impossible trinity, since rates of exchanges between EMS member states and Germany were fixed, these countries had to pursue the same monetary policy as the Bundesbank, requiring them to tighten their monetary policy. For speculators, this was yet another source of instability creating opportunities.

The Nyborg Agreement of September 13, 1987, contained a mechanism intended to address such situations, provided of course that this mechanism was called upon. As explained in an article in Le Monde of November 4, 1987, "Under the European Monetary System (EMS), currencies are allowed to fluctuate around central rates. At the last monetary adjustment, on January 12, 1987, the parity between the mark and the franc was set at 3.3538 French francs to 1 Deutsche mark. With a fluctuation band of 2.25%, the ceiling rate for the franc is currently 3.2792 francs per Deutsche mark, and the floor rate is 3.4305 francs per Deutsche mark. [...] Henceforth, countries whose currencies are under attack can ask for help from countries with strong currencies, even before the parity limits set under the EMS are reached. Under this new system, a central bank trying to defend its currency can ask for very short-term credit from the central banks of strong-currency countries, to have more ammunition on hand."[13]

It is interesting to note that the article explains that Germany and other European counties reached quite different interpretations of this agreement: "If necessary, France could mobilize some ECU3.4 billion, or around FRF23 billion.[14] How automatic is this mechanism? The assessments expressed the day after the Nyborg weekend differed considerably, with the European Commission and France claiming that this was a 'quasi-automatic' commitment, whereas the West German monetary authorities contended that there was no new commitment."[15]

The government led by John Major discovered at its own expense that the German authorities did not consider themselves bound by the Nyborg agreement. On September 16, 1992, sterling came under attack. Unlike Italy, whose currency was attacked on September 11, 1992, the United Kingdom complied with EMS rules and did not devalue its currency. The Bank of England raised its interest rates and waited for the Bundesbank to lend it marks needed to counter speculation. But the Bundesbank was not forthcoming and sterling was forced out of the EMS. The speculators won and the European Monetary Union lost sterling forever. Why didn't France demand that Germany respect the Nyborg agreement? How could the British trust the Continentals again and ever be fully convinced they were an integral part of the European Union?

Spurred on by their success against sterling, speculators continued to bet on the breakup of the EMS and attacked the French franc on September 17, 1992. Germany once again hesitated, but on September 22, two days after the French 'yes' vote in the

[13] Le Monde, November 5, 1987, *Les accords de Nyborg Un soutien préventif aux monnaies faibles*, source: https://www.lemonde.fr/archives/article/1987/11/05/les-accords-de-nyborg-un-soutien-preventif-aux-monnaies-faibles_4081473_1819218.html.

[14] Equivalent to €6.72 billion in 2024.

[15] Le Monde, November 5, 1987, *Les accords de Nyborg Un soutien préventif aux monnaies faibles*, source: https://www.lemonde.fr/archives/article/1987/11/05/les-accords-de-nyborg-un-soutien-preventif-aux-monnaies-faibles_4081473_1819218.html.

Maastricht Treaty referendum, Jean-Claude Trichet [1942-], head of the French Treasury,[16] succeeded in convincing Helmut Schlesinger, the President of the Bundesbank, to respect the Nyborg agreements. On September 23, the Banque de France raised its key policy rate from 10.5% to 13% and the Bundesbank lent it the marks needed to counter the speculation. Faced with the German response, speculation stopped the same day. The French franc did not suffer the same fate as sterling, remaining in the EMS, but British confidence in a common currency was shattered forever.

Balladur Loan and EMS Crisis

With the EMS crisis having pushed short rates up to 10% at the end of 1992, when inflation reached 3%, causing a recession that was exacerbated by the cycle downturn, the hour of reckoning for the government came with the March 1993 general elections. What ensued was a divided government French-style, François Mitterrand beginning his second cohabitation with Edouard Balladur as Prime Minister from March 1993 to May 1995.

The new government would pursue the same strategy as during the first cohabitation, pressing on with large-scale privatizations in the banking sector (Banque Nationale de Paris and Crédit Local de France, later to become Dexia), insurance sector (Union des Assurances de Paris), and oil and gas sector (Elf-Aquitaine), also privatizing the former State-owned tobacco monopoly Seita and selling a large block of shares in carmaker Renault.

But a new EMS crisis erupted after Edouard Balladur launched a FRF40 billion franc[17] government loan on June 25, 1993, consisting of four-year bonds offering a 6% coupon, placed directly with individual savers. The bonds were offered in FRF1000 denominations, the placement clearly targeting retail investors. As a further incentive, individuals purchasing the bonds were to be given priority for the upcoming privatizations. The holders of the bond were given the option to convert their holdings into shares in companies sold by the State on a priority basis immediately after employees of that company or of its directly or indirectly majority-owned subsidiaries, or by former employees having served at least five years with the company or any such subsidiary.

The so-called Balladur loan was a resounding success, raising FRF100 billion.[18] But speculators attacked the franc because they realized that to preserve its credibility among those having subscribed to this loan, Banque de France could not now offer more than 6% on government loans, and so would be unable to raise rates in the event of a speculative attack on the franc. In a well-intentioned but misguided

---

[16] From August 1987 to September 1993.

[17] Equivalent to €9.85 billion.

[18] Equivalent to €27.1 billion.

attempt to quell speculation, the Minister for the Economy[19] Edmond Alphandéry [1943-] declared in a radio interview that "the franc is at least as strong in the EMS as the mark, so we will be able to discuss with the Germans the conditions for easing credit."[20] In other words, the interest rate adjustment required by the EMS would come from the Bundesbank cutting its rates at France's request. To which the Bundesbank immediately replied that it was independent of the German and French political authorities…

To quash the speculation, Banque de France drew down FRF160 billion from its reserves and borrowed FRF180 billion from Germany.[21] On August 2, 1993, an agreement was reached to broaden the EMS fluctuation band from ± 2.25% to ± 15% for all participating currencies, much to the exasperation of France's European partners. On August 9, Banque de France cut its key policy rate by 25 basis points. On August 15, the Deutsche mark was worth FRF3.50, compared with FRF3.40 before the Balladur loan.

By an ironic twist of fate, it was the same Edmond Alphandéry who, in application of the Maastricht Treaty, pushed through the amendment to the statutes of the Banque de France in August 1993 to enshrine its independence. Jean-Claude Trichet was its Governor from September 1993 to November 2003. He was then President of the ECB from November 2003 to November 2011.

"In the Fight Against Unemployment, no Stone Was Left Unturned," Save for the OECD's Recommendations

The unemployment rate climbed from 6.5% in the second quarter of 1981 when François Mitterrand was elected for the first time, to 10.2% in the third quarter of 1993. By comparison, in 1993, the unemployment rate was 7.79% in Germany and 9.72% in Italy.[22] During an interview given by François Mitterrand on July 14, 1993, a journalist asked him whether he was satisfied with the government's economic policy, notably in combating unemployment. The opening remark in his reply has gone down in history: "Oh, you know, no stone has been left unturned in the fight against unemployment. In the twelve years I've been in office, everything has been tried. You know the outcome, which is a sad one, since in 1981 we had between 1.6

[19] From March 1993 to May 1995.

[20] Le Monde, June 27, 1993, *Marché monétaire et obligataire victoire technique, défaite diplomatique*, source: https://www.lemonde.fr/archives/article/1993/06/27/marche-monetaire-et-obligataire-victoire-technique-defaite-diplomatique_3954274_1819218.html.

[21] Equivalent to €39.31 billion and €44.34 billion, respectively.

[22] Source: https://data.oecd.org/unemp/unemployment-rate.htm.

million and 1.7 million unemployed and at the time of the last elections that figure had risen to 3 million."[23]

Mitterrand's diagnosis, still relevant today, did not make much of an impression. It has faded from memory, even though it is unfortunately still accurate and continues to apply to France: "As a result of the economic depression, technological change, and often the lack of vocational training, with young people ill-prepared for their new career, the whole of the Western industrial world is suffering from the same ills. This situation is nothing to rejoice about. I'm simply saying that we've tried everything, and the current government needs to persevere with everything that is being undertaken because we need continuity in our efforts."[24]

Unemployment would hold above 10% until the first quarter of 1995 before declining in the next three quarters to 9.9% first of all, then 9.8%, and 9.9%. In the first quarter of 1996, unemployment recovered back above 10% and would remain in double-digit territory until the third quarter of 1999.[25]

After that, unemployment continued to subside, but never pulled back below 7%, that is back to levels reached between the first quarter of 1975 and the fourth quarter of 1981.

In the second quarter of 1981, when François Mitterrand was elected, 10.5% of men and 22.6% of women aged between 18 and 24 were unemployed. When François Mitterrand addressed the nation on July 14, 1993, 18.6% of men and 27% of women aged between 18 and 24 were unemployed.

When the journalist pointed this out, François Mitterrand attempted to put things into perspective, but played fast and loose with the truth: "There are more young people unemployed in France than in other countries, but other countries have education and training systems that last longer, so comparisons are often distorted."[26] It is difficult to know which countries François Mitterrand was referring to because, in 1993, unemployment rates for this age group reached 14.9% for men and 14.3% for women in the United States, 21.1% and 14.1%, respectively, in the United Kingdom, 19.5% and 22% in Belgium, 11.3% and 9.5% in the Netherlands, 12.2% and 18.1% in Portugal, and 4.8% and 5.6% in Luxembourg. Youth unemployment has been an albatross around the neck of successive governments for thirty years.

During this period, France has been constantly beset by very high youth unemployment. In the fourth quarter of 2023, unemployment rates for people aged 18 to 24 reached 18.1% for men and 16.7% for women. In France, compared with 6.25% and

---

[23] Interview given by François Mitterrand, President of the Republic, to TF1, France 2 and Europe 1 on July 14, 1993, covering the new cohabitation, the Balladur loan and privatizations, the fight against immigration, constitutional reform and international issues, source: https://www.vie-publique.fr/discours/134439-interview-de-m-francois-mitterrand-president-de-la-republique-accorde.

[24] Ibid.

[25] INSEE, *Au quatrième trimestre 2023, le taux de chômage est stable à 7,5%*, source: https://www.insee.fr/fr/statistiques/7765269.

[26] Interview given by François Mitterrand, President of the Republic, to TF1, France 2 and Europe 1 on July 14, 1993, covering the new cohabitation, the Balladur loan and privatizations, the fight against immigration, constitutional reform and international issues, source: https://www.vie-publique.fr/discours/134439-interview-de-m-francois-mitterrand-president-de-la-republique-accorde.

5.47%, respectively, in Germany.[27] Furthermore, in France youth unemployment is very high compared with other age groups: for people aged 25 to 49, unemployment rates are 6.9% for men and 7.1% for women, while for people over 49, unemployment rates are 5.1% for men and 4.9% for women. The root of the problem is the mismatch between salary levels and skills and productivity levels, particularly among young people. As explained rather well by the OECD, one of the weaknesses of the French system is that the level of youth training in France does not correspond to the firm's expectations. This leaves firms having to train young hires.

Yet, in July 1993, at Edouard Balladur's request, the Mattéoli commission—named after Jean Mattéoli [1922–2008], the President of France's Economic and Social Council from 1987 to 1999—handed in a 135-page progress report to the Prime Minister on structural obstacles to employment (*Rapport d'étape à M. le Premier Ministre sur les obstacles structurels à l'emploi*). This report contained forty proposals aimed at introducing greater flexibility in labor law and lowering labor costs in order to reduce unemployment. The OECD Jobs Strategy published in 1994 went further. Its ten recommendations fit on one page.

To address unemployment among young people leaving the French education system, which had become less selective and therefore unable to provide companies recruiting with a clear picture of the situation, Parliament followed the recommendation of the Mattéoli Commission to "reduce the minimum wage during the first two years of employment" for young people. In December 1993, it voted in favor of a professional integration contract (*contrat d'insertion professionnelle*). This was a contract of employment for people under the age of 26, paying not less than 80% of the minimum wage. The implementing decree was published in February, but bowing to street protests, the law was repealed in August 1994.

Yet, in 1994, combating unemployment had become a global issue. In the communiqué released after the meeting of the OECD Council at ministerial level held on June 7 and 8, point 4 stated:

> "Ministers endorse the main conclusions of the OECD Employment/Unemployment Study Policy Report. They agree to implement its employment strategy recommendations within the context of their particular economic circumstances. They recognise that the present situation is attributable both to the effects of the recent recession and, significantly, to serious structural deficiencies, especially the inadequate and sluggish adjustment of Member country economies to the rapid changes associated with technological progress, competition and globalisation."[28]

Point 13 stated that:

> "Member country governments also resolve to promote measures that can increase sustainable employment and help achieve both social equity and economic efficiency. With these ends in mind, they will seek:
>
> - to further improve education and training systems, in each national institutional context and, where appropriate, in close co-operation with social partners, local authorities and private

[27] Source: https://data.oecd.org/unemp/unemployment-rate.htm.

[28] OECD, Communiqué, OECD Council at ministerial level of June 7 and 8, source: https://one.oecd.org/document/SG/PRESS(94)41/En/pdf.

initiatives, so as to ensure that people can, throughout their lifetime, develop their knowledge and skills, thereby contributing to improved productivity and sustained high levels of growth;

- to improve the functioning of labour markets by making them more flexible, with a view to achieving a better match between the supply of and demand for jobs, and by reducing impediments to labour mobility;

- to make employment services more effective and, more generally, give high priority to active labour market policies and programmes including those targeted to the long-term unemployed and youth;

- to amend laws and regulations that discourage firms from taking on workers, or people from taking up work;

- to co-operate closely with regional and local authorities towards enhancing employment opportunities at all skill levels, without neglecting services activities which can absorb unemployed workers in large numbers."[29]

The *1994 OECD Jobs Strategy* is a seminal document. It contains 10 proposals:

"1. Set macroeconomic policy such that it will both encourage growth and, in conjunction with good structural policies, make it sustainable, i.e., non-inflationary.

2. Enhance the creation and diffusion of technological now-how by improving frameworks for its development.

3. Increase flexibility of working-time (both short-term and lifetime) voluntarily sought by workers and employers.

4. Nurture an entrepreneurial climate by eliminating impediments to, and restrictions on, the creation and expansion of enterprises.

5. Make wage and labour costs more flexible by removing restrictions that prevent wages from reflecting local conditions and individual skills levels, in particular of younger workers.

6. Reform employment security provisions that inhibit the expansion of employment in the private sector.

7. Strengthen the emphasis on active labour market policies and reinforce their effectiveness.

8. Improve labour force skills and competencies through wide-ranging changes in education and training systems.

9. Reform unemployment and related benefit systems - and their interactions with the tax system - such that societies' fundamental equity goals are achieved in ways that impinge far less on the efficient functioning of the labour markets.

10. Enhance product market competition so as to reduce monopolistic tendencies and weaken insider-outsider mechanisms while also contributing to a more innovative and dynamic economy."[30]

Edouard Balladur did not have the necessary clout to apply this program successfully in France, but he did manage to get structural measures adopted in the area of pensions. It is the progress in European construction that would eventually lead to France's modernization.

---

[29] Meeting of the OECD Council at Ministerial Level, Communiqué, source: https://one.oecd.org/document/SG/PRESS(94)41/en/pdf.

[30] OECD, *Implementing the OECD Jobs Strategy*, source: https://read.oecd-ilibrary.org/employment/implementing-the-oecd-jobs-strategy_9789264173682-en#page11.

Balladur Government's Fiscal Policy and 1993 Recession

The EMS crisis, which pushed short rates in France up to 10% at the end of 1992 when inflation reached 3%, caused a recession that was exacerbated by the cycle downturn. Better management of German reunification could have mitigated the impact. The average yield at issue for French government bonds was 8.1% in 1992 when inflation reached 2.4%. It fell to 5.6% in 1993 with inflation at 2.1% before rising to 8.3% in 1994 with inflation at 1.6%. Financing the deficit was costing more than potential growth. In this context, a rebalancing of the public accounts became imperative.

In 1992, the government deficit was already 3.2%, when to comply with the convergence criteria for Stage 2 of the Economic and Monetary Union (EMU), the deficit must not exceed 3% of GDP. This deficit reached 6% in 1993, but the economic cycle was responsible for only 20% of this deficit, the structural deficit accounting for 80%.

To plug this gaping hole in the country's public finances, Edouard Balladur concentrated his efforts on the social security deficit by increasing the rate for the generalized social contribution (*Contribution Sociale Généralisée—CSG*) from 1.1% to 2.4% in the spring.

Then in the summer, the government also pushed through four structural reforms to the pension system:

- The number of contribution quarters required for a full pension was increased gradually (by one-quarter per year until January 1, 2004), from 37.5 years to 40 years in total;
- The reference wage was reduced by gradually raising the number of years required for its calculation with each generation from the ten best years to the twenty-five best years;
- Pensions were indexed on consumer prices instead of wages;
- A separate fund (*Fonds de solidarité de vieillesse*) was created to finance non-contributory benefits such as the guaranteed minimum income to the elderly (*minimum vieillesse*).

Despite this successful reform of the pension system, France's debt continued to rise inexorably, from 39.7% of GDP when Balladur was appointed Prime Minister in March 1993 to 49.4% when he left two years later. France still met the convergence criterion, requiring government debt to be less than 60% of GDP, but the rate of increase in the debt-to-GDP ratio was accelerating.

Economic Policy During the Chirac Era

Mitterrand's 14-year 'reign' came to an end on May 17, 1995. Jacques Chirac [1932–2019], mayor of Paris since 1977, twice prime minister, each time for two years, twice a presidential candidate, is elected President of the Republic. As the term of office of the French President was reduced from seven years to five years by referendum in September 2000, Jacques Chirac's second term of office lasted five years, the first seven years. He remained in office until May 16, 2007. In the history of the Fifth Republic, only Mitterrand served a longer term of office than he did. As the French Constitution was amended once more in 2008, with a limit of two consecutive terms being introduced, no other president under the Fifth Republic is likely to emulate them.

Chirac defeated Balladur, who was initially the favorite but started his campaign too late and not energetically enough compared to Chirac's voluntarism. The satirical puppet show *Les guignols de l'info*, which aired from 1988 to 2018, a parody of the television news show, helped to endear Chirac by caricaturing him as your average Joe whose slogan was "*Mangez des pommes*" (Eat apples) and whose electoral program was a country-style buffet catering to all and sundry, while Balladur, the Prime Minister-candidate, was caricatured as an evil, self-important traitor. At the end of January 1995, Le Nouvel Observateur ran the headline "*Les Français en veulent-ils vraiment?*" (Do the French really want this) depicting Balladur as Louis-Philippe, France's penultimate monarch, on the front page. These depictions conveyed a harsh reality, which is that Chirac was more charismatic and dynamic than his companion of thirty years, Balladur.

Chirac's election was also helped by the announcement on December 11, 1994, that Jacques Delors, the European Commission President, had decided not to run for President. As he confided in a live primetime television interview, he feared that once elected he would not be able to muster a sufficient legislative majority to address his priorities, which were to: "renovate democracy, encourage citizen participation, combat unemployment and exclusion, […] re-establish the social bond, ensure the cohesion [of] the country," and ensure that "France remains the inspirer of a political Europe that is both powerful and generous." Jacques Delors had every chance of being elected.

How many presidential candidates think more about what they can actually do after their election than about being elected? The 1972 American feature film "The Candidate," starring Robert Redford, is a good example. Bill McKay, who has just won an improbable victory in the Senate election, turns to his campaign manager and asks: "Marwin, what do we do now?".[31]

---

[31] Source: https://www.youtube.com/watch?v=myEpap3TxVs.

Chirac's Volte-Face and the 1995 Strikes

On May 17, 1995, Jacques Chirac appointed Alain Juppé [1945-] Prime Minister, a position he held until June 2, 1997. His general policy statement of May 23, 1995, is the longest in the Fifth Republic, running to twenty-one pages. The policy statement was influenced heavily by his mentor. It is reminiscent of the country-style buffet in the satirical TV show "*Les guignols de l'info.*" There was something for everyone, intended to pave the way for a consumption-driven economic recovery.

In his General Policy Statement (*Déclaration de politique générale*), Alain Juppé announced that: "On July 1, the minimum hourly wage (*salaire minimum interprofessionnel de croissance—Smic*) will be raised by a significant percentage, to be set after consultation with the social partners and which, in my view, could be up to double the legal minimum requirement."[32]

The Prime Minister promised to heal the "social divide" by combating all forms of exclusion:

> "The government will take urgent action against all forms of exclusion.
>
> - First and foremost, long-term unemployment. This scourge currently affects 1.2 million people and has risen by a further 10% in the last year. To reduce it, we are going to institute the employment initiative contract (*contrat initiative-emploi*), the general features of which you are familiar with: for a salary at the level of the SMIC, a complete exemption from employers' social charges and a bonus of FRF2,000[33] per month for two years. [...]
>
> I have asked the ministers concerned to prepare a similar proposal to promote the professional integration of young people leaving work-study programs. Paid the minimum wage, the youth employment access contract (*contrat d'accès à l'emploi pour les jeunes - CAEJ*) will be the subject of in-depth consultation with the social partners and aid will be extended to employers. [...]
>
> - The second particularly unacceptable form of exclusion is homelessness, which afflicts tens of thousands of our compatriots. In 1995, the government will launch a program for the construction of ten thousand social integration housing units (*logements d'insertion*) in addition to the twenty thousand affordable social housing units (*logements très sociaux*) already planned. [...]
>
> - Third form of exclusion: living conditions in the problem neighborhoods of our cities and suburbs. [...]
>
> - The social isolation and poverty of the elderly. [...] The creation of a dependency allowance (*allocation de dependence*) could create 50 thousand new jobs while making our society more welcoming to a large number of elderly people. [...]
>
> - Public health policy, after that, where major reforms are now needed."[34]

---

[32] *Déclaration de politique générale de M. Alain Juppé, Premier ministre* to the National Assembly and Senate on May 23, 1995, source: https://www.vie-publique.fr/discours/151564-alain-juppe-23051995-declaration-de-politique-generale.

[33] Equivalent to €475.65.

[34] *Déclaration de politique générale de M. Alain Juppé, Premier ministre* to the National Assembly and Senate on May 23, 1995, source: https://www.vie-publique.fr/discours/151564-alain-juppe-23051995-declaration-de-politique-generale.

Five months later, under pressure from his European partners in the run-up to the adoption of the euro, Jacque Chirac turned off the tap, announcing a U-turn in the government's economic policy in a live TV interview on the evening of October 26, 1995, and explaining that "the priority was the reduction of public deficits."[35]

Jacques Chirac mentioned the "single currency" six times during the interview, defining it thus: "What is the single currency? Quite simply, it is the modern expression of a stable system of exchange rates, and so is an opportunity."[36]

He pointed out that "Franco-German policy in its entirety is based on one reality: it can only work if France and Germany are in the same state of health."[37]

He went on to explain that "France has a problem which is not an economic problem—our economy is doing well, it is dynamic, it is vigorous, it is exporting - but it has a financial problem, it has deficits. The priority, therefore, is to reduce the deficits; to do this we need to take measures that may be in contradiction with what we want to do later, so as to restore balances. It is a two-year effort. [...] Irrespective of any other consideration, we will have to balance public finances two years from now, if only to adopt the European single currency pursuant to the commitments we have made. So we will succeed."[38]

To Alain Juppé falls the task of refocusing economic policy, summarized by Jacques Chirac during the interview as follows: "What I'm simply saying is that, as far as expenditure is concerned, the State must set an example by drastically reducing spending that it allowed to grow excessively. As far as receipts are concerned, it must be clearly understood that in France it has reached a level—taxes, social security contributions—that is becoming paralyzing, and while we may have been forced to make adjustments to reduce deficits, it is essential to aim for a situation, in two years at the latest, which will be one where we start to lower taxes and social security contributions."[39] In other words, it was going to be necessary to cut spending and raise taxes to begin with.

Three weeks later, on November 15, the Prime Minister went to task on social security spending in the broadest sense, announcing:

- an increase in the number of contribution quarters required for a full pension in the public sector to forty years in total, in line with the private sector;
- the requirement for the passing of a law each year on the financing of the social security system, setting targets for the evolution of medical expenses and introducing penalties for doctors who exceed them;

---

[35] Interview given by Jacques Chirac, President of the Republic, to France 2 on October 26, 1995, on the priority given to reducing public deficits, controlling healthcare spending and combating social exclusion, source: https://www.elysee.fr/jacques-chirac/1995/10/26/interview-de-m-jacques-chirac-president-de-la-republique-a-france-2-le-26-octobre-1995-sur-la-priorite-a-la-reduction-des-deficits-publics-et-a-la-maitrise-des-depenses-de-sante-et-sur-la-lutte-contre-lexclusion-sociale.

[36] Ibid.

[37] Ibid.

[38] Ibid.

[39] Ibid.

- an increase in health insurance contributions paid by pensioners and the unemployed;
- the delegation of the supervision of the reform of the hospitals to regional hospital service agencies (*agences régionales de l'hospitalisation—ARH*), while increasing hospital admission fees;
- the freeze and taxation of family allowances.

On November 24, 1995, trade unions organized a first day of strikes, which would lead to the biggest social movement in French history after May 1968, with "six million days lost to strikes, four million in the civil service and two million in the private and semi-public sector."[40] The civil service accounted for some 64% of days lost to strikes.

On December 12, two million strikers took to the streets demanding the withdrawal of the Juppé plan. On December 14, The General Framework Agreement for Peace in Bosnia and Herzegovina initialed in Dayton on November 21, 1995, was signed at the Élysée Palace in Paris on December 14, 1995. Trains, subways, and buses in the capital had come to a standstill. Traffic jams were so bad that, for the heads of state and governments to reach the Élysée Palace for the signing ceremony, they had to be flown by helicopter from the airport to the Esplanade des Invalides. This was the last straw for Jacques Chirac, whereas Alain Juppé was not for turning. The next day, Chirac withdrew the Juppé plan and announced that a major social summit would be held on December 21.

Some of the measures proposed by Alain Juppé were implemented, such as the requirement to pass a law each year on the financing of the social security system setting targets for the evolution of medical expenses, also the delegated supervision of hospitals, and the creation of an administrative body (*Caisse d'amortissement de la dette sociale—CADES*) tasked with extinguishing the accumulated debt of the social security general system, funded by the social debt repayment contribution (*Contribution pour le remboursement de la dette sociale—CRDS*), a new tax applied to the same tax base as the generalized social contribution (*Contribution sociale généralisée—CSG*).

Placing hospitals under the supervision of regional hospital service agencies added yet another administrative layer to the health system, while the CRDS was another addition to a long list of taxes. As Colbert explained: "The art of taxation consists in so plucking the goose as to obtain the largest possible amount of feathers with the smallest possible amount of hissing." Having weathered the strikes, Alain Juppé accomplished just that with the CDRS. All in all, the tax burden increased from 42.7% in 1995 to 43.9% in 1996 and 44.1% in 1997, the final year of the Juppé government, helping lower the general government deficit from 5.5% of GDP in 1995 to 3.1% in 1996 and 3% in 1997. At the same time, the strikes of 1995 impacted growth and the level of the public debt, which increased from 55.7% of GDP in 1995 to 58% in 1996, and then to 59.3% in 1997. One factor driving up the level of the debt was that

[40] Direction de l'animation de la recherche, des études et des statistiques (Dares), *Les conflits du travail en 1995: un niveau élevé*, source: https://dares.travail-emploi.gouv.fr/publication/les-conflits-du-travail-en-1995-un-niveau-eleve.

it was being refinanced at high interest rates, though these were starting to subside. The average yield at issue declined from 6.6% in 1995 to 5.8% in 1996 and 5.3% in 1997, compared with inflation of 1.8%, 2%, and 1.2%, respectively. While France had succeeded in reining back inflation, the debt-to-GDP ratio was perilously close to the 60% ceiling set by European convergence criteria.

Historic 1995 Madrid Summit

> "Question: Are you yourself a confident European or a wary European?
> - The President: I'm a realist European. I've always thought that, faced with the development of very large blocks in the world, Europe would only safeguard its values, its very existence and its independence if it constantly strengthened the ties that unite its constituent parts. And I'm in favor of an enlarged Europe, representing the whole of our continent, in other words, a return to the European family."[41]
> Jacques Chirac, 1995

The European Council meeting held in Madrid on December 15 and 16, 1995, has gone down in history for the many key decisions that were taken, marking the culmination of a long process of European construction that began after the Second World War.

The Council confirmed the date for the adoption of the single currency and its name: "The European Council adopted the scenario for the changeover to the single currency, confirming unequivocally that this stage will commence on 1 January 1999. The European Council decided to name the currency, to be used from 1 January 1999, the 'Euro'."[42]

'Ecu' was the name proposed by Giscard d'Estaing at the European Council held in Bremen in 1978. The name, an acronym formed from the English term European Currency Unit, appealed to Giscard d'Estaing because the écu was a family of gold coins minted in France in the Middle Ages during the Valois dynasty.

Paragraph 7 of the section dealing with the scenario for the changeover to the single currency, which would be respected scrupulously, stated: "By 1 January 2002 at the latest, Euro banknotes and coins will start to circulate alongside national notes and coins. At most 6 months later, the national currencies will have been completely replaced by the Euro in all participating Member States, and the changeover will

---

[41] Interview given by Jacques Chirac, President of the Republic, to France 2 on October 26, 1995, on the priority given to reducing public deficits, controlling healthcare spending and combating social exclusion, source: https://www.elysee.fr/jacques-chirac/1995/10/26/interview-de-m-jacques-chirac-president-de-la-republique-a-france-2-le-26-octobre-1995-sur-la-priorite-a-la-reduction-des-deficits-publics-et-a-la-maitrise-des-depenses-de-sante-et-sur-la-lutte-contre-lexclusion-sociale.

[42] Madrid European Council 15 and 16 December 1995, Presidency Conclusions, source: https://www.europarl.europa.eu/summits/mad1_en.htm.

be complete. Thereafter, national banknotes and coins may still be exchanged at the national Central Banks."[43]

On the matter of enlargement, the Council concluded that: "Enlargement is both a political necessity and a historic opportunity for Europe. It will ensure the stability and security of the continent and will thus offer both the applicant States and the current members of the Union new prospects for economic growth and general well-being. Enlargement must serve to strengthen the building of Europe in observance of the acquis communautaire which includes the common policies. [...] The European Council takes note of the Council report on relations with the associated CCEE[44] during the second half of 1995. [...] The representatives of those countries of Central and Eastern Europe which have concluded Europe Agreements, and of Malta and Cyprus, will be briefed regularly on the progress of discussions and will be able to put their points of view at meetings with the Presidency of the European Union to be held, in principle, every two months."[45]

Jacques Chirac supported enlargement and was the French president who welcomed the most Central European countries into the European Union in what was the fourth wave, coming before Putin resurrected his dreams of recreating the Soviet Union. Between 2004 and 2007, the Czech Republic, Estonia, Hungary, Latvia, Lithuania, Poland, Slovakia, Slovenia, Bulgaria, and Romania joined the European Union. Faced with Russia, there was no time to lose. Cyprus and Malta joined the European Union in 2004.

A few months after the Madrid European Council meeting, the Franco-German Financial and Economic Council (*Conseil économique et financier franco-allemand - CEFFA*)[46] held a meeting on March 26, 1996, in the French city of Laval. France stuck to the position of the European Commission, which wanted the Stability and Growth Pact to be based on the fiscal rules set out in the Maastricht Treaty, imposed at the time by France when the Germans wanted balanced public finances. There followed that planned or actual government deficit must not exceed 3% of GDP for countries to be admitted to the European Monetary Union, although at the Madrid European Council meeting, Germany had made the case that public deficits should not exceed 1% during the accession phase.

Return of Socialist Government in 1997

"Finding one's place in society

---

[43] Ibid.

[44] Countries of Central and Eastern Europe, including the Baltic States.

[45] Ibid.

[46] CEFFA was created on January 22, 1988, on the occasion of the 25th anniversary of the Élysée Treaty.

means first and foremost having a job".[47]

Lionel Jospin, 1997

The Socialist Party and its allies won the general elections held on May 25 and June 1, 1997. France therefore entered a third cohabitation, but this time between a President from the Right and a Prime Minister from the Left. Lionel Jospin [1937-] was appointed Prime Minister on June 2, 1997, and stayed in office until May 6, 2022. In terms of the European agenda, his premiership stretched from the signing on October 2, 1997, of the Treaty of Amsterdam[48] to euro banknotes and coins being put into circulation on January 1, 2002.

Lionel Jospin's victory came when Europe was lurching to the left, with the appointment on May 2, 1997, of Labour leader Tony Bair [1953-] as Prime Minister in the United Kingdom. He would remain at 10 Downing Street until 2007. Gerhard Schröder [1944-], the leader of the Social Democratic Party, had been Germany's Chancellor since 1988 and would remain at the Bundeskanzleramt until 2005. Although French socialism had evolved since the Mitterand era, it remained more Keynesian than in the rest of Europe, where public deficits are now considered damaging for the economy and as placing an unfair burden on future generations.

Amsterdam European Council Meeting

The European Council met in Amsterdam on June 17 and 18, 1997, when it laid down the firm commitments of the Member States, Commission and Council regarding the implementation of the Stability and Growth Pact (SGP), with a twofold objective: reduce general government deficits in the run-up to EMU accession and require Euro Area Member States to maintain close to or in surplus positions. Until a country joins the Euro Area, it must comply with the Maastricht criteria, thereafter it is the requirements of the Stability and Growth Pact that apply. It is France, on the occasion of the Dublin European Council meeting in December 1996, that asked for the term 'growth' to be added to the Stability Pact so that it might integrate not only monetary but also economic objectives. The objectives are for GDP growth of 3% in volume plus 2% inflation, with stability to be maintained by a general government deficit-to-GDP ratio of at most 3% and a general government debt-to-GDP ratio of at most 60%.

The Stability and Growth Pact calls for the annual control of the public finances of Euro Area Member States to prevent lax fiscal policies and to coordinate fiscal policies such that overall budget balances would tend towards a close to or in surplus position. The Maastricht Treaty regulated EMU access but not what followed. Germany

[47] *Déclaration de politique générale de M. Lionel Jospin, Premier ministre, sur les axes de travail du gouvernement* on June 19, 1997, published in the La Lettre du Gouvernement of June 24, 1997, source: https://www.vie-publique.fr/discours/163833-declaration-de-politique-generale-de-m-lionel-jospin-premier-ministre.

[48] Which came into force on May 1, 1999.

wanted assurances that, upon joining the Euro Area, countries would not then become free-riders.

The Pact consisted of two main building blocks: the preventive arm and the corrective arm. At the core of the preventive arm is the requirement for country-specific medium-term objectives (MTO). The Council of Ministers responsible for Economic and Financial Affairs (ECOFIN) can address a recommendation to the Member State whose policies are not consistent with the broad guidelines or risk jeopardizing proper EMU functioning. At the core of the corrective arm is the Excessive Deficit Procedure (EDP), when the general government deficit exceeds 3% of GDP. The European Commission will address a warning to the Member State concerned, and suggest to the Council of Ministers responsible for Economic and Financial Affairs that it issue a recommendation, which must be approved by a qualified majority. If the Member State then fails to take appropriate action within the given deadline, a decision on no effective action and the imposition of sanctions are possible, in the form of an interest-bearing deposit at the European Central Bank, which can be transformed into a fine (between 0.25% and 0.5% of GDP) if there continues to be an excessive deficit.

The first weeks of his premiership were all about European construction, with the Amsterdam European Council meeting, but shortly after, in his general policy statement on June 24, Lionel Jospin made it clear that he remained a Socialist through and through. He announced that "an exceptional program to renovate one million [social] housing units will be carried out before the end of the legislature," and that "the back-to-school allowance, budgeted by the previous government at FRF420 will be raised to FRF1600[49]" and that the legal minimum hourly wage would be increased by 4%, despite the fact that inflation was 1.2% in 1997, which he said "represents the biggest increase in purchasing power in fifteen years."[50]

Reduction in Working Hours

> "The existence of a leader is observed
> more often than it is proclaimed."
> Lionel Jospin, 2003

In his General Policy Statement (*Déclaration de politique générale*), Lionel Jospin also announced that: "It is necessary, at the same time, to begin negotiating a reduction in working hours, giving priority to employment. Reducing working hours, without loss of pay, represents both economic progress—likely to create many jobs - and

[49] From €96 to €369.

[50] *Déclaration de politique générale de M. Lionel Jospin, Premier ministre, sur les axes de travail du gouvernement* to the National Assembly on June 19, 1997, published in the La Lettre du Gouvernement of June 24, 1997, source: https://www.vie-publique.fr/discours/163833-declaration-de-politique-generale-de-m-lionel-jospin-premier-ministre

social progress. That is why, with the agreement of the social partners, it is the intention to reduce the legal working week from 39 to 35 h. It will be the task of the National Conference on Wages, Employment and Working Time (*Conférence nationale sur les salaires, l'emploi et le temps de travail*) to establish a general framework and debate all aspects of this process. The Conference will convene in September. To ensure its success, in-depth preparatory work must be carried out this summer with the social partners. At the end of the Conference, a framework law will be presented, reducing the legal working week to 35 h before the end of the legislature, limiting abusive recourse to overtime and encouraging voluntary part-time work. Negotiations will then be conducted on a branch-by-branch and company-by-company basis. The State will provide support, particularly financial, to businesses that conclude innovative agreements, as well as to labor subcontracting firms, so that their competitiveness is not undermined."[51]

It was the Law of June 13, 1998 (*Loi n° 98–461 du 13 juin 1998 d'orientation et d'incitation relative à la réduction du temps de travail*), also known as the Aubry I Law (*Loi Aubry I*) after Martine Aubry [1950-], the Minister for Employment and Solidarity from June 1997 to October 2000, that reduced the legal working week from 39 to 35 h from January 1, 2000, for businesses with more than 20 employees, and from January 1, 2002, in all other cases.

The effects are positive not only in terms of well-being, but also in terms of job creation: "By seeking to strike a balance between shorter working hours, wage moderation, productivity gains and State aid, the reduction in working hours has led, according to the estimates [produced by DARES and INSEE] to a rapid acceleration in job growth, with almost 350 thousand job creations over the period 1998 to 2002, and this without any apparent financial imbalance for firms."[52]

On February 22, 1996, Jacques Chirac announced his decision to drum out conscription in favor of a professional army, which entailed shedding 130 thousand jobs between 1997 and 2002. Because this coincided with the reduction in working hours, these job losses did not have a dramatic impact.

The country's output did not suffer from the switch to a 35-h week. The added value for "Aubry 1" early adopters rose by 5% more than that of comparable businesses having continued to work 39 h. On the other hand, as far as wage growth was concerned, reducing working hours did not go hand in hand with wage increases: "Between the end of 1998 and the end of 2001, the gap observed between the average wage of 39-h businesses and the corresponding index for all businesses was 0.9 points."[53] In general, compared with estimates obtained applying usual determinants, wage growth for all businesses remained slightly lower due to the effect of wage moderation at businesses switching to a 35-h working week.

---

[51] Ibid.

[52] Gubian,Alain, Jugnot, Stéphane, Lerais, Frédéric, and Passeron, Vladimir, *Les effets de la RTT sur l'emploi: des simulations ex ante aux évaluations ex post*, published June 1, 2005, source: https://www.insee.fr/fr/statistiques/1376464?sommaire=1376476.

[53] Ibid.

Earned Income Tax Credit and Universal Health Cover

Taking the view that the labor market was suffering from supply-side problems, Laurent Fabius [1946-], Minister of the Economy, Finance, and Industry from March 2000 to May 2002, created the earned income tax credit (*prime pour l'emploi—PPE*) as part of a series of reforms designed to make the transition from non-employment to employment more rewarding. The law of May 30, 2001 (*Loi n° 2001–458 du 30 mai 2001 portant création d'une prime pour l'emploi*) establishing this tax credit, described its purpose as follows: "In order to encourage people to return to work or to remain in work, an entitlement to a tax refund or earned income tax credit (*prime pour l'emploi—PPE*) is being introduced for the benefit of natural persons domiciled in France." This is a government scheme designed to encourage employment and improve the remuneration of the lowest earners. According to Laurent Fabius, ten million people were to benefit in the first year. Introduced in 2001, it benefited tax households in which one member has earned income from work, but whose hourly wage is low.

In 2008, INSEE published a study on the earned income tax credit paid on the basis of income for 2001, concluding that the motivational effects of this tax credit were difficult to assess: "No significant effect of the PPE on employment emerged, including when there was a focus on the employment of married women. These results, in line with those of previous studies, which highlighted the reform's weak motivational power, can be explained, on the one hand, by the small sums distributed under the PPE in 2001 and, on the other, undoubtedly by the considerable time-lag between returning to the workplace and the PPE actually being paid (up to 18 months), which made it less visible. […] the scheme was probably still not very well known just one year after being introduced."[54]

The scheme, which still exists today but has been modified several times, has a dual purpose: it is redistributive and is intended to be motivational.

Another social advance was the introduction of universal health coverage (*couverture maladie universelle—CMU*) on January 1, 2000, in application of the Law of July 27, 1999 (*Loi n° 99–641 du 27 juillet 1999 portant création d'une couverture maladie universelle*). This scheme has two components: basic CMU and complementary CMU. One year after implementation, the basic universal health coverage benefited 1.1 million people. It also provided complementary coverage for almost 5 million people, or 8% of the French population (7.5% in mainland France and 36% in the overseas departments).

Over time, the number of basic CMU beneficiaries rose steadily, from 1.1 million in 2000 to 1.7 million in 2006. Between 2007 and 2010, the number of beneficiaries rose from 1.4 million to 2.2 million.

---

54 Arnaud Franck, Cochard, Marion, Junod-Mesqui, Bérengère, and Vermare, Sébastien, *The Motivating Effects of the French Tax Credit for Low-Earners: a Difficult Evaluation.*, INSEE, Economie et Statistique, n° 412, published October 1, 2008, source: https://www.insee.fr/en/statistiques/1377237?sommaire=1377243.

Lisbon European Council Meeting

"Don't confuse education,
general culture and professional competence."
Lionel Jospin, 2002

In the Presidency Conclusions to the Lisbon European Council of March 23 and 24, 2000, the first section dealing with employment, economic reform, and social cohesion set out what it terms "a strategic goal for the next decade," going on to describe "the new challenge" as follows:

> "1. The European Union is confronted with a quantum shift resulting from globalisation and the challenges of a new knowledge-driven economy. These changes are affecting every aspect of people's lives and require a radical transformation of the European economy. The Union must shape these changes in a manner consistent with its values and concepts of society and also with a view to the forthcoming enlargement.
>
> 2. The rapid and accelerating pace of change means it is urgent for the Union to act now to harness the full benefits of the opportunities presented. Hence the need for the Union to set a clear strategic goal and agree a challenging programme for building knowledge infrastructures, enhancing innovation and economic reform, and modernising social welfare and education systems."[55]

The Council stated that achieving its goals required an overall strategy aimed at "preparing the transition to a knowledge-based economy," towards "an information society for all." It explained that "the shift to a digital, knowledge-based economy, prompted by new goods and services, will be a powerful engine for growth, competitiveness and jobs. In addition, it will be capable of improving citizens' quality of life and the environment. To make the most of this opportunity, the Council and the Commission are invited to draw up a comprehensive eEurope Action Plan to be presented to the European Council in June this year, using an open method of coordination based on the benchmarking of national initiatives, combined with the Commission's recent eEurope initiative as well as its communication 'Strategies for jobs in the Information Society'."[56]

Although all European Councils mention the environment, and some even pat themselves on the back for the progress in this area, the environment is not yet really on the agenda. As for the knowledge-based economy, having fully embraced it, California's GDP has surpassed France's GDP since 2015. Yet California has a population of 38.9 million, to France's 66.5 million in 2015.

---

[55] Lisbon European Council, March 23 and 24 2000, Presidency Conclusions, source: https://www.europarl.europa.eu/summits/lis1_en.htm.
[56] Ibid.

The Father of the Euro

The European Monetary Institute (EMI) was established in January 1994 by the Maastricht Treaty as an intermediate but crucial step towards establishing the European Central Bank (which replaced it in 1998). Unlike the Committee of Governors that preceded it, the European Monetary Institute had its own legal personality. Its main focus was on establishing the European System of Central Banks, including the European Central Bank, and the new single currency.

In July 1997, when the European Monetary Institute (EMI) was about to be transformed into the European Central Bank, its President, the Hungarian-born Belgian economist Alexandre Lamfalussy [1929–2015] was replaced by Willem Frederik Duisenberg [1935–2005]. The Dutch economist and politician would go on to become the first President of the European Central Bank on June 1, 1998. Yet an agreement had been reached that, in return for the central bank having its seat in Frankfurt, its first president would be French. The members of the Executive Board are appointed for a non-renewable eight-year term. France accepts the appointment of Willem Frederik Duisenberg at the head of the European Central Bank, but on the condition his term of office is halved. He would in fact serve five years and five months until November 1, 2003, because before replacing him, Jean-Claude Trichet sought to clear his name in the Crédit Lyonnais near-bankruptcy trial in 1992–1993. As a result, it was Duisenberg's signature that can be found on the first euro banknotes put into circulation, for which reason he was regarded by the Americans as "the father of the euro."

What Determines EMU Accession…

> "Germans are not French people who speak German.
> They have a very different psychology."
> Laurent Fabius, 2012

… Not much sometimes. While France has to scrape the bottom of the barrel to demonstrate its compliance with the convergence criteria, Greece engaged in creative accounting, while Italy issued a mea culpa for its inflation and devaluations. Already being of the view that the convergence criteria are too accommodating, Germany would like to see the rules respected to the letter but is forced into one compromise after another. As German reunification placed a considerable financial burden, Germany was no longer in a position of strength, and so inclined to be more lenient with its European partners. This might have been a good thing at the time, but was the root cause of the public debt crisis that would rock the Euro Area from 2010 to 2012.

Of the twelve EU Member States (out of fifteen) wishing to join initially, eleven submitted their candidacy to join the Euro Area to the Commission on February 27,

1998, for examination by the European Council at the meeting held on May 3, 1998, in Brussels. Why did all these countries want to adopt the euro and not others?

The United Kingdom adopted the Maastricht Treaty under John Major and enacted a law giving the Bank of England operational independence over monetary policy in 1997, but Tony Blair, though profoundly pro-European, preferred to abstain. With sterling having been forced out of the EMS for lack of direct support from Germany and indirect support from France (who could have demanded that Germany respect the Nyborg Agreement), this gave the British pause for thought. The fact that their economy was highly correlated with the American economy was another argument for a national monetary policy.

Following the rejection of the Maastricht Treaty, Denmark preferred not to tempt fate once more, opting against further European integration.

A member of the European Union since 1995, Sweden felt it was not ready economically.

The fourth country is Greece, whose application was submitted when it was not even a member of the European Monetary System. No matter! In March 1998, by devaluing its currency by 13.8%, the drachma joined the EMS. In April 1998, Greece applied to join the euro. Its candidacy was rejected, whereas Italy's application was accepted.

The whole matter of accession was tainted by a beggar-thy-neighbor attitude: Greece could not abide Italy joining the euro before it, for it considered it was the birthplace of European civilization. As for Italy, as one of the founding members of the European Union, it was unimaginable that Spain should enter the Euro Area before it.

Under the Maastricht Treaty, the four convergence criteria to measure progress in countries' preparedness to adopt the euro were: price stability (so low inflation), sound and sustainable public finances, exchange rate stability (participation in ERM II for at least two years without severe tensions, in particular without devaluing the currency of another Member State), and durability of convergence (low long-term interest rates reflecting low inflation and public debt levels).

The improvement in Italy's deficit was spectacular. It was halved between 1996 and 1997 to reach the 3% required by the Maastricht criteria. But Italy's public debt was still 116.8% of GDP in 1997, when the debt-to-GDP ratio should not have exceeded 60%. The Italian lira only re-entered the EMS in November 1996, after losing half its value against the Deutschmark. Nevertheless, Italy's candidacy was admitted.

According to the World Bank, Greece's debt-to-GDP ratio reached 109.6% in 1997, 108.1% in 1998, 109% in 1999, 119.4% in 2000, and 123.6% in 2001.[57] However, in its candidacy, by dint of some creative accounting, this ratio was expected to reach 104.4% in 1999 and then pass below 100% in 2001, suggesting that the debt was on a downward trend, when it was quite the opposite. The deficit was expected

[57] Central government debt, total (% of GDP)—Greece, International Monetary Fund, source: https://data.worldbank.org/indicator/GC.DOD.TOTL.GD.ZS?end=2021&locations=GR&start=1997&view=chart

to improve from 10.2% of GDP in 1995 to 1.6% in 1999, so comfortably below the 3% ceiling imposed by the convergence criteria. Greece is a better pupil than Italy when it comes to the deficit. The durability of convergence is such that Greece's candidacy cannot but be approved. As it would turn out, it was the Trojan horse that would be EMU's undoing, triggering the 2010 public debt crisis.

As for France, as Talleyrand said: "When I examine myself, I am concerned. When I compare myself, I am reassured." The country's debt-to-GDP ratio soared from 46.2% in 1993 to 49.4% in 1994, then to 55.7% in 1995 and 58% in 1996. In 1997, it reached 59.3%, rising to 59.4% the following year, before dropping to 58.8% in 1999. But as it held below 60%, France met this Maastricht convergence criterion.

Keeping the general government deficit below 3% in 1997 required creativity, which in the world of finance is not a positive attribute... Dominique Strauss-Kahn [1949-] was Minister of the Economy, Finance, and Industry from June 1997 to November 1999. The deficit improved from 5.9% in 1993 to 5.4% in 1994, but then deepened to 5.5% in 1995, before improving to 4.1% in 1996. In 1997, the deficit was cut to 3%, not by a reduction in public spending, but by an exceptional budget receipt, which worked out down to the last franc to what was needed for France's deficit to land at 3%. The balancing cash payment came as a godsend.

However, as the balancing cash payment was not calculated to compensate for the difference between the public and private pension schemes, it was not correct. On December 20, 2011, the European Commission ordered Orange (formerly France Télécom) to pay almost €150 million in additional employer contributions for the pensions of employees who were civil servants. On February 26, 2015, the European Court of Justice in Luxembourg, having heard the appeal filed by Orange, upheld the European Commission's decision: "The operator thought it had settled the question of the civil servants' pensions in 1996, when it was transformed from an administration into a public limited company. At that time, its employer's contribution to the State was aligned with that of private companies. To compensate for the difference between the public and private systems, the former France Télécom made a balancing cash payment of €5.7 billion to the State. A welcome payment that enabled France to meet the Maastricht criteria...".[58]

Reelection of Jacques Chirac: Just Delaying the Inevitable

> "Because of the growth enjoyed these past two years, the State's coffers are full. It takes all the talent of the Ministry of Finance to mask this phenomenon. We need to give back to the French a share of what we've taken from them."
>
> Jacques Chirac, 1999

[58] Henni, Jamal, *Retraites: Orange perd son procès contre Bruxelles*, published February 26, 2015, source: https://www.bfmtv.com/economie/entreprises/services/retraites-orange-perd-son-proces-contre-bruxelles_AN-201502260118.html.

Up against the Far Right candidate in the runoff, Jacques Chirac was re-elected as President with 82.21% of the votes on May 5, 2002. On May 6, he appointed Jean-Pierre Raffarin [1948-] as Prime Minister, a position he held until May 31, 2005, when he was replaced by Dominique Galouzeau de Villepin [1953-].

"Bold reforming spirit" in the Areas of Public Finance, Healthcare and the Environment: "a matter of destiny"

In the General Policy Statement (*Déclaration de politique générale*) delivered on July 3, 2002, Jean-Pierre Raffarin's diagnosis of the state of public finances is accurate but not acted upon: "In this situation, the road ahead is straight but the slope is steep. A sentence from the audit report on the state of the country's public finances submitted to me by Messrs Bonnet and Nasse says it all, and we must grasp the nettle: 'Fundamental reforms are necessary, the simple search for savings without changes to the organization and structures is no longer enough given the immensity of the problem'. For France in the twenty-first century, a bold reforming spirit is a matter of destiny."[59]

The diagnosis is much the same when it comes to the state of the healthcare system: "Our healthcare system is our pride and joy, but today it is in a very, very difficult situation. Our population is demanding more and more care. Progress in science and medicine is accelerating all the time, and here, it is obvious that hopes are high—fortunately! But the fact that healthcare spending is rising too fast is a cause for deep concern about the future of the system: healthcare professionals are telling us loud and clear that they are going through a serious crisis of confidence."[60]

The Prime Minister went on: "As for hospitals, which are of grave concern to me as a minister and person, we need to give them new prospects for the future and create the necessary flexibility to combine proximity, permanent availability, a welcoming attitude, performance and safety. This action calls for new answers to the questions posed by the demographics of the healthcare professions. We will introduce a new form of governance for the healthcare and health insurance system. It will be based on three principles: greater clarity in the roles and funding of the State and the health insurance system, accountability on the part of all and, lastly, the desire to be closer to the population. [...]. We aim to avoid both a rationing of care and worrying uncontrolled expenditure overruns. [...]. With the Minister for Health, the Family and the Handicapped, I want to craft a modern healthcare policy."[61]

---

[59] *Déclaration de politique générale de M. Jean-Pierre Raffarin, Premier ministre, sur la restauration de l'autorité de l'État, la démocratie sociale et la relance de la décentralisation, la politique économique et sociale et sur la politique européenne de la France* to the National Assembly July 3, 2002, source: https://www.vie-publique.fr/discours/131219-jean-pierre-raffarin-03072002-declaration-de-politique-generale.

[60] Ibid.

[61] Ibid.

In terms of economic policy, what is astounding is that every French government is hell-bent on lowering social security contributions to support employment. While there is no evidence of such a correlation, what is certain is that reducing social security contributions weakens the financing of the social security system in a context where, as pointed out by Jean-Pierre Raffarin himself, expenditure is increasing. The general social security system is financed for 80% by contributions and taxes deducted from earnings, with social security contributions accounting for 82% of total financing in 1993 but only 49% in 2021.[62] Social security contributions are calculated by applying percentage rates decided at the national level and are borne partly by employers and partly by employees. The increase in tax exemptions, which began in the early 1990s, contributed to a considerable drop in the proportion of the financing provided by social security contributions, weakening everything that depends on these contributions.

In his general policy statement, Jean-Pierre Raffarin sets as an objective the creation of 200 thousand new businesses each year. In this respect, in 2003, the OECD invited the French authorities to "continue to support the reduction of administrative complexity by extending one-stop internet solutions for registering a new business."[63] Fast forward two decades later, and still the functioning of this one-stop counter is far from optimal.

Jean-Pierre Raffarin also declared: "We will also participate in everything that needs to be done to place France at the very heart of the information society." In this respect, the OECD recommends "ensuring that a certain proportion of revenues from licenses goes directly to the discoverers."[64]

The right diagnostic in all cases, but measures did not follow. Jean-Pierre Raffarin's five-year term was a far cry from the "bold reforming spirit" and need to "grasp the nettle" mentioned at the very start of his general policy statement.

When Jacques Chirac addressed the World Summit on Sustainable Development on September 2, 2002, he stated: "Our house is burning down and we're blind to it." And yet, no environmental objectives were set in the general policy statement of his Prime Minister in July 2002. In 2003, in its overview of progress implementing structural reform since 2000, in the section dealing with the environment,[65] the OECD warned that no measure had been taken in a number of areas in the interval and urged France to implement the following recommendations:

- "Better align environmental taxes with costs of externalities," put another way apply the polluter pays principle (PPP). Another recommendation along the same lines was to "cease attributing the revenues from water to finance local depollution efforts."
- "Subject diesel fuel to similar tax treatment as petrol."
- "Increase tax levels on emissions from sea and air transport."

---

[62] https://www.cleiss.fr/docs/regimes/regime_france/an_0.html.

[63] OECD, *OECD Economic Surveys: France 2003*, p. 105, source: https://read.oecd-ilibrary.org/economics/oecd-economic-surveys-france-2003/policies-to-raise-potential-output_eco_surveys-fra-2003-4-en#page56.

[64] Ibid, p. 106.

[65] Ibid, pp. 106–108.

- "Introduce tolls to limit peak-period traffic levels in major urban areas."
- "Implement tax on excess nitrogen."
- "Subject agricultural nitrogen inputs to taxation," with the following comment: "Implement the recommendation taking into account that at present tax levels on nitrogen content of commercial fertilizers are much lower than the environmental cost that their use imposes."[66]

The OECD warned about the use of pesticides in France, urging the authorities to "reform regulatory limits on pesticides." It pointed out that no measures have been taken since its last survey and that "current regulations do not distinguish adequately between the toxicity of different pesticides." It recommended authorities "implement different limits for different molecules and adjust tax rates in line with the environmental damage caused."

Non-Compliance with European Commitments

In 2001, growth slowed to 2% on account of the cycle downturn. Growth was just 1.1% in 2002 and then 0.8% in 2003. From 1998 to 2002, when France enjoyed stronger economic growth than the Euro Area, Lionel Jospin's government did not take advantage of the cycle peak to put public finances on an even keel. Laurent Fabius looked to cut taxes by FRF12 billion[67] over three years, without reducing public spending. The tax burden fell from 44.9% in 1999 to 44.1% in 2000, 43.8% in 2001, and 43.1% in 2002. As a result, France's public deficit deepened, while at the level of the Euro Area, it remained stable at 2.2%.

Once re-elected, Jacques Chirac continued this policy of lowering taxes without cutting spending, even though growth had tapered off. In 2003, the tax burden was reduced by 0.6%. From 58.8% in 2002, the debt-to-GDP ratio climbed to 62.4% in 2003, passing above the 60% ceiling imposed by the Stability and Growth Pact (SPG). This ratio continued to rise, reaching 64.3% in 2004, then 66.2% in 2005, 63.7% in 2006, and 64.2% in 2007.

In addition to the debt-to-GDP ratio passing above 60% in 2003, France's general government deficit passed the 3% mark, the country running up deficits of 3.2% in 2002 and then 4.1% in 2003. Germany and the UK were also black sheep, Germany running up deficits of 3.2% in 2002 and 3.9% in 2003, the United Kingdom deficits of 1.6% in 2002 and then 4.2% in 2003. As the United Kingdom had not joined the Euro Area, and its deficit was not far off 3%, its situation was less problematic than that of France and Germany.

These three countries failed to comply with the SPG deficit criterion but were in the minority. Many European countries—Spain, Ireland, Belgium, Sweden, Denmark, and Finland—posted a surplus in 2003. The deficits in Austria, Luxembourg, the Netherlands, and Portugal were below 3%. On paper, Greece's deficit reached 1.7%, but in reality exceeded 3%. This would all unravel later.

---

[66] Ibid, pp. 106–108.

[67] Equivalent to €2.69 billion.

In his general policy statement, Jean-Pierre Raffarin asserted: "We want a strong European project, a Europe of people, a Europe that respects our humanist heritage. But also a strong economic Europe, a Europe now built on the success of the euro. It must be a Europe that deepens the single market. Also, a Europe that must make progress in harmonizing tax systems, and which must be committed to strengthening its social role."[68]

Not only did France make no effort to these ends, but it destabilized European integration at a time when the European Union was being enlarged with the addition of ten new Member States on January 1, 2004. Instead of setting an example in its management of public finances and complying with European rules, France forced the European Commission's hand and circumvented these rules. On October 7, 2002, France promised to start reducing its structural deficit by 0.5 percentage point a year, starting in 2004, with the intention of achieving a balanced budget by 2007. Unlike Germany, which had the excuse of reunification, there was no justification for France requesting such a delay.

Germany quickly set about tackling its general government deficit. On March 14, 2003, in a Policy Statement to the German Bundestag, Gerhard Schröder presented a series of measures to implement the recommendations of the *Kommission für moderne Dienstleistungen am Arbeitsmarkt* chaired by Peter Harz, the Human Resources Director at Volkswagen. Harz gave his name to four laws designed to liberalize the labor market and stimulate growth, notably:

- The requirement for those unemployed to take up a reasonable offer of work even if the salary was inferior to their unemployment benefits;
- The creation of part-time job opportunities with a low monthly salary of less than €400 (so-called mini-jobs and midi-jobs) and the offer of grants to those unemployed to encourage business start-ups;
- The introduction of tougher eligibility criteria for unemployment benefits, which were now restricted to 12 months for older workers;
- The merger of long-term unemployment benefits with social welfare benefits.

With the so-called Harz-Reform, the former East Germany swung from one extreme to another. In the command economy that lasted for forty-five years until 1989, everyone had a job. With the Harz reforms, job insecurity was much greater, compounded by unemployment benefits not providing much protection. As a result, the birth rate in the former East Germany plummeted. The birth rate in the former West Germany also declined.

In addition to these measures, Angela Merkel [1954-], who would serve as Chancellor for sixteen years from November 2005 to December 2021, decided at the start of her mandate to increase the VAT rate from 16 to 19%, with 2% to go towards reducing the public deficit and 1% to offset the reduction in social security contributions.

---

[68] *Déclaration de politique générale de M. Jean-Pierre Raffarin, Premier ministre, sur la restauration de l'autorité de l'État, la démocratie sociale et la relance de la décentralisation, la politique économique et sociale et sur la politique européenne de la France* to the National Assembly July 3, 2002, source: https://www.vie-publique.fr/discours/131219-jean-pierre-raffarin-03072002-declaration-de-politique-generale.

Jacques Chirac did not take this fast track to rebalancing public finances. In 2003, with the agreement wrested from Gerhard Schröder, the French President fought hard to ensure that the budget for the Common Agricultural Policy (CAP) remained virtually unchanged. This budget came in for a slight downward revision from €44.3 billion to €41.66 billion, with a subsequent increase of 1% per year in value until 2013. This went against the advice of the Economic Advisory Group chaired by Belgian economist André Sapir, who considered that the EU budget does not correspond to the Lisbon strategy, but "is a historical relic," as €44.3 billion out of €97.5 billion or about "half of its spending goes on supporting a sector whose economic significance is declining",[69] namely agriculture, instead of promoting innovation as a driver of change, a knowledge-based economy and societal and environmental renewal for sustainable growth. Chirac put off the modernization of the CAP until 2013, at the cost of the European Union falling far behind in cognitive capitalism and organic farming, two areas where it trails to this day. The United States and China meanwhile forged ahead.

Having succeeded in putting off the CAP reform, Jacques Chirac sought to put off the inevitable, not tackling head-on the yawning government deficit. In the report published on July 22, 2003, Jean-Claude Trichet, who was serving out his final months as Governor of the Banque de France, considered that pursuing a "sound fiscal policy" was one of the three conditions necessary "to achieve robust growth and sustainable job creations." For the future President of the European Central Bank, breaking the "European consensus not to change the Stability and Growth Pact" was out of the question, this coming even as Jacques Chirac was calling for a temporary relaxation of SGP criteria. Jean-Claude Trichet also drew attention to the fact that, despite the economic slowdown in 2002, five of the twelve members of the Euro Area had maintained a close to or in surplus position. The two other conditions mentioned for stronger growth and lower unemployment were "the strengthening of policies aimed at reducing production costs" and "accelerated" structural reforms in the fields of education, training, labor law, and social protection. The report praised the pension reform implemented by Social Affairs Minister François Fillon [1954-] in 2003. Among changes made, the number of contribution quarters required for a full pension in the public sector was increased to 40 years in total, in line with the 1993 reform of private-sector pensions. Also, the pay-as-you-go pension scheme was completed by creating the popular retirement savings plan, an individualized funded pension scheme. But as the saying goes, one swallow doesn't make a spring.

At the start of 2003, the European Commission initiated the Excessive Deficit Procedure for France and Germany. Whereas Germany liberalized the labor market to stimulate growth and devoted part of the receipts generated by the hike in the VAT rate to reducing the general government deficit, France was content to aggressively challenge the rules of the Stability and Growth Pact and call for its reform. It is after all easier to question others than to question oneself. The European Council was due

[69] *An Agenda for a Growing Europe, Making the EU Economic System Deliver*, Report of an Independent High-Level Study Group established on the initiative of the President of the European Commission.

to impose sanctions in November 2003, but Jacques Chirac 'convinced' the Council to hold in abeyance the Excessive Deficit Procedure on November 25.

On November 26, 2003, shortly after his appointment at the head of the European Central Bank on November 1, 2003, Jean-Claude Trichet reiterated the importance of the Stability and Growth Pact, suggesting that failure to comply with its criteria would threaten price stability and could therefore lead to a rise in interest rates: "By contrast, non-disciplined fiscal policies, wage increases in excess of productivity growth and higher taxes would undermine confidence and thus reduce potential output and longer-term growth. Such a situation could soon lead to unwelcome inflationary pressures if not counteracted by monetary policy."[70]

To prevent smaller Member States or new Member States drawing the conclusion that the large founding member states can circumvent the rules they impose on others, the European Commission brought an action before the European Court of Justice, which, in its judgment of July 13, 2004, annulled the European Council's decision to put in abeyance the Excessive Deficit Procedure: "The Court hereby: [...] Annuls the Council's conclusions of 25 November 2003 adopted in respect of the French Republic and the Federal Republic of Germany respectively, in so far as they contain a decision to hold the excessive deficit procedure in abeyance and a decision modifying the recommendations previously adopted by the Council under Article 104(7) EC".[71]

Nevertheless, the Court observed that no party concretely possessed the possibility of forcing these two governments into reducing their deficits to remedy the situation of their public finances.

Chirac's criticisms of Brussels and Frankfurt resonated among French electors. In the referendum held on May 29, 2005, they voted at 54.87% against the second Treaty of Rome establishing a European constitution.

On June 27, 2005, a new version of the Stability and Growth Pact was adopted, the main objective being the prevention of structural deficits. The Maastricht convergence criteria for EMU accession remain unchanged, still for a deficit-to-GDP ratio of at most 3% and a debt-to-GDP ratio of at most 60%.

In 2005, Thierry Breton [1955-], Minister of the Economy, Finance and Industry from 2005 to 2007, commissioned a report on the state of the country's public finances from Michel Pébereau, the Chairman of BNP Paribas. The commission of twenty experts set up by Michel Pébereau produced a report[72] that was handed to Thierry Breton on December 13, 2005. The report, which said it was time to break with the easy option of public borrowing and to harness public finances in the service of the

[70] *The ECB's monetary policy strategy after the evaluation and clarification of May 2003*, speech by Jean-Claude Trichet, President of the European Central Bank, delivered at the Center for Financial Studies' key event, Frankfurt am Main, November 20, 2003.

[71] Commission v Council, Judgment of the Court (Full Court), July 13, 2004, in Case C-27/04, source: https://eur-lex.europa.eu/legal-content/EN/TXT/PDF/?uri=CELEX:62004CJ0027.

[72] *Rompre avec la facilité de la dette publique, Pour des finances publiques au service de notre croissance économique et de notre cohésion sociale*, report of the commission chaired by Michel Pébereau, source: https://www.vie-publique.fr/files/rapport/pdf/054004454.pdf.

country's economic growth and social cohesion, contained four recommendations that brought into question Jacques Chirac's economic policy:

"Recommendations:

1. Be back in balance within at most five years by stabilizing spending in current euros and modulating the intensity of the effort according to the economic situation.

2. No reduction in the level of the global tax burden while bringing public finances back in balance.

3. Allocation of all exceptional receipts to debt repayment, subject to transfers to the pension reserve fund (*fonds de réserve des retraites - FRR*).

4. Once back in balance, utilization of public finances to regulate the economic cycle."[73]

The report provides a rundown on how to adapt fiscal policy to the economic cycle:

"Four principles should therefore guide the State's fiscal policy once public finances are in balance:

- Insofar as possible, when at the peak of the cycle, avoid reducing the overall level of the tax burden, although this does not preclude a review of its structure.

- Continue reducing all government expenditure at a slower pace than while bringing public finances back in balance, but still guaranteeing a reduction in constant euros. This rule would apply to all expenditures, including the gradual provisioning of the future funding shortfall for the civil servants' pension scheme.

- Build up reserves at the peak of the cycle, thanks to the gap between expenditure (which would increase more slowly than inflation) and receipts (which would broadly track GDP).

- Use this room for maneuver to mitigate the effect of a slowdown in growth, through cuts in taxation and/or rises in expenditure, without breaching the country's European commitments.

It goes without saying that, once the fiscal leeway required for cyclical regulation has been restored, it will be up to the public authorities to set the level and structure of both the tax burden and public expenditure, in keeping with the principle of balanced public finances. This decision stems from a set of political choices and a societal choice."[74]

Following this report, Dominique de Villepin did declare that the government debt would be cut to 60% of GDP, but after declining slightly from 66.2% in 2005 to 63.7% in 2006, the debt recovered to 64.2% in 2007, the final year of Jacques Chirac's presidency and his government.

Dominique de Villepin's attempt to liberalize the labor market by introducing two new types of employment contracts also proved futile. The new employment contract (*contrat nouvelle embauche—CNE*), introduced in August 2005 and reserved for companies with fewer than twenty employees, which allows dismissal without prior notice for the first two years, was declared contrary to international law by the International Labour Organization on November 14, 2007. Under pressure from the street, the first employment contract (*contrat première embauche—CPE*), a modified version of the new employment contract reserved for young people under the age of 26 (nearly 25% of whom were unemployed that year), was not implemented. Eleven

[73] Ibid.

[74] Ibid.

days after the law providing for its creation was promulgated, Dominique de Villepin announced that "the conditions are not in place" for the CPE's application.

Chapter 11
2008 Financial Crisis and 2010 Sovereign Debt Crisis

> "There is one reality that everyone must understand and accept: sovereignty can only be exercised with others. Europe does not mean less sovereignty, but more sovereignty, because it means more capacity to act. You can defend your sovereignty better with allies than single-handed. That's the big lesson of twentieth-century history."[1]
>
> Nicolas Sarkozy, 2011

After the Chirac era, another president from the right of the political spectrum was elected in May 2007. Nicolas Sarkozy [1955-] would serve just one five-year term. François Fillon [1954-] would be the Prime Minister throughout this period.

In 2007, the French economy was in good shape: GDP reached 2.4% and 358 thousand jobs in total were created by the French economy, including 275 thousand in the service sector. Although the jobs created were in lower-value-added sectors, including temporary work, they reflect the continuation and acceleration of the recovery in employment that began in 2004. The construction sector recorded an increase of 4.3%, on par with 2006. On the other hand, there were further job losses in the industrial sector. The pace of job losses did slow, however, with 46 thousand jobs lost in 2007, compared with 59 thousand in 2006 and 87 thousand in 2005.

As mentioned above, a new version of the Stability and Growth Pack was adopted on June 27, 2005, with as main objective not to have a structural deficit. The structural budget balance is a nominal budget balance adjusted by the cyclical component, excluding one-off and temporary policy measures.[2] Nicolas Sarkozy inherited a structural deficit of 2.6%.

---

[1] Le Figaro, *Le discours de Nicolas Sarkozy à Toulon en 2011*, source: https://www.lefigaro.fr/politique/le-scan/2014/03/27/25001-20140327ARTFIG00086-le-discours-de-nicolas-sarkozy-a-toulon-en-2011.php.

[2] European Parliament, Briefing, Structural budget balances in EU Member States—November 2019, source: https://www.europarl.europa.eu/RegData/etudes/BRIE/2017/587388/IPOL_BRI(2017)587388_EN.pdf.

C. Peicuti, *A Monetary and Economic History of France since 1944*, Contributions to Economics, https://doi.org/10.1007/978-3-032-17596-0_11

Deepening of Government Deficit Ahead of Subprime Crisis

"Captain Bordure:

'Oh, come on. Pa Ubu, don't you see that the people are awaiting the fruits of your joyous accession[3]?'

Ma Ubu:

'If you don't hand out meat and gold you'll be dethroned within two hours.'"[4]

Alfred Jarry [1873-1907]. *Ubu roi* (1868)

Nicolas Sarkozy does not see the clouds gathering on the horizon, announcing the greatest financial crisis since 1929. Worse still, instead of thinking about how to bring the structural deficit close to zero, the new President remained faithful to the French tradition of lavish handouts at the start of his term, only later did he take stock of the situation. So, even before the subprime crisis worsened the persistent imbalance in France's public finances, the government of François Fillon was already doing exactly that, notably with the Law of August 21, 2007, in favor of work, employment and purchasing power (*Loi n° 2007–1223 du 21 août 2007 en faveur du travail, de l'emploi et du pouvoir d'achat*, the so-called *Loi TEPA*). With this law, the government resumed the crusade to lower taxes and social security contributions, with a flagship measure concerning overtime (exemption from income tax and payroll taxes). The law also lowered the tax shield (*bouclier fiscal*) to 50% applicable to direct taxes, including the wealth tax. The law encouraged geographical mobility by removing or reducing the transfer tax (*droits de mutation*) and the purchase of a main residence by allowing mortgage interest to be deducted for income tax purposes.

The tax deductibility of mortgage loan interest took the form of a tax credit equivalent to 40% of interest paid in the first year and 20% of interest paid in the next four years. Real estate financing was the root cause of the 2008 crisis, just as it was for the 1929 crisis. By supporting the real estate sector before the crisis began, Nicolas Sarkozy prevented real estate prices from collapsing when the crisis broke out, whereas prices nosedived in the United States. To succeed is an undertaking the Greek philosopher Aristotle warned that one cannot be sparing in one's efforts: "Fire a thousand arrows and you will end up catching something." One problem created by the crisis was nipped in the bud thanks to the so-called TEPA Law, but the volleys of arrows let off by the government led to a premature and exorbitant debt escalation.

According to the Senate's Information Report of October 26, 2011: "The cost of the TEPA Law [from 2007 to 2011], after taking into account direct and indirect mitigations, is of the order of €9.3 billion, half of which on account of the measure

[3] In French *don de joyeux avènement*, referring to gifts to and by the king on his accession to the throne. At coronation ceremonies knighthoods or higher honors would be bestowed, gifts lavished, feasts held for the nobility and, sometimes, conduits of wine provided throughout the city in which the coronation was taking place. Source: https://thehundredyearswar.co.uk/coronation-of-king-charles-vi-of-france/.

[4] Jarry, Alfred (1973), Ubu Rex, a new translation by David Copelin, Pulp Press, Vancouver, Canada, source: https://coldreads.files.wordpress.com/2018/07/ubu-roi-copelin.pdf.

relating to overtime, the remainder being almost entirely divided between the income tax credit in respect of mortgage loan interest and the reduction in taxes on transfers not for onerous consideration."[5]

In 2007, the cost of these measures totaled €1.3 billion, of which €0.9 billion in respect of the exemption of overtime from income tax and payroll taxes. In 2008, the cost rose to €6.2 billion, of which €3.3 billion in respect of this exemption. These tax cuts, which were not accompanied by spending cuts, caused the structural deficit to deteriorate to 3%. Nicolas Sarkozy promised to break with the previous government. Yet with this law, it was all about continuity, with no departure from Jacques Chirac's economic policy. Like the President, he was not sparing in his criticism of the European Central Bank and its President, Jean-Claude Trichet.

The pension reform can be put in the plus column, so too the General Review of Public Policies (*Revue Générale des Politiques Publiques—RGPP*), aimed at reducing public spending while increasing the efficiency and quality of public action. This last measure would generate €8 billion of savings.

As part of the pension reform, the retirement age was raised to 62 for the general scheme (*régime général de la sécurité sociale*). Sarkozy's ambition is to succeed where Juppé and Chirac failed: to align retirement eligibility conditions for the public sector with those of the private sector. Two decrees reforming the special schemes (*régimes spéciaux de la sécurité sociale*) were published on January 15, 2008, for SNCF and RATP, a third on January 22, 2008, for the electricity and gas industries. On December 31, 2006, the SNCF pension fund (*Caisse de prévoyance et de retraite du personnel de la SNCF*) had 165,280 contributors and 297,751 pensioners, the RATP pension fund (*Caisse de retraite du personnel de la RATP*) 44,180 contributors and 43,733 pensioners, and the pension fund for the electricity and gas industries (*Caisse nationale des industries électriques et gazières*) 145,520 contributors and 145,341 pensioners. But this alignment did not go all the way: for example, in the case of the SNCF, the retirement age is maintained, but the number of years of contributions required to receive a full pension is aligned with the general scheme. As part of this reform, civil servants gradually increased their contribution period from 37.5 years to 40 years in 2008. Thereafter, the contribution period was extended for everyone to more than 40 years: the period was gradually raised to 41 years in 2012, at the end of Nicolas Sarkozy's presidency. The reform also provided for the indexation of civil servant pensions to prices, as in the private sector following the Balladur reform.

Three other special schemes are concerned by the 2008 reform: the pension and provident fund for notaries' clerks and employees (*Caisse de retraite et de prévoyance des clercs et employés de notaires*), which had 49,475 contributors and 55,782 pensioners, and the Comédie française pension fund (*Caisse de retraite de la Comédie française*) and Opéra de Paris pension fund (*Caisse de retraite de l'Opéra de Paris*). It is hard to imagine that the 382 Comédie française pensioners and the 1,633 Opéra de Paris pensioners were destabilizing France's pension system! Nicolas Sarkozy

[5] French Senate, Information Report n° 64 (2011–2012), *Prélèvements obligatoires 2007–2012: un quinquennat d'incohérences et d'injustices*, filed October 26, 2011, source: https://www.senat.fr/rap/r11-064/r11-0642.html#fn8.

reformed the special scheme for the dancers of the Opéra de Paris, which had been set up by Louis XIV… Every little helps when it comes to savings, but then there are also huge heads of expenditures!

In December 2009, Nicolas Sarkozy declared: "On June 22, before the Congress of the French Parliament (*Congrès*),[6] I announced that the first task of the government after the reshuffle would be to reflect on our national priorities and to arrange a loan to finance them."[7] Is it necessary to live through a crisis like that of 2008 to reflect on 'priorities for the future' before spending on credit? The expression 'priorities for the future' should be a pleonasm in economic policy, but as French presidencies often begin by financing current expenditure on credit, it is unfortunately not. After Chirac's 'kitty' (*cagnotte*), we have Sarkozy's 'investment for the future' (*investissements d'avenir*). There is no kitty, only funds accumulated at the top of the cycle, which should be utilized to tide the economy through the cycle downturn. As for priorities and investments, they should all be with the future in mind…

American Causes of Subprime Crisis and Response of French Economic Policy

> "Financiers flourish only
> when nations decline."[8]
> Talleyrand [1754–1838]

In the 1990s, subprimes—mortgage loans extended to borrowers who exhibit characteristics that indicate a significantly higher risk of default than prime customers and charge three percentage points above the rate for equivalent maturity Treasury securities—were still a niche market in the United States. This changed when securitization allowed subprime loans to be repackaged into investment products that were then sold, enabling these loans to be taken off the lenders' balance sheets. Exposure to the default risk in respect of subprime borrowers was thus transferred from the banks to the buyers of products invested in subprime loans. With lenders no longer exposed to the credit risk, hence no longer having to tie down capital to cover this risk, they gradually became less stringent in selecting subprime borrowers, with an increasing number able to benefit from variable-rate mortgages, bearing in mind these generate a far greater margin than prime mortgage loans.

---

6 The Congress of the French Parliament is the name given to the body created when both houses of the present-day French Parliament—the National Assembly and the Senate—meet at the Palace of Versailles to notably listen to an address by the President of the French Republic.

7 Press conference by Nicolas Sarkozy, President of the Republic, on the priorities financed by the national loan, Paris, December 14, 2009, source: https://www.vie-publique.fr/discours/177597-conference-de-presse-de-m-nicolas-sarkozy-president-de-la-republique.

8 Bernard, J. F. (1973), *Talleyrand: A Biography*, Putnam.

"In the United States, securitization experienced an extremely rapid boom. In ten years, the market for mortgage-backed securities and asset-backed securities tripled, reaching $10,000 billion in 2007, equivalent to 40% of the US bond market. In Europe, the securitization market consisted for 50% of mortgage-backed securities and 50% of asset-backed securities. At European level, the market for asset-backed securities remained modest at €100 billion in the second quarter of 2007, while by then the US market exceeded €238 billion."[9]

Yet, as early as November 2002, the Federal Reserve warned of the risk faced by institutions purchasing high-margin but also high-risk loans from lenders and dealers:

"As they evaluate expected profits, institutions that purchase subprime loans from other lenders or dealers must give due consideration to the cost of servicing these assets and to the loan losses that may be experienced. For instance, some lenders who sell subprime loans charge borrowers high up-front fees, which are usually financed into the loan. This provides incentive for originators to produce a high volume of loans with little emphasis on quality, to the detriment of a potential purchaser. Further, subprime loans, especially those purchased from outside the institution's lending area, are at special risk for fraud or misrepresentation (that is, the quality of the loan may be less than the loan documents indicate)."[10]

The mechanism that would trigger the subprime crisis was described by the Federal Reserve Board's Division of Supervision and Regulation as early as November 2002. Yet nothing was done in terms of regulation or monetary policy to stop the formation of a speculative bubble that ballooned so large that its bursting reverberated across the world. Worse still, investment products from repackaging subprime mortgages were highly rated by US credit rating agencies, with these products being sold around the world, disseminating the risk, much as a powder trail, ensuring that the crisis would spread like wildfire. Demand was strong, as yields were higher than that of other products, and these investment vehicles were highly rated. Yet these were opaque vehicles that the sellers and buyers did not fathom. And in finance, anything that is not simple, transparent, and easy to understand is bound to be unhealthy.

"There was certainly a degree of social pressure on the Fed's monetary policy, insofar as low interest rates provide access to housing for the less privileged social classes. Moreover, the higher property prices rise, the more important it is to keep interest rates low to facilitate access to home ownership. But delaying rate hikes fueled the upward spiral in real estate prices. Fed members were well aware of this. Nevertheless, many considered the Federal Reserve's track record to be positive, as can be seen, for example, in Governor Edward M. Gramich's speech on May 21, 2004, at the Financial Services Roundtable Annual Housing Policy Meeting in Chicago, when he emphasized that because of this monetary policy nearly 9 million new homeowners were now able to live in their own homes, more than half of whom are minorities."[11]

Many subprime borrowers lost their homes in the crisis. Banks and savers' deposits were saved, but subprime borrowers benefited from no measures enabling them to

---

[9] Peicuti, Cristina (2010), *Crédit, déstabilisation et crises*, L'Harmattan.

[10] Article 2133.1 of the Commercial Bank Examination Manual. Effective date November 2002, source: http://www.federalreserve.gov/boarddocs/supmanual/cbem/200810/2000.pdf.

[11] Peicuti, Cristina (2010), *Crédit, déstabilisation et crises*, L'Harmattan.

extend their loans, refinance at rates of less than 6%, stagger repayments, or negotiate a payment holiday, even though these were financially vulnerable people to begin with. Foreclosures were decreed and the mortgaged property sold at the worst moment of the crisis, when worth far less than when purchased, pushing subprime borrowers into bankruptcy. Ultimately, it is the poor who paid for the greed of the banks and the errors of the financial system. The aftermath of this crisis would lay the foundations for Donald Trump's presidency. On a global scale, by impoverishing populations, the 2008 crisis led to a wave of populism (responsible for Brexit) that is still sweeping across Europe.

The magnitude of the crisis was all the greater given that all the progress of the previous economic cycle was wiped out by an unprecedented easing of monetary policy and a highly expansionary fiscal policy. As a result, the adjustments that should have taken place when the cycle turned were postponed until the next cycle. To prevent those having ordered the September 11, 2001, terrorist attacks from taking credit for an economic slowdown in fact caused by a cycle downturn and claiming that their attacks had succeeded in destabilizing the US economy, Alain Greenspan, Chairman of the Federal Reserve, and George Bush, President of the United States, decided to overcompensate for the cycle downturn with a highly expansionary fiscal policy and by rushing to cut the Federal Reserve's key policy rate from 5.5% before the attacks to 1.75% in January 2002. This decision made it easier for more and more subprime borrowers to buy a main residence. Low rates also encouraged investors to buy more and more subprime products, which yielded higher returns than other products in a context of artificially low rates and abundant liquidity. As the ensuing downturn combined the adjustments of two cycles and was coupled with the bursting of the speculative subprime bubble, which had not stopped ballooning, this triggered a crisis that would be global. Saving the short term at the expense of the long term comes at a steep cost.

France's growth rate fell from 2.2% in 2007 to 0.8% in 2008, with GDP going on to contract by 2.5% in 2009. Following the economic downturn in the second quarter of 2008, the unemployment rate rose sharply. After improving for two consecutive years to 7.4% in 2008, the unemployment rate averaged 9.1% in 2009, at its highest level since 1999. In metropolitan France, almost 2.6 million people were unemployed in 2009, almost 508 thousand or 25% more than in 2008.

Nicolas Sarkozy's response to the crisis was to launch a stimulus plan. On December 5, 2008, the President appointed a minister to serve under the Prime Minister, specifically responsible for implementing the stimulus plan. On August 26, 2009, a large national loan (*Grand Emprunt*) was launched, with the establishment of an ad-hoc commission charged with strategic investment priorities and the national loan, co-chaired by Alain Juppé and Michel Rocard. On December 14, 2009, following the submission of the commission's report, he declared in his press conference on the decisions taken regarding the national loan and the priorities of the future:

> "We have therefore decided to mobilize €35 billion, which will be devoted exclusively to the priorities of the future [...]. This means that we will be embarking on €60 billion of

investments, public and private, in five priority areas that largely coincide with the Commission's recommendations: higher education and training, research, industry and small and medium-sized enterprises, digital technology and, finally, sustainable development.

First priority, higher education and training, to which will be devoted €11 billion. [...]

Second priority, research, €8 billion [...]

Third priority, industry and small and medium-sized enterprises, €6.5 billion [...]

Fourth priority, sustainable development. €5 billion of additional investment, on top of the €7 billion of state investment planned each year until 2020 further to the Grenelle Environment Round Table (*Grenelle de l'Environnement*). A major technological effort is required. We will therefore launch the development of fourth-generation nuclear reactors (€1 billion), which by recycling uranium and plutonium will produce much less waste. But the bulk of the effort will be focused on renewable energies, with €2.5 billion earmarked for ADEME, which will then select the best projects presented by research units dedicated to renewable energies at the Institut français du pétrole (IFP), Centre national de la recherche scientifique (CNRS), Commissariat à l'énergie atomique (CEA) and universities.

The CEA has unrivaled technological know-how in the field of nuclear energy, but what is less well known is that, thanks to this organization, France is at the forefront of world research in solar energy, biofuels and energy storage. Tomorrow, I would like to see this research organization further develop this focus on alternative low-carbon energies. After all, the aim here is to respect the government's commitment to absolute parity in research efforts between nuclear and renewable energies. The CEA will thus become the Commissariat à l'énergie atomique et aux energies alternatives (CEA^2).

Digital economy, to which will be devoted €4.5 billion. [...] Of this €4.5 billion, €750 million will be earmarked for the digitization of the content of our museums, libraries and cinematographic heritage."[12]

Subprime Crisis and French Presidency of European Council in 2008

The presidency of the Council rotates among the EU Member States every six months. France assumed the presidency from July 1 to December 1, 2008, when the international financial crisis was in full swing. For this reason, great attention was paid to the speech given by Nicolas Sarkozy in Toulon on September 25, 2008[13] on the international financial crisis and France's economic policy, this speech receiving media coverage throughout the 27 EU Member States. The first part of the speech was addressed to France's EU partners.

At the very start of the crisis, at the height of the financial meltdown, Nicolas Sarkozy mapped out the road ahead and what had to be done. His undeniable merit is that he did not make the wrong diagnosis. He understood from the outset that this was

[12] Press conference by Nicolas Sarkozy, President of the Republic, on the priorities financed by the national loan, Paris, December 14, 2009, source: https://www.vie-publique.fr/discours/177597-conference-de-presse-de-m-nicolas-sarkozy-president-de-la-republique.

[13] Address by Nicolas Sarkozy, President of the Republic, on the international financial crisis and France's economic policy, Toulon, September 25, 2008, source: https://www.vie-publique.fr/discours/172360-declaration-de-m-nicolas-sarkozy-president-de-la-republique-sur-la-cr.

a deficiency in the global financial system that could be corrected by regulation, and that this financial crisis did not signal a failure as such of the market economy and global trade: "Then we need to tighten regulation of the banks to regulate the system, because banks are at the heart of the system. We need to stop imposing prudential rules on banks that encourage creative accounting rather than rigorous risk management. What we need to do in the future is to monitor much more closely the way they do their business, their risk assessment and management, the effectiveness of their internal controls…".[14]

The call for more stringent regulation in response to the 2008 crisis would lead to the creation of the Banking Union. This is a considerable breakthrough for European taxpayers. There are three pillars: the Single Supervisory Mechanism (SSM), the Single Resolution Mechanism (SRM), and the European Deposit Insurance Scheme (EDIS). The Single Supervisory Mechanism is an EU-level system for prudential supervision of the largest credit institutions in the Euro Area, while the Single Resolution Mechanism is intended to ensure an orderly resolution of ailing banks with minimal costs to taxpayers and to the real economy.

As Nicolas Sarkozy spoke with candor about the crisis and insisted that it had not called capitalism into question, but an amoral financial system that had betrayed the values of the market economy, the French President managed to restore confidence. This is essential in the context of a financial crisis, for as Franklin Delano Roosevelt explained in his inaugural speech on March 4, 1933: "The only thing we have to fear is fear itself."[15] Nicolas Sarkozy being well aware of this, he made the same point in his speech: "As everywhere else in the world, the French are afraid for their savings, for their jobs, for their purchasing power. Fear is suffering. Fear prevents us from undertaking, from committing. When you are afraid, you have no dreams, you cannot project yourself into the future. Fear is the main threat to the economy today. This fear must be overcome. This is the most urgent task. We will not overcome fear, we will not restore confidence by shrinking from the truth, but by telling the truth. The French want the truth, and they are ready to hear it. If they feel that something is being hidden from them, doubts will grow. If they are convinced that nothing is being hidden from them, they will draw upon their inner strength to overcome the crisis."[16]

In the second part of his speech, he addressed the French people. Once again, he was at pains to restore confidence by asserting that the State would guarantee the bank deposits of customers and take the necessary measures to ensure the continued financing of productive investment. To better withstand the crisis, he announced an increase in the research tax credit to 30% to support innovation-based growth.

---

[14] Ibid.

[15] Franklin D. Roosevelt, Inaugural Address, March 4, 1933, as published in Samuel Rosenman, ed., The Public Papers of Franklin D. Roosevelt, Volume Two: The Year of Crisis, 1933 (New York: Random House, 1938), pp. 11–16.

[16] Address by Nicolas Sarkozy, President of the Republic, on the international financial crisis and France's economic policy, Toulon, September 25, 2008, source: https://www.vie-publique.fr/discours/172360-declaration-de-m-nicolas-sarkozy-president-de-la-republique-sur-la-cr.

In his speech, Nicolas Sarkozy insisted on the need for a global response to the international financial crisis. On October 12, 2008, he hosted a summit of Euro Area heads of state and government at the Élysée Palace. Instead of blaming the United States for triggering the crisis, the French President, accompanied by José Manuel Barroso, the President of the European Commission, traveled to Camp David to convince President Bush of the need for a global response to the financial crisis. In his political memoir, *La France pour la vie*, Nicolas Sarkozy explained that: "Still President-in-office of the European Union, I had to try to organize the reaction, at least of our continent, by convening a summit of the Euro Area heads of state or government at the Élysée Palace on Sunday October 12, 2008, the first such meeting in the nine years since the euro's adoption, and by adopting the rescue plan for European banks, which served as a model for the rest of the world, notably the United States. However, since the crisis originated in the United States, it was impossible to do it without this country. I therefore decided to convince the President of the United States, George Bush, to take the initiative in the counter-offensive."[17]

He describes his meeting with George Bush as follows: "I wanted to convince him that we needed to bring together in Washington, as a matter of urgency, the representatives of the world's largest economies to try to coordinate their economic policies, influence the course of events, and begin to regulate world finance, which was in great need of it. George Bush was initially reluctant. The very principle of a regulatory response was not really part of the American DNA, especially among Republicans, but also Democrats. His abiding fear was that he would be put in the dock. I extolled the merits of a meeting at fourteen, namely the G8 plus the G5 of major emerging countries, with the addition of an Arab country, which could be Saudi Arabia or Egypt. Eventually, he agreed in principle to a meeting in Washington, but on condition that there would be twenty of us, not fourteen. He wanted longstanding US allies—Australia, Turkey, Saudi Arabia, South Korea, Mexico, and Argentina—to be added to the guest list. And so was born the G20, which since 2008 has managed the world's major economic issues."[18]

Market's Gamble on Euro Area Achilles' Heel

On October 4, 2009, ten million Greeks went to the polls. The Socialist Party won the general elections. On October 21, the government of George Papandreou [1952-], Greece's Prime Minister from October 2009 to November 2011, announced that the 2009 government deficit, forecast by the previous government at 3.7%, had in fact risen to 12.7% of GDP, far above the European Union limit of 3%. The Greek Deputy Finance Minister reported that the government debt stood at 113% of GDP at the end of 2009, far above the European Union limit of 60%. Greece's debt towered at €300 billion. On December 8, Fitch Ratings downgraded Greece from A− to BBB+

[17] Sarkozy, Nicolas (2016), *La France pour la vie*, Plon.

[18] Ibid.

. The same US government-sponsored credit rating agencies that had rated subprime mortgage securities so highly even though they were toxic were now, three years later, taken seriously enough to undermine trust in Greek debt and, implicitly, the euro. This was the beginning of a descent into hell.

In France, with no let-up in public spending since the start of Nicolas Sarkozy's presidency, this diminished the country's negotiating clout with Germany, which was running a government deficit of 3.3% in 2009, the structural deficit reaching 2%, whereas France's government deficit for the same year was 7.2%, the structural deficit reaching 5%. After the Chirac era and two years into Sarkozy's presidency, France's credibility in terms of fiscal discipline and compliance with EU commitments had hit rock bottom. One crisis can hide another… and with its public finances in such dire straits, France's voice was drowned out.

On December 14, 2009, even as Nicolas Sarkozy, believing that the crisis was now behind, was happily detailing how the proceeds of the Grand Emprunt would be applied, George Papandreou presented a raft of reforms to put the country's finances on a sound footing. His ambition is to prevent Greek government debt from reaching 130% of GDP by 2010. George Papandreou warned that some changes called for would be painful. "We must all lose our comfort",[19] he said. Measures included a 10% cut in healthcare spending, the taxation at 90% of bankers' bonuses and a curb on civil servant pay increases. Rightly blaming corruption and tax evasion for having ruined Greece, he announced: "We need to move immediately to a new social deal. We must change or sink."[20] Not only are the Greeks up in arms over the measures, but the austerity plan fails to restore investor confidence. If Athens had been London, the 90% tax on City bankers' bonuses might have done the trick, but in the case of Greece this measure fell flat. Investors see these as one-off measures, whereas structural reforms were expected. In reaction, interest rates on Greek debt climbed above 10%.

As early as December 12, 2009, investor wariness had started to spread to all the PIGS, a rather unflattering acronym coined by investors to designate Portugal, Ireland, Greece, and Spain. The euro, which had only been in circulation since 2002, is a young currency whose first years of existence have been a success. In 2010, the euro accounted for 28% of international foreign currency reserves. Would it have matched the US dollar had it not been for the mismanagement of the European sovereign debt crisis? The fact that, because of the state of its public finances, France no longer had the credibility needed to convince Germany to save Greece would force the latter to seek an IMF bailout. This dealt a final blow to the euro's ambition of becoming the leading reserve currency. By the end of 2023, its share of international foreign currency reserves was just 20%. The 2010 sovereign debt crisis left its imprint. Shame on the European Union for failing to deal with the Greek crisis on its own, leaving Greece, though part of a strong monetary area, to go hand in cap to the IMF as would an emerging country.

---

[19] *Greek PM says Greece needs new social deal*, Reuters, source: https://www.reuters.com/article/greece-economy-speech-idUSLDE5BD2B220091214/.

[20] Ibid.

On May 9, 2010, the Executive Board of the International Monetary Fund gave the go ahead to a first rescue plan for Greece, approving a €30 billion Stand-By Arrangement as part of a total €110 billion joint Euro Area/IMF financing package. Threatened with bankruptcy and unable to access financial markets, Greece was granted this substantial sum in order to honor its debt. In return, the IMF imposed drastic austerity measures. Confidential documents divulged by the Wall Street Journal[21] have revealed that nearly a third of the IMF Executive Board, representing more than forty non-European countries, raised major objections to the Greek bailout's design. "The alternative of a voluntary debt restructuring should have been on the table," said Argentina's executive director at the IMF, Pablo Andres Pereira. He warned that the IMF risked merely "postponing, and maybe worsening the inevitable"—a Greek debt default. The scale of the fiscal adjustments required of Greece would be "a mammoth burden that the economy could hardly bear," India's director at the IMF, Arvind Virmani, told the meeting. He fretted that these adjustments "could trigger a deflationary spiral of falling prices, falling employment, and falling fiscal revenues that could eventually undermine the program itself." This is exactly the trap in which Greece found itself in 2011 and 2012.

On February 21, 2012, Euro Area countries agreed a Second Economic Adjustment Programme for Greece to stave off bankruptcy, which combined €130 billion in new financing along with a €107 billion debt write-off by private creditors, banks, and investment funds.

In return, ten days before the meeting of Euro Area countries, a new austerity package was passed by the Greek Parliament despite more than 100 thousand Greeks taking to the streets of Athens and Salonika in protest. This called for a 22% reduction to the standard minimum monthly wage, to €586 gross over 14 months, with an even more brutal 32% cut for those under 25. The austerity plan also called for a reduction in the number of civil servants, bearing in mind that one in five people in employment was a civil servant or much the same proportion as in France. The pay of certain public sector employees benefiting from special regimes was cut by 10%. Cuts are to be made to the highest pensions. State-owned enterprises in the gaming, water, oil, and gas sectors are to be privatized. The objective was to achieve €3.3 billion of savings in 2012.

But the new austerity plan and Second Economic Adjustment Programme failed to reassure the markets. On July 26, 2012, to restore market confidence, Mario Draghi [1947-], the President of the European Central Bank from 2011 to 2019, announced: "Within our mandate, the ECB is ready to do whatever it takes to preserve the euro. And believe me, it will be enough."[22] Shortly after, the European Central Bank (ECB) went on to announce a new programme of open-ended, unlimited buying of government bonds, what it termed outright monetary transactions, but it was never activated as Mario Draghi's intervention had instantly restored confidence! 18 s was all it took.

[21] Wall Street Journal, *IMF Document Excerpts: Disagreements Revealed*, source: https://www.wsj.com/articles/BL-REB-20793.

[22] Video: https://www.youtube.com/watch?v=W97hM8eCE5g.

Central banks develop strategies, proffer guidance through commitments relating to future decisions, which can be conditional or unconditional, like this one. Mario Draghi's intervention has proved the most effective commitment in the history of central bank communication, and has become a textbook case. If only this unconditional commitment had come two years earlier from the other Euro Area institutions! Of course, better late than never, but as the Roman poet Publilius Syrus explained in the first century BC: "*Bis dat, qui dat celeriter*" ("He who gives quickly gives twice").

The Accomplishments of Nicolas Sarkozy's Presidency

Proof that Nicolas Sarkozy succeeded in restoring confidence and quelling the political risk in the short term was when France next went to the ballot box. In the 2012 presidential elections, neither the far right nor the far left qualified for the second round. Marine Le Pen obtained 17.9% and Jean-Luc Mélenchon 11.1% of the votes in the first round of the 2012 presidential election.[23]

Although governments and central banks looked on as the dynamics built up that would lead to the subprime crisis and shake the global economy, the crisis itself was more ably managed. European countries did not succumb to protectionism in a knee-jerk reaction, nor did they withdraw into their shell as they did after the 1929 crisis. Nicolas Sarkozy deserves some of the credit for this.

As for France, the Senate produced the following assessment of Nicolas Sarkozy's five-year presidency:

> "On the one hand, costly measures amounting to €17 billion (TEPA Law €10 billion, reduction of VAT on food services €3 billion, reduction in business tax €4 billion);
>
> - On the other hand, measures that more than offset these costly measures, to the tune of €28 billion (including €1 billion in direct or indirect mitigations of the TEPA Law), almost all of it concentrated in 2011 and 2012;
>
> - [...] the stimulus plan, which cost €12.7 billion in 2009, but this cost was only temporary."[24]

In other words, even in the short term, it was taxpayers who lost out. Long term, France also, with debt rising from 64.4% of GDP in 2007 to 68.1% in 2008, 79% in 2009, 81.7% in 2010, 85.2% in 2011, and 89.3% at the end of the first quarter of 2012, shortly before the end of Nicolas Sarkozy's presidency.

The government deficit deteriorated from 2.5% of GDP to 3.2% in 2008, then to 7.2% in 2009, before improving slightly to 6.8% in 2010 and 5.1% in 2011. Back in Toulon on December 1, 2011, Nicolas Sarkozy called for tighter control of deficits: "If we want more solidarity, we need more fiscal discipline. We need to discuss our fiscal policies together, not so that they are the same everywhere when situations

---

[23] Source: https://www.interieur.gouv.fr/Elections/Les-resultats/Presidentielles/elecresult__PR2012/(path)/PR2012/FE.html.

[24] Source: https://www.senat.fr/rap/r11-064/r11-064_mono.html.

are different, but so that they converge instead of drifting apart. Let us examine our budgets together. Let's introduce faster, more automatic and tougher sanctions for those who fail to meet their commitments. Let's strengthen preventive measures to ensure that the abuses we have seen do not happen again. Each country in the Euro Area must adopt a golden rule that enshrines the objective of a balanced budget in its legal system. It must be adopted by France."[25]

The golden rule means a balanced budget in its structural component. However, in June 2010, the French National Audit Office (*Cour des Comptes*) estimated the structural deficit at around 5% of GDP in 2009, excluding the stimulus plan.[26] Considering that a strong and rapid turnaround of public finances is essential to restore sustainable growth, preserve the State's ability to intervene and maintain confidence, it also recommended a structural effort to reduce the deficit by around €20 billion a year from 2011 onwards. To meet this recommendation, which became imperative in the wake of the Greek sovereign debt crisis, the Fillon government raised taxes by €12 billion in September 2011.

What would his successor do?

[25] Speech by Nicolas Sarkozy, President of the Republic, Toulon, 2011, source: https://www.lefigaro.fr/politique/le-scan/2014/03/27/25001-20140327ARTFIG00086-le-discours-de-nicolas-sarkozy-a-toulon-en-2011.php.

[26] National Audit Office, *Annual Report 2011 - February 2011*, source: https://www.ccomptes.fr/sites/default/files/EzPublish/1_finances_publiques_situation_ensemble.pdf.

Chapter 12
Tax Bludgeoning and Reduction in Structural Deficit

"Pa Ubu: '[…] but I have changed government and I had the newspaper print that everybody would pay all taxes twice. Those designated at our later convenience will pay three times.'"[1]
Alfred Jarry, *Ubu roi* (1868)

While François Hollande [1954-] declared his candidacy for the Socialist presidential primary on March 31, 2011, Nicolas Sarkozy only officially launched his campaign for the presidential election on February 15, 2012, less than three months before electors went to the poll. The dynamics of this presidential election were much as in La Fontaine's fable, *Le lièvre et la tortue*:

"To win a race, the swiftness of a dart
Availeth not without a timely start.
The hare and tortoise are my witnesses.
Said tortoise to the swiftest thing that is,
'I'll bet that you'll not reach, so soon as I
The tree on yonder hill we spy.'
'So soon! Why, madam, are you frantic?'
Replied the creature, with an antic;
'Pray take, your senses to restore,
A grain or two of hellebore.'
'Say,' said the tortoise, 'what you will;
I dare you to the wager still.'
'Twas done; the stakes were paid,
And near the goal tree laid--
Of what, is not a question for this place,
Nor who it was that judged the race.

[1] Jarry, Alfred (1973), Ubu Rex, a new translation by David Copelin, Pulp Press, Vancouver, Canada, source: https://coldreads.files.wordpress.com/2018/07/ubu-roi-copelin.pdf.

C. Peicuti, *A Monetary and Economic History of France since 1944*, Contributions to Economics, https://doi.org/10.1007/978-3-032-17596-0_12

Our hare had scarce five jumps to make,
Of such as he is wont to take,
When, starting just before their beaks
He leaves the hounds at leisure,
Thence till the kalends of the Greeks,
The sterile heath to measure.
Thus having time to browse and doze,
And list which way the zephyr blows,
He makes himself content to wait,
And let the tortoise go her gait
In solemn, senatorial state.
She starts; she moils on, modestly and lowly,
And with a prudent wisdom hastens slowly;
But he, meanwhile, the victory despises,
Thinks lightly of such prizes,
Believes it for his honour
To take late start and gain upon her.
So, feeding, sitting at his ease,
He meditates of what you please,
Till his antagonist he sees
Approach the goal; then starts,
Away like lightning darts:
But vainly does he run;
The race is by the tortoise won.
Cries she, 'My senses do I lack?
What boots your boasted swiftness now?
You're beat! and yet, you must allow,
I bore my house upon my back.'"
The Hare and the Tortoise[2]
Jean de la Fontaine [1621-1695]

The term most often used to describe François Hollande's fiscal policy is '*matraquage fiscal*,' the reference to a bludgeon being derived from '*matraq,*' a Maghrebi Arabic word for "stick, club," which originally referred to the large stick used by camel-drivers in North Africa to drive their animals. Is this a fair assessment? If so, with what results?

[2] *The Fables of La Fontaine*, Translated from the French by Elizur Wright, A New Edition, With Notes By J. W. M. Gibbs, 1882, source: Project Gutenberg's The Fables of La Fontaine, by Jean de la Fontaine.

When François Hollande was elected in 2012, the government deficit reached 5% of GDP. This deficit was gradually reduced to 4.1% in 2013, 3.9% in 2014, 3.6% in 2015 and 2016, and 3% in 2017.[3]

The Treaty on Stability, Coordination and Governance in the Economic and Monetary Union (TSCG) negotiated by Nicolas Sarkozy was ratified by the two houses of the French Parliament in October 2012, but during François Hollande's presidency, France did not comply with the quintessential part of this treaty, namely the Fiscal Compact, which states:

> "(a) the budgetary position of the general government of a Contracting Party shall be balanced or in surplus;
>
> (b) the rule under point (a) shall be deemed to be respected if the annual structural balance of the general government is at its country-specific medium-term objective, as defined in the revised Stability and Growth Pact, with a lower limit of a structural deficit of 0.5 % of the gross domestic product at market prices. […]"[4]

The "annual structural balance of the general government" is defined as "the annual cyclically-adjusted balance net of one-off and temporary measures."

Jean-Marc Ayrault [1950-] was appointed Prime Minister in May 2012, a position he would hold until March 2014. During the early part of François Hollande's presidency, it would be all about walking back the measures of the previous government.

Whereas Nicolas Sarkozy awarded himself an increase in his net monthly allowance as President of the Republic from €7084 to €19,331 at the first cabinet meeting on May 17, 2012, François Hollande, Jean-Marc Ayrault and all the ministers agreed to cut their compensation by 30%. This was enacted by the decree of August 23, 2012, which was applied retrospectively from the date they took office on May 15.

On July 11, 2012, addressing the French National Assembly, Jean-Marc Ayrault passed judgment on the legacy of the Sarkozy presidency, pointing out the "debt increased by €600 billion in five years." He announced the repeal of the VAT hike from 19.6% to 21.2% decided by Nicolas Sarkozy in return for a €13.2 billion reduction in employers' social security contributions earmarked to finance the family scheme and paid by private-sector businesses. This VAT increase, dubbed social VAT (*TVA sociale*), was to have come into force on October 1, 2012.

As part of Nicolas Sarkozy's pension reform, the retirement age was raised to 62. With the decree of July 2, 2012, François Hollande "opens up the right to early retirement at sixty to those insured persons with the required length of insurance contributions for their generation and having begun working before the age of twenty. This amounts to a two-year reduction in the retirement eligibility period required following the abolition of the eight-quarter increase previously in force. In addition, the condition relating to the working start date has been extended to include people

---

[3] Government balance, source: https://www.insee.fr/fr/outil-interactif/5367857/details/10_ECC/15_FIN/15A_Figure1.

[4] *Treaty on Stability, Coordination and Governance in the Economic and Monetary Union*, source: https://www.consilium.europa.eu/media/20399/st00tscg26_en12.pdf.

who started work before the age of 20, and not just before the age of 18. Finally, the number of quarters "deemed to have vested" has been extended: in addition to the four quarters of national service and four quarters of sickness, maternity and industrial accidents previously retained, the new system adds two quarters when the insured was in the receipt of unemployment benefits and two additional quarters for maternity leave. [...] To finance this extension of early retirement options, articles 5 to 13 gradually increase old-age insurance contributions by half a percentage point in progressive steps. Both employees' and employers' contributions will therefore eventually each be increased by a quarter of a percentage point."[5]

Jean-Marc Ayrault criticized the former government for the cost of the TEPA law and went on to deprive it of all substance. Considering that the cost of exempting overtime from income tax and social security contributions was excessive and that the measure was contributing to rising unemployment, part of the reduction in social security contributions for overtime under full-time employment contracts (*heures supplémentaires*) and part-time employment contracts (*heures complémentaires*) introduced by the TEPA law of August 21, 2007, was repealed: "The payroll tax exemptions for overtime and complementary working hours are abolished, as is the flat-rate deduction for employers' contributions on overtime for businesses with at least twenty employees."[6]

On September 9, 2012, in a live address on the 8 o'clock news, François Hollande declared that his ambition was to "reverse the unemployment curve within a year." This promise, repeated time and time again throughout his five-year term, when extending his New Year greetings or addressing the European Parliament in Brussels, would become one of his mantras. In 2012, at the start of his presidency, unemployment stood at 9.8%. The unemployment rate increased 10.3% in 2013 and 2014, then to 10.4% in 2015, before dropping to 10.1% in 2016 and 9.4% in 2017 at the end of his five-year term. France's unemployment rate was above the European average of 7.6% in 2017. In Germany, the unemployment rate was 3.8% in 2017.

During the election campaign, on February 27, 2012, François Hollande promised that annual income over €1 million would be taxed at 75% for two years. This was another flagship promise. On December 29, 2012, France's Constitutional Council (*Conseil constitutionnel*) threw out this "exceptional solidarity contribution." François Hollande promised to come up with a new version. On March 28, 2013, he announced that this contribution would be paid by firms. Employers were up in arms, denouncing the measure as "singling out business." Capped at 5% of company sales in 2013, it is payable for two years on amounts paid by way of a salary exceeding €1 million. Its rate is 50%, but it comes close to the initial promise if social security contributions are added. There is a drop in the number of taxpayers declaring a gross salary in excess of €1 million between 2012 and 2013, which

[5] *Décret no 2012–847 du 2 juillet 2012 relatif à l'âge d'ouverture du droit à pension de vieillesse*, source: https://www.legifrance.gouv.fr/jorf/id/JORFTEXT000026106324.

[6] *Décret no 2012–1074 du 21 septembre 2012 relatif à la réduction générale de cotisations patronales de sécurité sociale et à la déduction forfaitaire de cotisations patronales sur les heures supplémentaires*, source: https://www.legifrance.gouv.fr/download/pdf?id=1ZyQlgusUV3ocZz65WJJ1uN7Pce5JP_lubW2AuKlCjU=.

suggests that some taxpayers took steps to evade this tax in 2013. Over the two years of application of this measure, it generated €420 million in tax receipts but harmed France's attractiveness.

In his speech at Le Bourget on January 22, 2012, before his election, François Hollande declared: "If finance is the adversary, then we must confront it with our means and first of all here at home, without weakness but without shying from reality, in the belief that it will be a long fight, a tough test, requiring that we put our cards on the table. Controlling finance will begin here, by passing a law on banks that will force them to separate lending from their speculative activities. No French bank will be allowed to have a presence in tax havens. [...] I will create a public investment bank which, in addition to regional funds, will support the development of companies of strategic importance."[7] While the first part of this promise was never acted upon, Banque publique d'investissement (BPI, better known as BPI France) was created by the law of December 31, 2012, by combining OSEO, CDC Entreprises and the Fonds stratégique d'investissement. In 2023, BPI France injected €63 billion into the French economy. In September 2020, BPI France and Banque des Territoires launched a joint climate plan (*Plan Climat*) amounting to almost €40 billion through 2024.

Another recurring theme in Jean-Marc Ayrault's communication is the erosion of France's competitiveness. In answer to a question put by one opposition leader at the National Assembly on July 11, 2012, the Prime Minister refers to the fact that his government inherited "a foreign trade deficit of €70 billion, which reflects the difficulty in which our industry finds itself. Some 750 thousand jobs lost in the industrial sector in ten years; that is the reality. So please do not lecture us. But we are here above all to contribute to the country's recovery, and the measures we have taken, starting with the amending finance law (*loi de finance rectificative*), are to this end. But I would like to correct an astonishing fallacy that you have tried to propagate. You say that we have committed €20 billion in spending in this Finance Act. How can you stoop to such falsehood! You must bear the responsibility you assumed five years ago, when in August 2007 you pushed through the TEPA law, which resulted in a €20 billion levy on middle-class and working-class households, for which we are still paying the bill! That is the reality."[8]

On July 11, 2012, Jean-Marc Ayrault set out the terms of reference for Louis Gallois [1944-], Airbus director from 2007 to 2012 and France's general commissioner for investment (*commissaire général à l'investissement*) from 2012 to 2014,

[7] The full speech given by François Hollande at Le Bourget on January 22, 2012, source: https://www.nouvelobs.com/election-presidentielle-2012/sources-brutes/20120122.OBS9488/l-integralite-du-discours-de-francois-hollande-au-bourget.html.

[8] Statement by Prime Minister Jean-Marc Ayrault in answer to a question asked by opposition MP Catherine Vaudrin about the priorities of the 2012 amending finance bill, National Assembly, July 11, 2012, source: https://www.vie-publique.fr/discours/185471-declaration-de-m-jean-marc-ayrault-premier-ministre-en-reponse-une.

tasked with drawing up a national pact for competitiveness, growth, and employment[9] (*Pacte national pour la compétitivité, la croissance et l'emploi*) intended to trigger a "reaction."

The competitiveness and employment tax credit (*crédit d'impôt pour la compétitivité et l'emploi—CICE*), contained in the 2012 amending finance act and which came into force on January 1, 2013, was inspired by the work of Louis Gallois. The measure is the first of eight levers and thirty-five "concrete decisions" in the pact adopted at the government seminar:

> "Lever 1: implement a competitiveness and employment tax credit
>
> The state of our productive apparatus means that we cannot continue to compete internationally today, nor can we effectively prepare for the future by investing in the products of tomorrow. What is more, over the last ten years or so, labor costs in France and Germany have diverged.
>
> It is, therefore, necessary to restore to firms the means of repositioning themselves sustainably on the offensive, for those which are directly exposed to international competition, and for all firms, to ensure that they contribute to the competitiveness of the national economy through a moderation of their costs.
>
> 1st decision: Reduce company costs by €20 billion a year, with a gradual ramp-up over three years (€10 billion in the first year), via a tax credit for competitiveness and employment. The tax credit will be proportional to the company's gross payroll, excluding salaries above 2.5 times the minimum hourly wage (*salaire minimum interprofessionnel de croissance - Smic*). Companies will benefit from the tax credit for the first time against their 2013 tax liability. The economic impact will therefore be immediate."[10]

Although tantamount to a reduction in labor costs, the objectives of the competitiveness and employment tax credit went beyond increasing employment. For the companies concerned, the intention was "to finance an improvement of their competitiveness, notably through efforts in the areas of investment, research, innovation, training, recruitment, market prospection, ecological and energy transition, and working capital restoration."[11] According to France Stratégie, the effect on employment was positive, but came at a huge cost. For example, in 2016, "the total effect is still estimated at around 100 thousand jobs, which is low compared with the cost of the tax credit—around €18 billion in 2016."[12] As for improving competitiveness, the tax credit had no visible impact on the evolution of France's foreign trade balance.

As early as July 2016, an information report published by the French Senate's Finance Committee warned that, three years after the introduction of the competitiveness and employment tax credit, this public policy measure had come to account for almost 1% of the country's GDP and asked whether this was sustainable fiscally:

---

[9] *Pacte national pour la croissance, la compétitivité et l'emploi*, Appendix, Terms of reference, source: https://www.entreprises.gouv.fr/files/files/directions_services/politique-et-enjeux/simplifications/pacte-national-cce.pdf?v=1707407271.

[10] Ibid.

[11] *Article 66 de la loi de finances rectificative pour 2012 modifiant l'article 244 quater C.-I. du code général des impôts.*

[12] *Assessment of the competitiveness and employment tax credit*, source: https://www.strategie.gouv.fr/sites/strategie.gouv.fr/files/atoms/files/fs-2020-rapport-cice2020-16septembre-final18h.pdf.

"Tax credits in respect of 2013, per the records as of May 31, 2016, amount to €11,343 million […]

Tax credits in respect of 2014, per the records as of May 31, 2016, amount to €17,260 million."[13]

The report draws attention to the fact that the administration of this measure was proving very complex for both the beneficiaries and tax authorities. As a result, large enterprises found it easier to benefit from this measure than very small, small, and medium-sized enterprises. According to the Senate's report, the profile of tax credit beneficiaries revealed that the measure was not fit for purpose, missing its target, for though the industrial sector had been the intended target initially, it accounted for only 19.4% of the tax credits applied for.

Despite repeated warnings about its cost and effectiveness, the competitiveness and employment tax credit remained in force until 2019, when it would be abolished and replaced by a reduction in employers' contributions on low wages. When Jean-Marc Ayrault accused the opposition of stooping to untruths by claiming that the government was committing €20 billion of expenditure from the onset with the adoption of the 2012 Finance Law, he was right. It was much more…

Like his predecessors, François Hollande would make a social-liberal turn a year and a half into his presidency, which he saw as being part of the Social Democrat mainstream. He appointed Emmanuel Macron as Minister for the Economy, Industry, and Digital Affairs in August 2014. He raised value-added tax (VAT) in 2014 from 19.6% to 20% for the standard rate and from 7 to 10% for the intermediate rate. There was a sharp reduction in labor costs thanks to the competitiveness and employment tax credit.

In *Le Stage est fini* published in 2015, Le Monde political editor Françoise Fressoz recounts François Hollande telling her: "You often pay for the first amending finance law […]. For Sarkozy, it was the law in favor of work, employment and purchasing power, which was perceived as a tax giveaway. He paid for it throughout his five-year term. We paid for the €11 billion in new taxes raised when we took up office."[14]

And when asked if he had to do it all over again, "I wouldn't have gone so far,"[15] replied François Hollande.

"I would have kept the VAT increase decided by Nicolas Sarkozy to balance the budget he had left us. I would have introduced the competitiveness and employment tax credit for businesses. And I would have avoided the increases in subsequent budgets."[16] For all the criticism the measure attracted, François Hollande would still have kept the competitiveness and employment tax credit… why is it that French presidents do not learn from the mistakes of their predecessors? Each presidency begins with the same mistakes before it dawns on the head of the executive what

[13] French Senate, Information Report n° 789 (2015–2016), *Rapport d'information au nom de la commission des finances sur le profil des bénéficiaires du crédit d'impôt pour la compétitivité et l'emploi (CICE)*, filed July 13, 2016, source: https://www.senat.fr/rap/r15-789/r15-789_mono.html.

[14] Fressoz, Françoise (2015), *Le Stage est fini*, Albin Michel.

[15] Ibid.

[16] Ibid.

should have been done when taking up office, the bill for this 'on-the-job training' being footed by the French taxpayer.

The liberalization of the labor market was steered by Myriam El Khomri [1978-], the Minister of Labor, Employment, Vocational Training and Social Dialogue from September 2015 to May 2017. The government wanted to reform the Labor Code to "protect employees, encourage job creations, and give more scope to enterprise bargaining." The legislation was supported by the MEDEF (*Mouvement des entreprises de France*), the leading employers' federation in France, and its members, but led to street protests because it simplified redundancy procedures. Nonetheless, the Law of August 8, 2016, concerning work, the modernization of the social dialogue and safeguarding career paths (*Loi n° 2016–1088 du 8 août 2016 relative au travail, à la modernisation du dialogue social et à la sécurisation des parcours professionnels*) was published in the Official Journal the next day. With this law, François Hollande's popularity plunged to lows as never before for a President under the Fifth Republic. According to an Ipsos survey conducted from October 14 to 19, 2016, for Cevipof and Le Monde, the policies pursued by the French president achieved barely 4% of favorable opinions.[17]

---

[17] Berdah, Arthur, *Popularité: à 4% de bonnes opinions, Hollande touche le fond,* Le Figaro, October 25, 2016, source: https://www.lefigaro.fr/politique/le-scan/2016/10/25/25001-20161025ARTFIG00143-popularite-a-4-de-bonnes-opinions-hollande-touche-le-fond.php.

Part III
Resurrection of Inflationary Dirigisme

"All is in the end."
Gérard de Nerval [1808–1855]

In December 1812, Charles-Maurice de Talleyrand-Périgord, on news of Napoleon's disastrous retreat from Moscow and the battle and crossing of the Berezina River, said: "It is the beginning of the end." On November 10, 1942, following the victory at El-Alamein, Winston Churchill humorously adapted the words of Talleyrand and declared, "This is not the end, nor even the beginning of the end, but it may be the end of the beginning." Fast forward to 2024, Emmanuel Macron was still putting his signature to the economic history of his presidency, which began in 2017. What judgment will be passed when his second five-year term draws to a close? Like Napoleon's Russian campaign, will it have been a disaster in terms of public debt and the ecological and energy transition, or will it perhaps be "the end of the beginning" in the turnaround of France's public finances and transition towards a sustainable economy? As Gérard de Nerval would say: "all is in the end."

In December 1812, Charles-Maurice de Talleyrand-Périgord [1754–1838], on news of Napoleon's disastrous retreat from Moscow and the battle and crossing of the Berezina River, said: "It is the beginning of the end." On November 10, 1942, following the victory at El-Alamein, Winston Churchill humorously adapted the words of Talleyrand and declared, "This is not the end, nor even the beginning of the end, but it may be the end of the beginning."[1] Fast forward to 2024 when I was writing these pages, Emmanuel Macron [1977-] was still putting his signature to the economic history of his presidency, which began in 2017. What judgment will be passed when his second five-year term draws to a close? Like Napoleon's Russian campaign, will it have been a disaster in terms of public debt and the ecological and energy transition, or will it perhaps be "the end of the beginning" in the turnaround of France's public finances and transition towards a sustainable economy?

After serving as Élysée Deputy Secretary-General to President François Hollande from May 2012 to July 2014, then as Minister of the Economy, Industry and Digital

[1] Speech at the Lord Mayor's Day Luncheon, November 10, 1942.
From Churchill, Winston (1943), *The End of the Beginning*, Cassell and Company Ltd., London.

Affairs from August 2014 to August 2016, Emmanuel Macron [1977-] formed his own political movement, *En Marche*, in April 2016, which he defined as "neither to the Right, neither to the Left".[2] A few months later, in August, he resigned and later announced his candidacy for the presidential election. Whereas François Hollande had announced his candidacy more than one year before the 2012 presidential election, this time his former minister pulled the rug from under his feet. To avoid even the possibility of the Far Right winning by splitting the vote, and given that he was extremely unpopular, François Hollande did not stand for reelection. What might be the economic policy of a political movement that was "neither to the Right, neither to the Left"?

The year of Emmanuel Macron's election, the government deficit reached 3% of GDP. The deficit declined to 2.3% in 2018. With the Yellow Vests Movement (*mouvement des gilets jaunes*) erupting on November 17, 2018, the deficit went back on the rise, reaching 3.1% in 2019 and 9% in 2020, at the height of the COVID-19 pandemic. With Emmanuel Macron's famous "whatever the cost" uttered on March 12, 2020, France was more generous than its European neighbors, as a result of which the deficit deteriorated to 6.5% in 2021. On February 24, 2022, Russia invaded Ukraine. The electricity tariff shield from February 1, 2022, to January 31, 2023, had an impact on public finances, the deficit declining to 4.8% in 2022 and was expected to be stable at this level in 2023.

In 2017, Germany had a debt-to-GDP ratio of 65.2%, while in France this ratio climbed to 98.1%. The gap between the two countries would continue to widen, with this ratio declining by several percentage points to 61.9% in Germany in 2018, whereas in France it edged down by a few basis points to 97.8%. In 2019, Germany recorded another significant decrease to 59.6%, whereas France recorded another small decrease to 97.4%. In 2020, because of the pandemic, France's debt-to-GDP ratio soared to 114.6%, whereas Germany's ratio increased to just 68.7%. In 2021, this ratio edged down to 112.9% in France, whereas in Germany it edged up to 69.3%. In 2022, at the end of Emmanuel Macron's first term of office, of the 27 EU Member States, only Greece, Italy, Portugal, and Spain had higher debt-to-GDP ratios. In Germany, this ratio declined to 66.3%, while in France there was a very slight decline to 111.6%[3]. On September 30, 2023, France's government debt set a new record high, passing above €3,000 billion to €3,088.2 billion.

The Treaty on Stability, Coordination and Governance in the Economic and Monetary Union permits temporary imbalances, but only in "exceptional circumstances," the objective always being to achieve fiscal sustainability over the medium term: "the Contracting Parties may temporarily deviate from their respective medium-term objective or the adjustment path towards it only in exceptional circumstances […]."[4]

---

[2] *Emmanuel Macron lance un 'mouvement politique nouveau' baptisé 'En marche !'*, Le Monde, April 6, 2016, source: https://www.lemonde.fr/politique/article/2016/04/06/emmanuel-macron-lance-un-mouvement-politique-nouveau-baptise-en-marche_4897274_823448.html

[3] Weight of government debt in the European Union, source: https://www.insee.fr/fr/statistiques/2830286#tableau-figure1.

[4] *Treaty on Stability, Coordination and Governance in the Economic and Monetary Union*, source: https://www.consilium.europa.eu/media/20399/st00tscg26_en12.pdf.

In the treaty, exceptional circumstances are defined as "an unusual event outside the control of the Contracting Party concerned which has a major impact on the financial position of the general government or to periods of severe economic downturn as set out in the revised Stability and Growth Pact, provided that the temporary deviation of the Contracting Party concerned does not endanger fiscal sustainability in the medium-term."[5] All which begs the question of whether the measures taken by the governments of Édouard Philippe [1970-], Prime Minister from May 2017 to July 2020, and Jean Castex [1965-], Prime Minister from July 2020 to May 2022, have endangered fiscal sustainability in the medium term?

[5] Ibid.

Chapter 13
From Brexit to the Yellow Vests Movement in France

"I don't believe I'm over-dramatising things, I'm trying to be lucid. But just look at what is happening in the world Things that were unthinkable five years ago. To be wearing ourselves out over Brexit, to have Europe finding it so difficult to move forward, to have an American ally turning its back on us so quickly on strategic issues; nobody would have believed this possible. How did Europe come into existence? I'm trying to face the facts. Personally, I think Europe is a miracle. This continent has the greatest geographical concentration of cultural and linguistic diversity. Which explains why, for almost two millennia, Europe was rocked by constant civil wars. And over the past 70 years we've achieved a minor geopolitical, historical and civilisational miracle: a political equation free of hegemony which permits peace."[1]

Emmanuel Macron, 2019

Brexit: The First Major Victory of Populism in Europe Post-War

In the wake of the subprime crisis, the political risk was kept in check in the short term, but the impoverishment that resulted from this crisis would propel this risk on high over the medium term. German economist Otto Karl Pöhl [1929–2014] famously compared inflation to toothpaste, and much the same can be said of populism: "Once it's out, you can hardly get it back in again. So the best thing is not to squeeze too hard on the tube." It took the Second World War to eradicate the populism brought on by the Great Depression.

The risk of political and social fragility, one of the main components of political risk, has increased significantly since the subprime crisis, to the point of getting

[1] *Emmanuel Macron in his own words*, The French president's interview with The Economist, October 21, 2019, source: https://www.economist.com/europe/2019/11/07/emmanuel-macron-in-his-own-words-french.

C. Peicuti, *A Monetary and Economic History of France since 1944*, Contributions to Economics, https://doi.org/10.1007/978-3-032-17596-0_13

Donald Trump elected and bringing about a profound change to the political landscape in the United States. The even starker inequalities in the wake of the 2008 crisis are largely responsible for this state of affairs. In *The Great Escape, Health, Wealth, and the Origins of Inequality*, published in 2023, Angus Deaton [1945-], who was awarded the 2015 Sveriges Riksbank Prize in Economic Sciences, explained that: "All families shared in the rising prosperity until the mid- to late 1970s. Since then, incomes have pulled apart. As we already know from the poverty numbers, the bottom fifth of families gained very little. The growth in their average incomes was less than 0.2 percent a year over the past forty-four years and, even before the recession, their real incomes were no higher than they had been in the late 1970s. Average incomes of the top fifth, by contrast, grew more quickly, at 1.6 percent a year, though not as quickly as those of the top 5 percent, whose average incomes grew at 2.1 percent a year."[2]

Angus Deaton considers that life is "the story of mankind's escaping from deprivation and early death."[3] He explains that nothing guarantees there is a general relationship between growth and poverty unless Nation-States intervene in the redistribution of wealth in their country. For the British economist, progress in this area is non-linear. Without political will, poverty reduction will not go hand in hand with economic growth!

Deaton highlights the fact that there are almost unimaginable differences between countries in the average material standard of living and that the gap between the poor and the rich within each country is only slightly smaller. He warns that income inequality in many rich countries has soared in recent years. What has been observed by Deaton is a positive correlation between life expectancy and income: in other words, health and wealth often go hand in hand. But as he points out, "averages are no consolation to those who have been left behind" and "economic growth has been the engine of international income inequality."[4]

As with the election on November 8, 2016, of Donald Trump as the forty-fifth President of the United States, the 51.9% Leave vote in the Brexit referendum held on June 23, 2016, reflected the victory of populism fueled by rising inequality and poverty, also a political discourse constantly blaming the European Union for these woes. This wave of populism swept across the Anglo-Saxon world as well as other European countries (France, Germany, Austria, Poland, Hungary, and Greece). In these countries, when things are going well, politicians congratulate themselves; but, whenever things go wrong, they blame the faceless bureaucrats in Brussels.

An analysis of the Brexit vote by YouGov[5]shows that the higher the household income, the smaller the proportion of Leave votes. There was 62% support for leaving the European Union among voters from households with income of less than £20,000 a year, declining to 53% for the £20,000 to £40,000 bracket, then 42% for the £40,000

[2] Deaton, Angus (2023), *The Great Escape, Health, Wealth, and the Origins of Inequality*, Princeton University Press, Princeton and Oxford.

[3] Ibid.

[4] Ibid.

[5] yougov.co.uk/news/2016/06/27/how-britain-voted/.

to £60,000 bracket and only 35% among voters from households with income of more than £60,000 a year. The desire of younger generations was clearly to remain in the European Union: 71% of Britons aged 18 to 24 and 54% of those aged 25 to 49 voted Remain.

In 2016, 10% of all British children lived in persistent poverty (defined as being in income poverty in three of the last four years), with this reaching 38% among children in households that have been workless for at least three of the last four years. In other words, children are the collateral victims of persistent worklessness and intermittent increases in earnings for lone-parent households and families with more than three children.

The famous so-called zero-hours contracts led to an excessive liberalization of the labor market. Workers are at the beck and call of their employer, with no guarantee of being given work. With this contract, employees become the adjustment variable for businesses. Until the 2008 crisis, there were around 200 thousand contracts that did not guarantee a minimum number of hours. By 2017, 11.4% of UK workers were employed under zero-hours contracts according to the Office for National Statistics. Some 65.4% of people on these contracts worked part-time (compared with around one-quarter of people employed under contracts other than a zero-hours contract). Zero-hours contracts were rarely a choice on the part of the worker, but imposed by the employer. Contracts of this type foster poverty and uncertainty.

For poor voters who felt forgotten by the economic, social, and political system, the Leave vote was a way to express their discontent. Many held the misguided belief that their misfortune was due to immigration. Yet, before the 2008 financial crisis, wages grew despite the higher immigration. Immigrants are often seen as the personification of globalization. Scapegoating immigrants was easier than blaming the failings of financial regulation, although this is what triggered the financial crisis. Yet, the fact is that European immigrants are generally younger, better-educated, and less likely to claim welfare benefits than native-born Britons. Reducing immigration can be expected to hurt public finances and will not necessarily help to reduce inequalities. The entire British population is suffering economically from the consequences of Brexit. The deterioration in the standard of living of the most vulnerable social groups is driving them further into the quicksand of poverty.

The decade after Brexit is worse for most disadvantaged sections of the population than the one that followed the subprime crisis. The 2016 referendum has inspired a myriad of neologisms, the latest being Bregret, a contraction of Brexit and regret, which shows just how much sentiment has changed, 2024 surveys showing that between 55 and 60% of Britons regret leaving the European Union. The proportion is even higher among young people. There is still no question of a return to the European fold, though this would significantly strengthen the European Union on the international stage.

Yellow Vests or the Despair of France's Lower Classes

In France, Emmanuel Macron was elected in April 2017 thanks to a republican front (*front républicain*), voters of all stripes rallying behind the mainstream candidate to prevent a victory by the far-right candidate.

At the start of the previous presidency, the government of Jean-Marc Ayrault introduced an exceptional wealth tax (to counteract the decision of his predecessor, François Fillon, to lower the rate for the wealth tax in 2012) and then proceeded to reinstate the wealth tax as it was (in all aspects bar one, which was that the threshold for this tax remained set at €1.3 million). In an about-turn, plans to abolish the solidarity wealth tax were presented to the Council of Ministers at the meeting held on September 27, 2017, with the law being published in the Official Journal on December 30, 2017. It is replaced by a wealth tax on real estate assets (*impôt sur la fortune immobilière—IFI*). The tax concerns tax households possessing real estate assets with a net value of more than €1.3 million. In other words, the threshold is unchanged, but the tax base is narrower. Some 26% of households subjected to this wealth tax reside in Paris. In its last year of existence in 2017, the previous version of the wealth tax raised €4.2 billion. In its first year of existence, in 2018, the new wealth tax on real estate assets raised €1.29 billion. This would increase gradually, the tax bringing in €1.8 billion in 2022, up 10% compared with 2021.[6]

In the final report produced by the ad-hoc committee created by France Stratégie to look into the reforms affecting the taxation of capital (*Comité d'évaluation des réformes de la fiscalité du capital*), it considered what tax receipts would have been raised had there been no reform, concluding:

> "It's difficult to answer this question; at best we can give orders of magnitude. In 2017, the solidarity wealth tax (*impôt de solidarité sur la fortune - ISF*) raised €4.2 billion, and the committee in its first report in 2019 estimated that the replacement of this tax by the wealth tax on real estate assets (*impôt sur la fortune immobilière - IFI*) had led to a shortfall in tax receipts of €3.1 billion. In other words, in 2018, taxes raised by the wealth tax on real estate assets represented 29% of tax receipts that could potentially have been raised by the solidarity wealth tax. Assuming that tax receipts increased at the same pace for both taxes - in other words, that the ratio remained constant - the solidarity wealth tax could have been expected to bring in €6.3 billion, meaning that the shortfall in receipts due to its replacement by the wealth tax on real estate assets would have amounted to €4.5 billion.
>
> Since the replacement of the solidarity wealth tax by the wealth tax on real estate assets, in the case of households subject to the wealth tax, there has been a decline in the number of households moving out of France and an increase in the number of households moving into the country. Since 2018, the number of high-net-worth households returning to France has exceeded the number of high-net-worth individuals leaving France (on average, 380 returns to 260 departures each year from 2018 to 2021), whereas the opposite was true when the solidarity wealth tax was in force (on average, 370 returns to 950 departures each year from 2011 to 2016). However, this pattern is based on a small number of taxpayers, of the order of a few hundred, when 150 thousand taxpayers are subject to the wealth tax on real estate assets. In total, taxpayers who moved back to France in 2021 paid around €5.5 million in

---

[6] *DGFiP Statistiques, L'impôt sur la fortune immobilière en 2022*, source: https://www.impots.gouv.fr/dgfip-statistiques-limpot-sur-la-fortune-immobiliere-en-2022.

wealth tax in 2022, or around 0.3% of the total amount raised by this tax in France. The smaller number of taxpayers who left France in 2021 had paid around €3.8 million in wealth tax in 2019. [...]

Beyond the fiscal impact, there is also the matter of the impact on the productive fabric. In a study commissioned by France Stratégie, the Institut de Politique Publique (IPP) suggests that, on average, the economic activity of enterprises whose reference shareholder left France will underperform in the following years compared with other enterprises."[7]

One might add that, beyond the fiscal and entrepreneurial aspects, the perception of the public at large was that the first measures by the new government favored high- and very high-net-worth individuals.

Born in Motta di Livenza, Veneto, Corrado Gini [1884–1965] was an Italian statistician, demographer, ethnologist, and sociologist. The Gini coefficient was named after him. A Gini coefficient normally has a value of between 0 (perfect equality—everyone has the same) and 1 (perfect inequality - one person has everything). The Gini, as it is also known, measures how far people are apart on average from perfect equality. Looking at the evolution of this coefficient, what will be observed is that it reached 0.294 in 2021, very close to the level at the end of Nicolas Sarkozy's presidency (0.295 in 2012). During François Hollande's presidency, it reached 0.281 in 2013, 0.282 in 2014, 0.285 in 2015, 0.280 in 2016, and 0.281 in 2017. In 2018, the first full year of Emmanuel Macron's presidency, the Gini jumped to 0.290.[8] By 2021, it had increased to 0.294 while in Germany it was 0.2888. In his novel *Sérotonine* published on January 4, 2019, Michel Houellebecq [1956-] plunges his readers into the heart of rural France and appears to foretell the Yellow Vests Movement (*Mouvement des gilets jaunes*).

In addition to the abolition of the solidarity wealth tax, the new government introduced a 30% flat-rate tax (*prélèvement forfaitaire unique - PFU*) on capital income, which covered both income tax and social security contributions. The measure is perceived by the French population in the same way: the new government is prioritizing the rich, whom Emmanuel Macro termed the "*premiers de cordée*" for leading from the front, before looking after the poor. The report by France Stratégie points out that this adjustment brought France in line with its European partners: "For example, in the case of a taxpayer earning the equivalent of five times the average wage in dividends, the effective tax rate in France is 49%. Only Denmark and Spain have a higher rate of 54%. Germany, Belgium, and Italy are very close to France, with rates of 47% or 48%."[9] This same report indicates that, based on the research that was conducted, this flat-rate tax had no perceptible impact on investment.

---

[7] Comité d'évaluation des réformes de la fiscalité du capital, Final Report, source: https://www.strategie.gouv.fr/sites/strategie.gouv.fr/files/atoms/files/fs-2023-rapport-isf-quatrieme_rapport_complet_17octobre_2.pdf.

[8] INSEE, Gini coefficient, source: https://www.insee.fr/fr/outil-interactif/5367857/details/30_RPC/31_RNP/31G_Figure7.

[9] Comité d'évaluation des réformes de la fiscalité du capital, Final Report, source: https://www.strategie.gouv.fr/sites/strategie.gouv.fr/files/atoms/files/fs-2023-rapport-isf-quatrieme_rapport_complet_17octobre_2.pdf.

The same law increased the taxation of households. First, there was a 1.7% increase in the generalized social contribution (*contribution sociale généralisée—CSG*), except for pensioners with adjusted tax income (*revenu fiscal de reference*) of less than €14,404 per tax share. Second, there was an increase in fuel taxes, particularly on diesel, when previous governments had encouraged purchases of diesel cars by offering tax incentives. This measure crystallized the discontent of those who would later become the Yellow Vests. A video posted online on October 18, 2018, by Jacline Mouraud [1967-], one of the first figureheads of the Yellow Vests movement, denouncing the punitive taxation of diesel vehicles went viral, being viewed some six million times.

In return, employee health and unemployment contributions were abolished, which would a few years later be used as justification by the government to shorten the standard duration of unemployment benefits and their amount. The government also announced that the local residence tax (*taxe d'habitation*) would be phased out over three years, but in reaction, the property tax (*taxe foncière*) climbed sharply, up 52% in Paris for the tax paid in 2022 compared with the tax paid in 2021.

The Yellow Vests Movement erupted on November 17, 2018, when 300 thousand protesters clad in high-visibility safety vests occupied roundabouts and toll booths and erected roadblocks across France. The movement channeled the population's discontent and had public support even four months later. France became the scene of pitched battles between the protesters and the police force, with levels of violence rarely seen in the twenty-first century.

According to French daily Libération, in January 2019, "of the 143 seriously injured (including 17 women), 92 claim to have been hit by defensive flash-ball fire, in the vast majority of cases to the head, causing the loss of sight in one eye in fourteen cases."[10] On March 6, 2019, in light of the increasing number of mutilations and injuries linked to police brutality, the United Nations urged a "full investigation of all reported cases of excessive use of force."[11] On the anniversary of the movement, Amnesty International wrote: "2,500 injured in the ranks of the protesters and 1,800 in the ranks of the police: the figures released by the government reveal the unprecedented nature of the violence that has marred demonstrations in France over the past year."[12]

---

[10] Libération, *Gilets jaunes: le décompte des blessés graves*, January 13, 2019, source: https://www.liberation.fr/checknews/2019/01/14/gilets-jaunes-le-decompte-des-blesses-graves_1702863/.

[11] France 24, *UN calls for probe into 'excessive' force by French police at Yellow Vest protests*, March 16, 2019, source: https://www.france24.com/en/20190306-un-france-investigate-excessive-force-yellow-vests.

[12] Amnesty International France, *Gilets jaunes en France: un bilan inquiétant*, source: https://www.amnesty.fr/liberte-d-expression/actualites/gilets-jaunes-un-bilan-inquietant.

An opinion survey[13] revealed that 57% of Yellow Vests protesters were holding down a job, that they had a monthly income of €1486 on average, with 65% declaring they struggled to make ends meet each month, that 47% are women and 53% men, that 30% are aged between 50 and 64, 28% between 35 and 49, and 16% between 25 and 34.

The survey also revealed that in the first round of the 2017 presidential election, 29% of Yellow Vest protesters voted for Marine Le Pen, 27% abstained, voted blank or were not registered to vote, and 17% voted for Jean-Luc Mélenchon. 87% felt they lived in an unfair society, 83% were pessimistic about the future of French society, and 51% considered taxes unnecessary.

Although this was a nationwide movement, protesters are over-represented in the so-called empty diagonal (*diagonale du vide*), a wide strip of French territory stretching from the Meuse to the Landes, where population densities are lower than in the rest of France. Three out of four protesters used a motor vehicle every day. Incidentally, the movement began on May 29, 2018, when Priscillia Ludosky, a resident of Savigny-le-Temple in the Seine-et-Marne, put a petition online calling for a cut in fuel pump prices ("*Pour une baisse des prix du carburant à la pompe!*"). Then, on October 21, truck driver Éric Drouet took to social networks, calling for a nationwide blockade of roads, freeways, and oil depots.

As early as December 5, 2018, the government announced the cancellation of the increase in the carbon tax planned for 2019 and of the alignment in the taxation of diesel with gasoline, also the suspension of roadworthiness inspections, and a freeze of gas and electricity tariffs for the first few months of the year.

Four weeks into the Yellow Vests Movements, on December 10, 2018, Emmanuel Macron decreed a "state of economic and social emergency" and presented the following measures for incorporation into the 2019 Finance Bill:

> "- Cancellation in 2019 of the increase in the generalized social contribution (*contribution sociale généralisée - CSG*) for pensioners in receipt of pensions amounting to between €1,200 and €2,000 a month (rate cut from 8.3% to 6.6%, back to its previous level);
>
> - Exemption of overtime (time worked in excess of the legal 35-hour working week) from income tax and social security contributions;
>
> - An increase of €100 per month in the minimum wage (*salaire minimum interprofessionnel de croissance - Smic*), 'without it costing the employer a single euro more', achieved by increasing the in-work benefit (*prime d'activité*);
>
> - Exemption from income tax of any year-end bonus that might be paid by employers."[14]

Emmanuel Macron confirmed that he would not row back on the abolition of the wealth tax.

---

[13] Survey of 10,010 people conducted between December 14, 2018, and January 8, 2019, by Elabe, in partnership with Institut Montaigne.

Institut Montaigne, *Les Gilets jaunes: la partie émergée de la crise sociale française ?*, source: https://www.institutmontaigne.org/expressions/les-gilets-jaunes-la-partie-emergee-de-la-crise-sociale-francaise.

[14] Yellow Vests Movement: announcement by the President of the Republic, source: https://www.vie-publique.fr/en-bref/20065-mouvement-des-gilets-jaunes-les-annonces-du-president-de-la-republique

These were costly measures. Nevertheless, mobilization was halved on December 15 compared with December 8, with the number of protesters put at 66 thousand across France. In 2019, the movement picked up again and continued until the fall. Lassitude and the Great Debate (*grand débat*) launched on December 18, 2018, throughout the country and open to all and sundry put an end to the movement. The total cost of the measures announced by Emmanuel Macron in response to the Yellow Vests movement amounted to nearly €17 billion, with €10 billion in respect of the measures announced in December and listed above.

Beyond pushing for one-off measures, protesters questioned how public money was being spent. They called for structural solutions that taxpayers' money be better employed for the benefit of all. If their call remains largely left unanswered, a victory of the far-right in the 2027 elections cannot be ruled out. The far-right has always thrived on the precariousness and fear of social demotion haunting the most disadvantaged in society.

The carbon tax is certainly the most effective way of combating global warming, but if it is to be accepted, it must not be a tax on top of all others. It must replace income tax, and receipts must really be applied to achieving this objective.

Chapter 14
COVID-19 Pandemic

The COVID-19 pandemic is not unprecedented in its severity. The Black Death in the fourteenth century killed half of Europe's population in a few years. The Spanish flu in 1918 and 1919 killed over 40 million people worldwide, compared with 7 million for COVID-19 according to WHO data as of February 25, 2024.[1] What is striking is the disproportion between the cause, a health emergency, and the economic effects. As a result, during the COVID-19 pandemic, state dirigisme was reborn from its ashes with three full nationwide lockdowns, a first in the country's history:

- From March 17 to May 11, 2020, not included, 1 month and 25 days;
- From October 30 to December 15, 2020, not included, 1 month and 15 days;
- From April 3 to May 3, 2021, not included, 28 days.

This unprecedented restriction of liberties in peacetime came at a hefty cost to the country's public finances.

State dirigisme is synonymous with inflation. It was when economic activity resumed after the lockdowns that inflation reared its head, driven by the huge injections of liquidity into the economy. The war in Ukraine, by driving up energy prices and leading to shortages of agricultural commodities, also stoked inflation. In the words of Eugène Ionesco in his 1959 play Rhinoceros: "Take a circle, caress it, and it will turn vicious."

The address to the nation (*Adresse aux Français*) on March 12, 2020, has gone down in history as France's "whatever the cost" answer to the COVID-19 pandemic. A decade after Mario Draghi's famous "whatever it takes" instantly quelled market panic, there was Emmanuel Macron's "whatever the cost" shortly before the first full lockdown from March 17 to May 11, 2020.

However, whereas Mario Draghi's pledge cost nothing, the new program of open-ended, unlimited buying of government bonds never being activated, it was quite

[1] World Health Organization (WHO), Number of COVID-19 deaths reported to WHO, source: https://data.who.int/dashboards/covid19/deaths?n=c.

C. Peicuti, *A Monetary and Economic History of France since 1944*, Contributions to Economics, https://doi.org/10.1007/978-3-032-17596-0_14

otherwise in the case of Emmanuel Macron. The measures would drive up the government debt for far longer and to an extent dwarfing increases in other European countries. In his address to the nation on March 12, 2020, "whatever the cost" is uttered three times:

> "Health is priceless. The government will mobilize all necessary financial resources to provide assistance, treat patients, and save lives, whatever the cost. [...]
>
> We will not compound distress over the health situation by adding the fear of bankruptcy for entrepreneurs and anguish over unemployment and difficult month-ends for employees. Every effort will therefore be made to protect our employees and to protect our companies, whatever the cost. [...] In the next few days, an exceptional large-scale short-time working scheme will be implemented. [...] The State will bear the cost of indemnifying employees forced to stay at home. [...] I also want us to be able to protect those who are self-employed. We will take all necessary measures to honor this guarantee at the economic level."[2]

Emmanuel Macron declared that European governments will help the economy absorb the shock of the current crisis. The "whatever the cost" will not only be French but also European:

> "We must also provide a European response. Earlier today, the Central Bank announced a first series of decisions. Will they be enough? I do not think so. It will be up to the bank to take further decisions. But I want to be very clear with you this evening: we Europeans will not allow a financial and economic crisis to spread. We will react aggressively and swiftly. All European governments must take decisions to support economic activity and recovery, whatever the cost. France will do so and I will make the case for this policy on your behalf at the European level. I already did so at the special council held yesterday. I do not know how the financial markets will respond in the next few days and I will be just as clear on this. Europe will respond in an orderly manner and on a massive scale to protect its economy."[3]

On March 18, 2020, six days after Emmanuel Macron's address, the European Central Bank announced the launch of the Pandemic Emergency Purchase Programme (PEPP), with an envelope of €750 billion, with purchases to be conducted until the end of 2020. On December 10, 2020, the central bank announced that, given the resurgence of the pandemic and the economic fallout, the envelope would be increased further to €1850 billion, with net purchases under the PEPP until at least the end of March 2022.

The revival of state dirigisme reached its apogee in 2020. The price paid in terms of government debt and inflation is high and can be expected to destabilize the economy over the medium term. Given the aid package, the rise in unemployment and job losses was kept in check. The aid mobilized for households succeeded in preserving their overall financial situation.

In July 2021, the National Audit Office (*Cour des comptes*) drew up a report on public spending during the crisis and the operational assessment of its use. It concluded:

> "The COVID-19 crisis and its economic and social consequences have led to a sharp rise in public spending. It represented 61.8% of GDP in 2020, compared with 55.4% in 2019. [...]

---

[2] *Adresse aux Français*, source: https://www.elysee.fr/front/pdf/elysee-module-15339-fr.pdf.

[3] Ibid.

There was an increase of €96.4 billion or 6.5%, of which 86% was crisis-related. Ordinary expenditure, unrelated to the crisis, accounted for 14% of the rise in public spending, or €13.7 billion. The rise in public spending mainly concerned the central government (+11.0%) and social security administrations (+5.6%). By contrast, spending by local government was little affected by the health crisis (−0.9%).

In 2020, additional spending due to the crisis mainly concerned, in the health sector, the funding of COVID-19 screening tests, compensation for loss of revenue and additional staff and equipment costs for health and medico-social establishments, as well as aid to healthcare professionals affected by restrictions to their activity during the initial lockdown. Otherwise, support for businesses came mainly from the solidarity fund, short-time working scheme, state-guaranteed loans, and reductions and deferrals of social security contributions."[4]

The National Audit Office considered that, overall, these measures achieved their short-term objectives, helping to protect the country from the economic and social fallout of the crisis. However, it considered that in comparison with France's partners, support measures for businesses and households, as well as healthcare spending, were oversized and insufficiently targeted. This led to a rise of almost 20 percentage points in the government debt-to-GDP ratio compared with 2019.

If the additional government debt taken on because of the pandemic is measured in relation to GDP and the situation in 2021 compared with the situation in 2019, the debt-to-GDP ratio increased by just 2.4 points in Sweden, 12.5 points in Germany, and 9 points in the Netherlands. Only Spain, Greece, and Italy recorded bigger increases in government debt because of the pandemic than France. It is interesting to note that the European countries which oversized their support to the economy during the pandemic are those which were the most indebted before the pandemic. In the case of Spain, Italy, and Greece, the deterioration in public finances can also be explained by the downturn in tax receipts generated by tourism, which is a major economic sector in these countries. Before the pandemic, tourism accounted for 20.3% of GDP in Greece, 14.1% in Spain, and 13.1% in Italy, and the pandemic laid waste to this sector of the economy. As tourism represented only 8.4% of France's GDP pre-pandemic, the huge amount of government debt taken on by France in response to the pandemic cannot be blamed to the same extent on the collapse of tourism.

The National Audit Office also drew attention to "significant" windfall effects and risks of fraud due to the generosity of the schemes. This refers mainly to windfall effects in the case of short-time working, where companies that could have continued their activity instead opted to take advantage of the scheme. According to France Stratégie, though firms had to be 'forced' to reduce their activity in order to benefit from the scheme, around 8% of the one million companies having benefited from the short-time working scheme in 2020 in fact experienced a significant increase in sales. In addition to windfall effects, there were doubts over the efficiency of the scheme in that "short-time working may have benefited firms whose viability was uncertain. What can be observed is that payments of €138 million were made to firms which,

[4] Cour des comptes, *Les dépenses publiques pendant la crise et le bilan opérationnel de leur utilisation*, source: https://www.ccomptes.fr/fr/publications/les-depenses-publiques-pendant-la-crise-et-le-bilan-operationnel-de-leur-utilisation.

in December 2020, had entered legal proceedings. At the same time, these amounts are relatively low in relation to total payments (around 0.6%)."[5]

In addition, businesses that were not viable were kept afloat by state-guaranteed loans and the deferred payments of social contributions and taxes. The "whatever the cost" approach meant that the number of business failures declined to 31 thousand in 2020, down from 50 thousand in 2019. Between March 2020 and October 2021, 40 thousand bankruptcies were 'avoided,' their number decreasing by 45% compared with the equivalent period before the crisis.

Concerning state-guaranteed loans (*prêts garantis par l'État—PGE*), the National Audit Office considered that there are risks of optimization by companies, as no specific mechanism was set up to check that these loans were not substituted for pre-existing debts. Defined by the law and order published on March 23, 2020, in compliance with the State Aid Temporary Framework to support the economy in the context of the COVID-19 outbreak adopted by the Commission on March 19, 2020, state-guaranteed loans were one of the main schemes to support businesses through the health crisis. "These loans were granted by banks until June 30, 2022, guaranteed at between 70 and 90% by the State, and capped at 25% of annual sales—or, for new firms, two years' payroll. During the first lockdown, a huge number of these loans were taken out: of the €137 billion of state-guaranteed loans that had been granted by banks as of December 31, 2021, over 70% were granted between March and June 2020. [...] Compared with other countries, France offered firms one of the most advantageous schemes in cost terms, with an interest rate (including the guarantee premium) of 0.25% in the first year and 1% to 2.5% in subsequent years."[6]

The National Audit Office's report also pointed out that "the combined recourse to various forms of aids, notably to the Solidarity Fund (*fonds de solidarité*) and short-time working scheme, may in some cases have led to an improvement in a firm's situation compared with the previous year. Aid under the Solidarity Fund aid is intended to compensate for lost sales, while the short-time working scheme is designed to reduce payroll costs. So, for example, a firm that was closed by order of the administration in November 2020 and had sales of €10,000 in November 2019 could receive the same amount from the Solidarity Fund, even though its payroll costs were reduced under the short-time working scheme. Furthermore, unlike company sales, subsidies received from the Solidarity Fund are not subject to taxation."[7]

Moreover, the various government schemes failed to anticipate the emergence of frauds such as claiming relief for short-time working while asking employee to work from home. The report pointed out that, in addition to attempting to benefit fraudulently from the various schemes, frauds in general developed during the pandemic, as "the initiation of new inspections was suspended during the initial lockdown,

---

[5] Ibid.

[6] Cour des comptes, *Les prêts garantis par l'État*, source: https://www.ccomptes.fr/fr/publications/les-prets-garantis-par-letat.

[7] Cour des comptes, *Les dépenses publiques pendant la crise et le bilan opérationnel de leur utilisation*, source: https://www.ccomptes.fr/fr/publications/les-depenses-publiques-pendant-la-crise-et-le-bilan-operationnel-de-leur-utilisation.

and then, despite a gradual resumption from May 2020, inspections targeted solely taxpayers who were little affected by the crisis. As a result, the number of field tax audits and of controls (all categories) by the Organisation for the Collection of Social Security and Family Benefit Contributions (*Union de recouvrement des cotisations de Sécurité sociale et d'allocations familiales—URSSAF*) was halved in 2020, with many controls being postponed until 2021. There was a substantial reduction in field audits by the Family Allowances Fund (*Caisse d'allocations familiales*) [...]. Controls of amounts billed by healthcare establishments were suspended entirely."[8]

Other European countries decided to actively combat abuses securing short-term financial support during the pandemic. For example, the United Kingdom's March 2021 budget included a €117 million investment in a specialist taskforce to tackle fraud across all COVID-19 support packages, with the furlough scheme, business subsidies, and state-guaranteed loans of particular concern for the government. In countries such as Germany, the Netherlands, and Denmark, penalties for the fraudulent use of aid schemes during the pandemic have gone as far as prison sentences.

The response to the COVID-19 pandemic was not only national but also European. The European Commission is empowered by the EU Treaties to borrow on the international capital markets on behalf of the European Union. All EU bond issues by the European Commission are denominated exclusively in euros. The European Commission uses the proceeds of EU bond issues to finance EU policy programs such as the NextGenerationEU stimulus package. With a maximum value of around €800 billion, it is designed to support economic recovery from the pandemic and build a greener, more digital, and resilient future. The inaugural issue by the European Commission under NextGenerationEU took place in June 2021.

The pandemic put pay to the first pension reform, namely plans to switch to a points system, and the strikes staged in protest. In addition to aid payments, the French hospital system needs to be reorganized by changing regulations to arrive at a situation where there are more frontline nursing staff than administrative staff. In this area, taxpayers feel they are not getting their money's worth and want a structural reform.

---

[8] Ibid.

Chapter 15
The War in Ukraine

"I pushed European defence issues to the forefront as soon as I took office, at the European level, at the Franco-German level. At the Franco-German Council of Ministers on 13 July 2017, we launched two major projects: the tank and the aircraft of the future. [...] The instability of our American partner and rising tensions have meant that the idea of European defence is gradually taking hold. It's the aggiornamento for a powerful and strategic Europe. I would add that we will at some stage have to take stock of NATO. To my mind, what we are currently experiencing is the brain death of NATO. We have to be lucid."[1]

Emmanuel Macron, 2019

Emmanuel Macron rightly traces the beginning of the United States' disengagement from the European Union to the presidency of Barack Obama [1961-], who was paradoxically much loved in Europe despite being the first American president to lose interest in the Old Continent:

"But their position has shifted over the past 10 years, and it hasn't only been the Trump administration. You have to understand what is happening deep down in American policy-making. It's the idea put forward by President Obama: 'I am a Pacific president.' So the United States were looking elsewhere, which was in fact very astute from their point of view at the time: they were looking at China and the American continent. President Obama then theorised it as a geopolitical strategy of trading blocs, signed treaties, and withdrew from the Middle East, saying: 'This is no longer my neighbourhood policy.' But that then created a problem and a weakness: the 2013-2014 crisis, the failure to intervene in response to the use of chemical weapons in Syria, which was already the first stage in the collapse of the Western bloc. Because at that point, the major regional powers said to themselves: "the West is weak." Things that had already begun implicitly became apparent in recent years."[2]

France had the rotating presidency of the Council of European Union when the subprime crisis broke out. It again took the rotating presidency on January 1, 2022,

[1] *Macron in his own words*, The French president's interview with The Economist, October 21, 2019, source: https://www.economist.com/europe/2019/11/07/emmanuel-macron-in-his-own-words-french.

[2] Ibid.

C. Peicuti, *A Monetary and Economic History of France since 1944*, Contributions to Economics, https://doi.org/10.1007/978-3-032-17596-0_15

shortly before Russia invaded Ukraine. The subprime crisis was an endogenous shock, because it originated in the financial system. The war in Ukraine was an exogenous shock as it originated outside the economic system. Both crises had global repercussions. In the first months of the conflict, Emmanuel Macron tried to negotiate the withdrawal of Russian troops from Ukraine and secure the Zaporizhzhia nuclear power plant.

All wars are inflationary. The war in Ukraine is no exception, especially as the Russian invader possesses the world's largest gas reserves. Inflation jumped from 1.6% in 2021 to 5.2% in 2022, the year of the invasion, before falling back to 4.9% in 2023.[3] Inflation had camped below 2.5% since 1992 save in 2008, the year the subprime crisis broke out, when it increased to 2.8% before falling back to 0.1% in 2009.

To combat inflation, the European Central Bank tightened its monetary policy. It raised the interest rate on the main refinancing operations for the first time to 0.5% on July 27, 2022, then to 1.25% on September 14, 2% on November 2, and 2.5% on December 21, 2022. It was then raised to 3% on February 8, 2023. Further increases followed, taking this rate to 4.5% in September 2023.[4]

To limit the exponential rise in energy prices, the French government took several measures. According to the Senate's Information Report of June 27, 2023, the cost of these measures was "estimated at €85 billion between 2021 and 2023, of which:

- €40 billion to fund the shields and buffers;
- €18 billion in lost tax receipts linked to the reduction in the excise tax rate for electricity in 2022 and 2023;
- €8 billion of costs assumed by EDF as a result of increasing volumes available under the Regulated Access to Incumbent Nuclear Electricity (*Accès régulé à l'électricité nucléaire historique - ARENH*) in 2022."[5]

So-called Resilience State-guaranteed loans (*prêt garanti par l'État Resilience—PGE Resilience*) were made available to support firms that had significant working capital requirements as a result of the conflict in Ukraine, for example due to a rise in the prices of certain raw commodities (cereals, metals, energy), the disruption of supply chains, the suspension of payments from Russia or Ukraine, or the loss of commercial outlets due to international sanctions. While the State-guaranteed loans for firms affected by the COVID-19 pandemic ended on June 30, 2022, the Resilience State-guaranteed loans lasted until December 31, 2023.

---

[3] INSEE, Inflation rate, source: https://www.insee.fr/fr/statistiques/2122401#tableau-figure1.

[4] European Central Bank key policy rates, source: https://www.banque-france.fr/fr/les-taux-monetaires-directeurs.

[5] French Senate, Information Report n° 779 (2022–2023), *Contrôle budgétaire sur les dispositifs de soutien aux consommateurs d'énergie: l'usine à gaz des aides énergie*, filed June 27, 2023, source: https://www.senat.fr/notice-rapport/2022/r22-779-notice.html.

From February 2022 to February 2024, EU support for Ukraine amounted to over €88 billion, of which:

€43.4 billion to support the global economic, social, and financial resilience of Ukraine;

€28 billion of military aid; and

Over €17 billion of aid to help EU Member States attend to the needs of Ukrainians war refugees.

The Athenian historian and general Thucydides [460–400 BC] recommended always impressing one's adversaries to keep them at bay. His advice: "If you want peace, prepare for war." Unfortunately, this has not been heeded by the European Union. The war in Ukraine and its consequences for France is a chapter of history that is still in the writing.

Chapter 16
Ecological Crisis and Energy Transition: "Europe is the Fastest-Warming Continent in the World"

The IPCC Sixth Assessment Report published in March 2023 highlighted the additional adverse observed impacts and/or projected risks linked to climate change, warning they will be multiple times higher, which will make their management that much more complex, difficult, and costlier. In theory, France is pursuing a four-pronged energy strategy based on: energy sobriety, energy efficiency, accelerating the development of renewable energies, and revitalizing the country's nuclear industry. In terms of its application, this includes notably the national low-carbon strategy, which aims to achieve carbon neutrality by 2050. In practice, however, France is not giving itself the resources it needs to limit the scale of global warming and the seriousness of its impact. The dynamics of the climate crisis are accelerating by the day.

The Result of Inaction

The specificity of the ecological crisis is that it is a multiplier of risks that could exacerbate existing risks and crises. The poorest people are always the most exposed in a crisis but in the present case their very lives could be at risk. As the fruits of all the efforts deployed fall into a common pot, no country is incentivized to make efforts first; everyone secretly hopes to be a free-rider and benefit from the efforts of others combating climate change. The result of this strategy is catastrophic in the truest sense of the word.

The report published by the European Environment Agency draws attention to the fact that, globally, 2023 was the warmest year on record and that Europe is the continent most affected by this phenomenon:

European Environment Agency, *European climate risk assessment*, March 11, 2024, source: https://www.eea.europa.eu/publications/european-climate-risk-assessment.

C. Peicuti, *A Monetary and Economic History of France since 1944*, Contributions to Economics, https://doi.org/10.1007/978-3-032-17596-0_16

> "Human-induced climate change is affecting the planet; globally, 2023 was the warmest year on record, and the average global temperature in the 12-month period between February 2023 and January 2024 exceeded pre-industrial levels by 1.5°C.
>
> Europe is the fastest-warming continent in the world. Extreme heat, once relatively rare, is becoming more frequent while precipitation patterns are changing. Downpours and other precipitation extremes are increasing in severity, and recent years have seen catastrophic floods in various regions. At the same time, southern Europe can expect considerable declines in overall rainfall and more severe droughts."[1]

The report identifies 36 climate risks with potentially severe consequences across Europe. The risks are evaluated in the contexts of risk severity and policy horizon to identify priorities for EU policy action and find an efficient response to the climate crisis, taking into account the need for social justice. The report concluded that "several climate risks have already reached critical levels. If decisive action is not taken now, most climate risks identified could reach critical or catastrophic levels by the end of this century. Hundreds of thousands of people would die from heatwaves, and economic losses from coastal floods alone could exceed EUR 1 trillion per year."[2]

The Price of Inaction

In 2006, *The Economics of Climate Change: The Stern Review* already demonstrated the economic impact of climate change. If we do not act, the overall costs and risks of climate change will be equivalent to losing at least 5% and possibly as much as 20% of global GDP each year, whereas the cost of action can be limited to around 1% of global GDP each year.

In December 2023, France's Environment and Energy Management Agency (*Agence de l'environnement et de la maîtrise de l'énergie—Ademe*) published the findings of a study that assessed climate risks and their costs for France.[3] In scenarios that looked at a delayed transition on the one hand and no action on the other hand, costs linked to climate change would be exorbitant for France: "The study's initial estimates, which are very probably understated, show that if temperatures were to rise leading to global warming of 3.5 °C, the damages caused by climate change could reduce economic activity by more than 10 percentage points compared with a fictitious scenario in which there would be no climate change by the end of the century. Damages would break down as follows:

> - Natural catastrophes in the rest of the world, affecting French exports (almost 6 percentage points in terms of economic activity);
>
> - Decrease in agricultural yields (3 percentage points);

---

[1] Ibid.

[2] Ibid.

[3] ADEME, *Les risques climatiques et leurs coûts pour la France*, source: https://librairie.ademe.fr/changement-climatique-et-energie/6712-les-risques-climatiques-et-leurs-couts-pour-la-france.html.

- Direct cost of natural catastrophes in France (0.5 point);
- Rise in sea level (0.5 point);
- All other damages taken in aggregate (0.5 point)."[4]

If the transition is delayed, but global warming is kept below 2 °C until the end of the century, the cost to France would be "almost $1100 billion in stranded assets accumulated over the period, i.e., almost $50 billion a year between 2030 and 2050. A delayed transition scenario would result in the loss of nearly 1.5 percentage point of GDP in 2030 and 5 percentage points of GDP in 2050. [...] By the end of the century, the inaction scenario would cost nearly 7 percentage points of GDP each year."[5]

Furthermore, the Environment and Energy Management Agency warns that the estimates in its study are understated, as they do not take into account population displacement, mitigation and reconstruction policies, the economic cost of biodiversity loss, and the costs of climate change adaptation.

On June 1, 2017, US President Donald Trump announced the withdrawal of the United States from the Paris Climate Agreement signed by 195 countries in December 2016. From the start of his campaign, Donald Trump latched on to Ronald Reagan's 1980 slogan and repeated it ad nauseam until his election on November 8, 2016. In response to the withdrawal of the United States, Emmanuel Macron launched an appeal on the same day under the slogan "Make Our Planet Great Again" to researchers, entrepreneurs, associations and non-governmental organizations, students, and the whole of civil society to mobilize and join France in leading the fight against global warming. Will France just lecture the world, or will it lead by example in the fight to combat global warming? The green chapter in France's history is very much a work in progress.

---

[4] Ibid.

[5] Ibid.

Chapter 17
Epilogue or Temporary Conclusions

High Expectations

"A Grasshopper gay
Sang the summer away,
And found herself poor
By the winter's first roar.
Of meat or of bread,
Not a morsel she had!
So a begging she went,
To her neighbour the ant,
For the loan of some wheat,
Which would serve her to eat,
Till the season came round.
'I will pay you,' she saith,
'On an animal's faith,
Double weight in the pound
Ere the harvest be bound.'
The ant is a friend
(And here she might mend)
Little given to lend.
'How spent you the summer?'
Quoth she, looking shame
At the borrowing dame.
'Night and day to each comer
I sang, if you please.'
'You sang! I'm at ease;
For 'tis plain at a glance,

C. Peicuti, *A Monetary and Economic History of France since 1944*, Contributions to Economics, https://doi.org/10.1007/978-3-032-17596-0_17

Now, ma'am, you must dance.'"
The Grasshopper and the Ant[1]
Jean de la Fontaine [1621–1695]

Throughout our studies, we learn about the laws of the market economy. As future craftsmen, members of the profession, entrepreneurs, executives, board members, or more generally human capital, we are trained, indeed formatted, to evolve in a market economy governed by rational choices, with competition at the heart of this economic system. In reality, economic policies limit our room for maneuver. Even if they are beyond our control, knowing the history of national economic policies and understanding the whys and wherefores of the European Union's construction will enable us to better grasp the economic challenges and issues of the day. Not being caught off guard and destabilized by government decisions allows us to derive maximum benefit from economic activities in our private and professional lives.

The economic policy of most French governments, whether to the left or right of the political spectrum, has followed the same pattern for eighty years. Governments start handing out money at the start of their term, before taking stock of the situation and seeing whether there in fact is anything in the state coffers to hand out, or at least to think about how best to distribute it for the benefit not only of pressure groups, but above all of future generations. No individual or firm would ever proceed in this manner, because it would defy common sense and would rapidly lead to bankruptcy. The height of nonsense is handouts funded by public debt to pay a generation's current expenditure. What bank would extend credit for you to pay your electricity bill? If it were so, why would government have to step in and fund a tariff shield for gas and electricity by taking on public debt?

The consequence of this expansionary economic policy in the early years of a government is an inexorable increase in public debt, meaning in fact that the current generation is living off the backs of future generations. For each government, after two years in office or less, the early consumption-driven stimulus is replaced out of necessity by austerity, which is all the more severe the greater the initial largesse, and if an endogenous or exogenous crisis and/or cyclical downturn aggravates the situation. This economic roller-coaster takes its toll on the economic agents and European partners, who lose their bearings or know not what to undertake on this shifting sand. This does not correspond to the natural course of economic life, which is thrown off course by these constant about-turns, damaging visibility and, consequently, the confidence of economic agents. The French economy has long suffered from this incessant stop-and-go.

French statesmen seem not yet to have really integrated the cyclicality of the market economy into their analyses and decision-making. Thus, another constant in French economic policy is that political leaders do not think about saving at the top of the cycle, in order to have the reserves needed to mitigate the effects of the downturn. What is more, they distribute and cut taxes throughout the cycle. Chirac

[1] *The Fables of La Fontaine*, Translated from the French by Elizur Wright, A New Edition, With Notes By J. W. M. Gibbs, 1882, source: Project Gutenberg's The Fables of La Fontaine, by Jean de la Fontaine.

is not alone in ignoring the fact that there is no such thing as a "kitty." He's the archetypal French president. It is as if our leaders still have not grasped that the market economy is cyclical by nature, that no period of prosperity lasts forever. They systematically position themselves as the grasshopper in La Fontaine's fable, forgetting that the "winter's first roar" will inevitably resonate. Fortunately, there are the ants, Germany especially, which share the same currency, the euro, so that France does not have to pay "double weight in the pound." As Homer (eighth century BC) wrote in the *Iliad*: "Union is strength, and weakness comes of division."

At the top of the cycle, like the grasshopper, France does not put aside even a morsel to cope with a cyclical downturn or a crisis, so a begging she goes, and when the downturn comes, in the panic, credit-financed measures are often poorly calibrated and excessive, increasing debt exponentially. As spending is not restricted to what is in the coffers and the euro is also the currency of Germany and others like it, France can sign the winter away. But in the wake of the government's knee-jerk reaction, the State's medium-term objectives recede into the distance.

As explained by Finn Erling Kydland [1943-], who shared the 2004 Sveriges Riksbank Prize in Economic Sciences with Edward Prescott [1940–2022] "for their contributions to dynamic macroeconomics: the time consistency of economic policy and the driving forces behind business cycles"[2]: "One thing we have learned is that business cycles are not that costly to people. The welfare implications are not that big—at least from normal business cycles. That's not to say, of course, that governments can't implement bad policies and make things much worse. But it may behoove us to devote more attention to longer-run questions where the benefits can be really great. As our understanding of economic theory improves and as computers improve, it is natural to turn our attention to things that matter over the life cycle, such as social security, immigration, age and wealth distribution, and so on."[3]

Greek proverbs advise not persevering in the errors of one's way: "It is disgraceful to stumble against the same stone twice"; also: "To blunder twice is not allowed in war." This advice is not heeded in the conduct of French economic policy. Errors are repeated in the pursuit of policies that fail to bring any real benefits to the economy, yet gradually destroy a system that works. An ingrained belief of the French state's economic policy is that lowering social security contributions supports employment. This is the wrong way to put the problem. The only certainty is that this cut weakens the financing of the social security system, at a time when expenditure is rising as a result of an aging population and advances in medicine. The general social security system is financed for 80% by contributions and taxes deducted from earnings, with social security contributions accounting for 82% of total financing in 1993 but only 49% in 2021.[4] Social security contributions are calculated applying percentage rates decided at the national level and are borne partly by employers and partly

[2] Royal Swedish Academy of Sciences, Press Release, October 11, 2004, source: https://www.nobelprize.org/prizes/economic-sciences/2004/press-release/.

[3] International Monetary Fund, *Nobel laureate Kydland reflects, talks about what's in store*, May 24, 2005, source: https://www.elibrary.imf.org/view/journals/023/0034/009/article-A010-en.xml.

[4] https://www.cleiss.fr/docs/regimes/regime_france/an_0.html.

by employees. The increase in tax exemptions, which began in the early 1990s, contributed to a considerable drop in the proportion of the financing provided by social security contributions, weakening everything that depends on these contributions. Against this backdrop, how could the French healthcare system have managed a pandemic like COVID-19?

In 2005, in a report commissioned by Thierry Breton, Minister of the Economy, Finance and Industry, Michel Pébereau, the Chairman of BNP Paribas, wrote:

> "Every time a new problem has arisen over the past twenty-five years, our country has responded with additional expenditure, without calling into question expenditure routinely incurred in other areas, and constantly postponing adjustments to its solidarity systems made necessary by demographics. Exceptions do exist, but they are rare. A 'spending culture' has thus replaced the search for more than just superficial efficiency and the setting of objectives in terms of utility for citizens and the economy. As a result, France has gradually accumulated public deficits, while failing to solve the problems of unemployment and poverty. It has run up debts in conditions that restrict its room for maneuver in regulating the economy, and jeopardize its medium-term future.
>
> To continue in this way would lead to a lasting paralysis of public action, and would severely test our ambitions for growth and solidarity in the years ahead.
>
> But France's fate is not yet sealed. By opting for a lucid analysis and a rational method, it is possible to restore the effectiveness of public action in the service of growth and employment and to build the future our country deserves."[5]

During Emmanuel Macron's two 5-year terms, there was no let-up in the propensity towards public indebtedness and in the 'spending culture,' whether in response to the Yellow Vests movement, the COVID-19 pandemic, or the surge in energy prices triggered by the war in Ukraine. The first sentence of the report by Michel Pébereau could be updated to read: "Every time a new problem has arisen over the past forty-five years...," which is not to say there cannot be high expectations for the future...

For Hayek, democracy is a means, not an end in itself: "Democracy is essentially a means, a utilitarian device for safeguarding internal peace and individual freedom."[6] Democracy must submit to a body of formulated laws. If the scope of the State's action is not limited, the population may constantly push for more and more expenditure, which could eventually threaten the market order. Hayek resurrected the archaic term 'demarchy'[7] to describe such a state of affairs, explaining that: "Unless we restore a situation in which governments (and other public authorities) find that if they overspend they will, like everybody else, be unable to meet their obligations, there will be no halt to this growth which, by substituting collective for private activity, threatens to suffocate individual initiative. Under the prevailing form of unlimited democracy, in which government has power to confer special material benefits on

---

[5] *Rompre avec la facilité de la dette publique*, report published on July 8, 2005 by the commission chaired by Michel Pébereau, source: https://www.vie-publique.fr/files/rapport/pdf/054004454.pdf.

[6] Hayek, Friedrich A. von (1944), *The Road to Serfdom*, Routledge Press.

[7] Hayek, Friedrich A. von (1993), *Law, Legislation and Liberty*, Routledge Press.

groups, it is forced to buy the support of sufficient numbers to add up to a majority."[8] Hayek perfectly sums up the current socio-economic situation, which can be more ably managed within the European framework, which calls for the convergence of economic policies to ensure the prosperity and well-being not only of current but also of future generations.

After Anne-Robert-Jacques Baron de Turgot [1727–1781] was appointed as Controller-General of Finance, he wrote on August 24, 1774, to Louis XVI to proffer advice, which not being heeded would lead the monarch to the scaffold: "In the present moment, I confine myself, Sire, to call to your recollection three ideas:

No national bankruptcy.

No increase of taxes.

No new loans.

No bankruptcy - neither avowed nor disguised under compulsory reductions.

No increase of taxes—the reasons for this measure Your Majesty will find in the situation of your people, and still more in your own heart.

No new loans - for every loan, by diminishing the amount of the free revenue, necessarily produces at last a bankruptcy, or an increase of taxes. In a period of peace, money should not be borrowed, unless to liquidate old debts, or to discharge others bearing a higher interest.

To obtain these three points there is but one method, that of reducing the expenditure below the receipt, and so much below it as to leave twenty millions [livres] every year for the redemption of former debts."[9]

The first piece of advice, "no national bankruptcy," has been heeded, but three centuries on, the third piece of advice, "no new loans," has not.

Shocks to growth often stem from oil shocks, which can be amplified by a downturn in the cycle or an endogenous crisis such as the subprime crisis. While it is the oil shocks of 1973 and 1979 (which marked the end of the Glorious Thirty) that always spring to mind, bear in mind that the price of a barrel of oil climbed from \$38.2 in 2004 to \$62.5 in 2005, \$65.1 in 2006, \$72.5 in 2007 and peaked at \$101 in 2008, the year when the 2008 crisis broke out. In the same way, the oil shock triggered by the war in Ukraine, which began on February 24, 2022, is not given the attention it might merit. The price of a barrel of oil, which was \$86.5 in January 2022, jumped to almost \$140 on March 6, 2022, averaging \$117.2 in March 2022. As today's economy is based on oil, the rise in the price of this commodity increases all other prices in its wake, eroding household purchasing power and fueling populism.

Switching to other forms of energy that would make us less dependent would pave the way for sustainable growth in every sense of the term, for it is indeed the dependence on oil and gas and the lack of innovation that have been decisive factors in the crises that have shaken economies and societies. If innovation had not been reduced to the securitization of high-risk mortgages and their sale to the entire world

---

[8] Hayek, Friedrich A. von (1999), from *Good Money, Part II Volume Six of the Collected Works of F.A. Hayek*, edited by Stephen Kresge, Routledge.

[9] Turgot, Anne-Robert-Jacques Baron de (1774), *Letter to the King on Finance*, from Soulavie, Jean-Louis (1802), *Historical and Political Memoirs of the Reign of Lewis XVI from His Marriage to His Death*, Translated from the French, in Six Volumes, vol. 3, London: G. and J. Robinson.

but had led to the invention of the renewable energies of tomorrow, the destiny of Europe and the United States would have been different, because populism feeds on poverty and social demotion. Taking advantage of the relative abundance of coal, oil, and gas, the Industrial Revolution has yielded all that can rightly be expected. It is time to turn that page and write the green economy of tomorrow.

France's biggest error in its conduct of economic policy was not investing sufficiently in institutional research arrangements that would encourage innovation, which would in turn stimulate endogenous growth. As Nobel Prize winner Paul Romer explains: "Human history teaches us, however, that economic growth springs from better recipes, not just from more cooking. New recipes generally produce fewer unpleasant side effects and generate more economic value per unit of raw material."[10] In other words, growth is not just about the quantity of labor, but also and above all about quality. In the global arena, France cannot surpass China in terms of the quantity of work, but it can in terms of quality. On the other hand, reducing working hours and not investing in research amounts to what the novelist Louis-Ferdinand Céline called "death on the installment plan".[11] Strongly linking research, knowledge, and information to growth is France's only option to position itself as a leader in today's knowledge-based economy. Moreover, only this positioning is capable of financing the welfare state, responding to major societal challenges—energy, climate, healthcare—and fostering sustainable growth. The United States has already made this shift. To stimulate a new knowledge-based economy, the European Council defined the Lisbon Strategy in 2000, which will run for a decade, until 2020. It calls for each country to devote 3% of its GDP to research, with private firms to finance two-thirds and the public sector one-third.

In 1990, France invested 2.27% of its GDP in research and development, of which 1.37% financed by private firms. In 1991, the research and development effort reached 2.28%, while at the level of the 27 EU Member States, it averaged 1.65%, of which 1.03% financed by European firms. In 2020, expenditure on research and development represented 2.28% of France's GDP, of which 1.46% financed by French firms, while at the level of the European Union, it averaged 2.18%, of which 1.41% financed by European firms.[12]

At the level of the European Union, expenditure on research and development as a percentage of GDP has risen on average, whereas in France it has stagnated on average for two decades. It remains below the OECD average of 2.72% and is surpassed by the United States and China where expenditure on research and development reaches 3.46% and 2.43%. In Europe, Germany devotes 3.13% of its GDP to research, Belgium 3.43%, Austria 3.26%, Sweden 3.40%, Finland 2.99%, and Denmark 2.76%. The dynamics of French research funding are unlikely to improve,

---

[10] Céline, Louis-Ferdinand, *Mort à crédi.*

Death on Credit for the British edition, *Death on the Installment Plan* for the American edition.

[11] Romer, Paul, *Economic growth*, The Concise Encyclopedia of Economics, source: https://www.econlib.org/library/Enc1/EconomicGrowth.html.

[12] INSEE, Expenditure on research and development, source: https://www.insee.fr/fr/statistiques/3281637?sommaire=3281778#tableau-figure2.

even though innovation is crucial in the current economic war and the only way to finance the French welfare state when working thirty-five hours a week. Yet, the decree of February 21, 2024 (*Décret n° 2024–124 du 21 février 2024 portant annulation de credits*) stipulates that of the ten billion euros in budget cuts planned by the government in 2024, €904 million will concern research and higher education. Strategic programs such as *Programme 172*, which funds research organizations such as CNRS, Inrae, Inserm, and Inria, will have to cancel almost 5% of their budgets. *Programme 193*, for space technologies and research, has been cut by 10%. To sum up what is happening in terms of research and development in France, and consequently, in terms of growth, Talleyrand would say: "If you don't have the means to fulfil your ambitions, you have every right to worry."

State dirigisme is another scourge from which France suffers, Turgot already warning of its limitations two-and-a-half centuries ago: "Thus our policy should surrender itself to the course of nature, and the course of commerce, which is no less necessary and no less irresistible than the course of nature, without seeking to direct this course. For, in order to guide it without disturbing it, and without injuring ourselves, it would be necessary for us to be able to follow all the changes in the needs, the interests, and the industry of mankind. It would be necessary to know these in such detail as would be physically impossible to obtain and in which even the most skilful, the most active and the most painstaking government will risk always to be wrong in half the cases."[13]

When the Second World War ended, States throughout Europe had become more powerful, while individual freedoms had been circumscribed. The Europe that existed before the two world wars, depicted in Stefan Zweig's 1942 autobiography, *The World of Yesterday: Memoirs of a European*, is no more.[14] Some four decades later, in his essay *The Art of the Novel* published in 1986, Czech writer Milan Kundera, lamented the Europe without walls or bureaucracy of yesteryear. He defined a "European [as] one who is nostalgic for Europe"[15] such as it was before the modern nation-state that, like the gods of old, became omnipresent and omnipotent in the daily lives of Europeans. From 1945 onwards, the French economy was under the sway of dirigisme: the State intervened systematically and arbitrarily in the economy, without ever abandoning the capitalist economy. This dirigisme, which extended from the end of the Second World War to the first oil crisis, was inflationary. It was exercised in many ways, for example, through credit control, price setting, and wage and investment policies.

---

[13] Turgot, Jacques (1773), *Letter to l'Abbé Terray on the "Marque des Fers"*, from the Turgot Collection, edited by David Gordon, Mises Institute, source: https://cdn.mises.org/The%20Turgot%20Collection%20Writings,%20Speeches,%20and%20Letters%20of%20Anne%20Robert%20Jacques%20Turgot,%20Baron%20de%20Laune_2.pdf.

[14] Zweig, Stefan (1943), *The World of Yesterday: Memoirs of a European*, New York, The Viking Press.

[15] https://www.lemonde.fr/en/opinion/article/2023/07/17/milan-kundera-outlined-a-certain-idea-of-europe_6056272_23.html.

France's reconstruction was given a formal framework on January 3, 1946, with the creation of the *Commissariat au Plan*, whose four-year plan was aimed at modernizing France, and increasing its production capacity as well as its productivity. In his memoirs, Jean Monnet recalls his rejection of state dirigisme, which conditioned his appointment as *Commissaire Général au Plan*, a post he held from January 3, 1946, until September 11, 1952:

> "'I have a high regard for the French civil service' I said, 'but it is not equipped to produce a plan for changing the face of France. On the contrary, its job is to maintain the state of affairs entrusted to it. The senior civil servants who run it have every quality - except the spirit of enterprise. To transform France, we must first transform the French Establishment, and perhaps also the training that produces it. I do not propose to entrust the Modernization Commissions to civil servants, and still less to accept civil-service tutelage over the Plan. The Commissariat will be attached to your office or it will be nothing.'
>
> 'I'll speak to André Philip,' said Gouin.
>
> I heard no more of the matter, for a year at least. And I must say that we were left completely free to appoint the non-Ministerial members of the Planning Council."[16]

Jean Monnet remained lucid, however, adding: "No additional State control was proposed; but existing regulations, which provided for the allocation of raw materials and credit, gave the Government powerful enough means of encouraging and monitoring what had to be done."[17]

In *René Mayer: Études, témoignages et documents*, it is clear that dirigisme is at the heart of the concerns of René Mayer, who served as Finance Minister in the Schumann government. In a speech given to the Radical Party on July 6, 1948, after outlining the measures he had taken and their results, he declared: "It's a question of knowing whether we'll change course and whether inflationary dirigisme will regain the upper hand. We can change the pilot and the helmsman; that is not important. What matters is that the north of the compass should rest in the same horizontal direction."[18] He puts his finger on the real issue, which is political.

In a confidential letter dated July 8, 1948, to Robert Schuman, President of the Council, René Mayer set out a program of rigor: fiscal discipline, removal of the last subsidies used to artificially maintain prices, stability of agricultural prices and wages, and even a reduction in social charges to break free from state dirigisme.

It is the European construction that forced France to open up its economy, in turn lessening dirigisme. But the COVID-19 pandemic, which began with lockdowns that put the entire economy in the hands of the State as never before in human history, and continued with Emmanuel Macron's famous "whatever the cost" (17.1% in terms of the government public debt) saw dirigisme rise from the ashes, and inflation with it. Will governments steer to the compass or flounder in the shifting sands of public debt and inflationary dirigisme? If there are high expectations, they lie with Europe, which has kept France on the straight and narrow.

---

[16] Monnet, Jean (1978). *Memoirs*, translated from the French by Richard Mayne, Doubleday & Company, inc., Garden City, New York.

[17] Ibid.

[18] *René Mayer: Études, témoignages et documents*, source: https://gallica.bnf.fr/ark:/12148/bpt6k4808809p.texteImage.

Webography

L'Institut national de la statistique et des études économiques collects, produces, analyses and publishes information about the French economy and society, source: https://www.insee.fr/fr/accueil

Le Vème Plan, source: https://www.strategie.gouv.fr/sites/strategie.gouv.fr/files/atoms/files/cinquieme-plan-1966-1970.pdf

Le VIème Plan, source: https://www.strategie.gouv.fr/sites/strategie.gouv.fr/files/atoms/files/sixieme-plan-1971-1975.pdf

Converter franc and old franc into euro, source: https://www.insee.fr/fr/information/2417794

Poids des prélèvements obligatoires Données annuelles de 1959 à 2022, source: https://www.insee.fr/fr/statistiques/2381412#graphique-figure1

The OECD Observer, July 1977, source: https://www.oecd-ilibrary.org/docserver/observer-v1977-3-en.pdf?expires=1703617001&id=id&accname=guest&checksum=8F0F6273EF9C8EBCC8F180FE6EDCA178

Aux origines de la Compagnie générale d'électricité, Bulletin d'histoire de l'électricité,1985, 6, pages 103–120, source: https://www.persee.fr/doc/helec_0758-7171_1985_num_6_1_949

Saint Gobain institutional site, source: https://archives.saint-gobain.com/ressource/xviie/1665/1665-louis-xiv-fonde-la-manufacture-royale-des-glaces-miroirs-linstigation-de

110 propositions pour la France, source: https://www.mitterrand.org/110-propositions-pour-la-France.html

Loi n° 82–155 du 11 février 1982 de nationalisation, source: https://www.legifrance.gouv.fr/loda/id/JORFTEXT000000503960

Adieu Rothschild, Guy de Rothschild, 30 October 1981, source: https://www.lemonde.fr/archives/article/1981/10/30/adieu-rothschild_2710921_1819218.html

La nationalisation de la banque m'a contraint à repartir d'une page blanche, source: https://www.lesechos.fr/finance-marches/banque-assurances/la-nationalisation-de-la-banque-ma-contraint-a-repartir-dune-page-blanche-1787995

Rothschild, les secrets d'une renaissance, François Vidal, Nicolas Barré and Guillaume Maujean, source: https://www.lesechos.fr/2018/04/rothschild-les-secrets-dune-renaissance-988893

Loi no 98–461 du 13 juin 1998 d'orientation et d'incitation relative à la réduction du temps de travail, source: https://www.legifrance.gouv.fr/jorf/id/JORFTEXT000000558109

Journal officiel de la République française. Lois et décrets (version papier numérisée) n° 0181 du 06/08/1982, source: https://www.legifrance.gouv.fr/download/securePrint?token=PS5xvve@2YYAZnXNGTb0&pagePdf=2.

Les lois Auroux font entrer la démocratie dans les entreprises, source: https://www.gouvernement.fr/partage/12414-les-lois-auroux-font-entrer-la-democratie-dans-les-entreprises

C. Peicuti, *A Monetary and Economic History of France since 1944*, Contributions to Economics, https://doi.org/10.1007/978-3-032-17596-0

La « facture » pétrolière de la France a diminué en 1983, Le Monde, 11 February 1984, source https://www.lemonde.fr/archives/article/1984/02/11/la-facture-petroliere-de-la-France-a-diminue-en-1983_3004964_1819218.html

Déclaration de M. Pierre Bérégovoy, ministre des affaires sociales et de la solidarité nationale, sur la trésorerie des Caisses de Sécurité sociale en 1983, Paris 5 January 1984, source: https://www.vie-publique.fr/discours/213078-declaration-de-m-pierre-beregovoy-ministre-des-affaires-sociales-et-de

La proportion de reçus est en baisse dans les séries générales et en hausse dans les séries techniques, source: https://www.lemonde.fr/archives/article/1984/08/11/la-proportion-de-recus-est-en-baisse-dans-les-series-generales-et-en-hausse-dans-les-series-techniques_3009007_1819218.html

Loi du 4 janvier 1984 relative à l'activité et au contrôle des établissements de crédit, source: https://www.legifrance.gouv.fr/download/securePrint?token=nTw5WM7iGS!Of7yC7ren&pagePdf=2

Session du Conseil européen, Fontainebleau, 25 and 26 June 1984, source: https://www.consilium.europa.eu/media/20670/1984_juin_-_fontainebleau__fr_.pdf

Déclaration de politique générale de M. Jacques Chirac, Premier ministre, sur le programme du gouvernement, à l'Assemblée nationale le 9 avril 1986, source: https://www.vie-publique.fr/discours/130093-declaration-de-politique-generale-de-m-jacques-chirac-premier-ministre

Ordonnance n°86–1243 du 1 décembre 1986 relative a la liberte des prix et de la concurrence, source: https://www.legifrance.gouv.fr/download/securePrint?token=aU2B7R9bBOO40xU$ceXn&pagePdf=9.

Press conference by Roy Jenkins (Brussels, 6 November 1978), source: https://www.cvce.eu/obj/conference_donnee_par_roy_jenkins_bruxelles_6_novembre_1978-fr-dff92cfb-0bb3-42ad-8300-ac39691d88ba.html

Acte unique européen, source: https://eur-lex.europa.eu/legal-content/FR/TXT/PDF/?uri=CELEX:11986U/TXT

The Plaza Accord, 30 years later, Jeffrey Frankel, Working Paper 21813, source: http://www.nber.org/papers/w21813

Remarks by Chairman Alan Greenspan at the Annual Dinner and Francis Boyer Lecture of The American Enterprise Institute for Public Policy Research, Washington, D.C. December 5, 1996, source: http://www.federalreserve.gov/boarddocs/speeches/19961205.htm

Discours d'Hans-Dietrich Genscher à l'occasion de la signature du traité « Deux plus Quatre » (Moscou, 12 septembre 1990), source: https://www.cvce.eu/obj/discours_d_hans_dietrich_genscher_a_l_occasion_de_la_signature_du_traite_deux_plus_quatre_moscou_12_septembre_1990-fr-c14baf8d-c613-4c0d-9816-8830a7f233e6.html

Conférence de presse conjointe de M. François Mitterrand, Président de la République et de M. Helmut Kohl, Chancelier de RFA, sur la préparation du conseil européen de Hanovre et du sommet de Toronto, la construction européenne et la rencontre entre M. Reagan et M. Gorbatchev, Evian, jeudi 2 juin 1988, source: https://www.vie-publique.fr/discours/139561-conference-de-presse-conjointe-de-m-francois-mitterrand-president-de-l

Déclaration de politique générale de M. Michel Rocard, Premier ministre, sur le programme du gouvernement, à l'Assemblée nationale le 29 juin 1988, source: https://www.vie-publique.fr/discours/146230-declaration-de-politique-generale-de-m-michel-rocard-29061988

Qu'est-ce que la CSG, https://www.vie-publique.fr/fiches/21973-quest-ce-que-la-csg-contribution-sociale-generalisee

Premier bilan de l'emploi et du chômage en 1991, 11 May 1992, Dares Résultats N°17, source: https://dares.travail-emploi.gouv.fr/publication/premier-bilan-de-lemploi-et-du-chomage-en-1991

Déclaration de politique générale de Mme Cresson, Premier ministre, sur le programme du gouvernement, à l'Assemblée nationale le 22 mai 1991, source: https://www.vie-publique.fr/discours/181620-declaration-de-politique-generale-de-mme-cresson-premier-ministre-sur

Olympe de Gouges, *Les droits de la femme. À la Reine*, source: https://gallica.bnf.fr/ark:/12148/bpt6k64848397/f5.item

Chronologie du droit de vote et d'éligibilité des femmes, source: https://www2.assemblee-nationale.fr/decouvrir-l-assemblee/histoire/le-suffrage-universel/la-conquete-de-la-citoyennete-politique-des-femmes/chronologie-du-droit-de-vote-et-d-eligibilite-des-femmes

Traité sur l'Union européenne, source: https://eur-lex.europa.eu/legal-content/FR/TXT/?uri=celex%3A11992M%2FTXT

Les accords de Nyborg Un soutien préventif aux monnaies faibles, source: https://www.lemonde.fr/archives/article/1987/11/05/les-accords-de-nyborg-un-soutien-preventif-aux-monnaies-faibles_4081473_1819218.html

Marché monétaire et obligataire: victoire technique, défaite diplomatique », le 27 June 1993, source: https://www.lemonde.fr/archives/article/1993/06/27/marche-monetaire-et-obligataire-victoire-technique-defaite-diplomatique_3954274_1819218.html

Interview de M. François Mitterrand, Président de la République, accordée à TF1, France 2 et Europe 1 le 14 juillet 1993, sur la nouvelle cohabitation, l'emprunt Balladur et les privatisations, la lutte contre l'immigration, la réforme de la constitution et sur les questions internationales, source: https://www.vie-publique.fr/discours/134439-interview-de-m-francois-mitterrand-president-de-la-republique-accorde

Taux de chômage, https://data.oecd.org/fr/unemp/taux-de-chomage.htm#indicator-chart

Au quatrième trimestre 2023, le taux de chômage est stable à 7,5 %, source: https://www.insee.fr/fr/statistiques/7765269

La stratégie de l'OCDE pour l'emploi, La mise en œuvre de la Stratégie de l'OCDE pour l'emploi, page 11, source: https://read.oecd-ilibrary.org/employment/la-mise-en-France-de-la-strategie-de-l-ocde-pour-l-emploi_9789264273689-fr#page11

Réunion du conseil de l'OCDE au niveau des ministres, Communiqué, source: https://one.oecd.org/document/SG/PRESS(94)41/Fr/pdf

Jacques Delors : sa non-candidature à la présidentielle, source: https://www.ina.fr/ina-eclaire-actu/video/i13150249/jacques-delors-sa-non-candidature-a-la-presidentielle

The Candidate (1972), source: https://www.youtube.com/watch?v=myEpap3TxVs

Interview de M. Jacques Chirac, Président de la République, à France 2 le 26 octobre 1995, sur la priorité à la réduction des déficits publics et à la maîtrise des dépenses de santé, et sur la lutte contre l'exclusion sociale, source: https://www.elysee.fr/jacques-chirac/1995/10/26/interview-de-m-jacques-chirac-president-de-la-republique-a-France-2-le-26-octobre-1995-sur-la-priorite-a-la-reduction-des-deficits-publics-et-a-la-maitrise-des-depenses-de-sante-et-sur-la-lutte-contre-lexclusion-sociale

Les conflits du travail en 1995 : un niveau élevé, source: https://dares.travail-emploi.gouv.fr/publication/les-conflits-du-travail-en-1995-un-niveau-eleve

Conseil européen de Madrid 15 et 16 décembre 1995, Conclusion de la présidence, source: https://www.europarl.europa.eu/summits/mad1_fr.htm?textMode=on

Nicolas, Boileau, Satire IV, *À M. l'abbé Le Vayer*, 1664, source: https://gallica.bnf.fr/ark:/12148/bpt6k5665585g/f84.item.r=A%20M%20%20l'abb%C3%A9%20Le%20Vayer

Déclaration de politique générale de M. Lionel Jospin, Premier ministre, sur les axes de travail du gouvernement, à l'Assemblée nationale le 19 juin 1997, parue dans "La Lettre du Gouvernement" du 24 juin 1997, source: https://www.vie-publique.fr/discours/163833-declaration-de-politique-generale-de-m-lionel-jospin-premier-ministre

Les effets de la RTT sur l'emploi : des simulations ex ante aux évaluations ex post, Économie et Statistique, n° 376–377–2004, Alain Gubian, Stéphane Jugnot, Frédéric Lerais et Vladimir Passeron, 1 June 2005, source: https://www.insee.fr/fr/statistiques/1376464?sommaire=1376476

Conseil européen Lisbonne, 23 et 24 mars 2000, Conclusions de la présidence, source: https://www.europarl.europa.eu/summits/lis1_fr.htm

Retraites : Orange perd son procès contre Bruxelles, source: https://www.bfmtv.com/economie/entreprises/services/retraites-orange-perd-son-proces-contre-bruxelles_AN-201502260118.html

Déclaration de politique générale de M. Jean-Pierre Raffarin, Premier ministre, sur la restauration de l'autorité de l'État, la démocratie sociale et la relance de la décentralisation, la politique économique et sociale et sur la politique européenne de la France, à l'Assemblée nationale

le 3 juillet 2002, source: https://www.vie-publique.fr/discours/131219-jean-pierre-raffarin-03072002-declaration-de-politique-generale

Études économiques de l'OCDE : France 2003, source: https://doi.org/10.1787/eco_surveys-fra-2003-fr

Jean-Claude Trichet au pied du mur, Le Monde, 26 November 2003, source: https://www.lemonde.fr/archives/article/2003/11/26/jean-claude-trichet-au-pied-du-mur_4288716_1819218.html

Arrêt de la Cour (assemblée plénière) du 13 juillet 2004, source: https://eur-lex.europa.eu/legal-content/FR/ALL/?uri=CELEX%3A62004CJ0027

Rompre avec la facilité de la dette publique, commission chaired by Michel Pébereau, source: https://www.vie-publique.fr/files/rapport/pdf/054004454.pdf

René Mayer : Études, témoignages et documents, source: https://gallica.bnf.fr/ark:/12148/bpt6k4808809p.texteImage

The Origins of Endogenous Growth, Paul M. Romer, The Journal of Economic Perspectives, Vol. 8, No. 1 (Winter, 1994), pp. 3–22, source: https://www.jstor.org/stable/2138148

Dépenses de recherche, source: https://www.insee.fr/fr/statistiques/3281637?sommaire=3281778#tableau-figure2

International Monetary Fund, *Nobel laureate Kydland reflects, talks about what's in store*, 24 May 2005, source: https://www.elibrary.imf.org/view/journals/023/0034/009/article-A010-en.xml

Bibliography

Alain Peyrefitte, *C'était de Gaule*, Quarto Gallimard, 2002.

Albert Aftalion, *Les trois notions de la productivité et ses revenus*, Revue d'économie politique, Revue d'économie politique, Vol. 25, No. 2, pages 145–184, Editions Dalloz, 1911.

Anne Robert Jacques Turgot, *Lettre d'Anne Robert Jacques Turgot à Louis XVI*, Compiègne, 24 August 1774.

Charles de Gaulle, *Discours et Messages*, t. II, Dans l'attente 1946–1958, Plon.

Charles de Gaulle, *Mémoires d'espoir*, t. I, Le Renouveau, 1958–1962, Plon.

Edgar Faure, *Mémoires*, t. II ; Si tel doit être mon destin ce soir…, Paris, Plon, 1984.

Florian, Jean-Pierre Claris de, *Choix des plus jolies fables de M. de Florian*, éditeur Delarue, 1865, notice du catalogue: http://catalogue.bnf.fr/ark:/12148/cb30443965p

Franz Kafka, *Nouvelles et récits. Œuvres complètes I*, sous la direction de Jean-Pierre Lefebvre. Bibliothèque de la Pléiade NRF. 2018.

Gabriel Ardant, *Histoire de l'impôt*, t. II, Paris, Fayard, 1972.

Georges Pompidou, directeur du général de Gaulle, juin 1958-janvier 1959, Lachaise, Bernard, Le Béguec, Gilles, et Turpin, Frédéric (dir.), 2006.

Georgette Elgey, *Histoire de la IVe république, De 1945 à 1957*, éditions Robert Laffont, 2018.

Georgette Elgey, *Histoire de la IVe république, De 1956 à janvier 1959*, éditions Robert Laffont, 2018.

Henry Kissinger, *Les Années de renouveau*, le dernier volume des Mémoires, Paris, Fayard, 2000.

Jean Fourastié, *La productivité*, Que sais-je ? 1952.

Jean Fourastié, *Les Trente Glorieuses*, Jean Fourastié, Pluriel, 2011.

Jean-Jacques Carré, Paul Dubois et Edmond Malivaud, *La croissance française*, Éditions du Seuil, 1973.

Jean Monnet, *Mémoires*, Fayard, 1976.

Jean-Pierre Rioux, *La France de la IVe République*, éd Histoire, Points, 1983.

Jean-Pierre Vesperini, *L'économie de la France : de la crise de mai 1968 aux résultats de l'expérience socialiste*, Economica, 1985.

Johann Wolfgang Von Goethe, *Faust,* Gérard de Nerval, traducteur, version complète tomes 1 et 2, Kindle édition, 2018.

Joseph Staline, *Le Marxisme et la question nationale et coloniale*, Paris, Éditions sociales, 1950, p. 206-207.

Milton Friedman et Anna Jacobson Schwartz, *L'Histoire monétaire des États-Unis, 1867–1960,* National Bureau of Economic Research, *Studies in Business Cycles*, Princeton University Press, 1963.

Mundell R. (1963), *Capital Mobility and Stabilization Policy under Fixed and Flexible Exchange Rates*, Canadian Journal of Economics, vol. 29475–85.

Pierre Poujade, *J'ai choisi le combat*, Saint-Céré, Société générale des éditeurs et des publications, page 19, 1955.

MIX
Papier aus verantwortungsvollen Quellen
Paper from responsible sources
FSC® C105338

If you have any concerns about our products, you can contact us on
ProductSafety@springernature.com

In case Publisher is established outside the EU, the EU authorized representative is:
Springer Nature Customer Service Center GmbH
Europaplatz 3, 69115 Heidelberg, Germany

Printed by Libri Plureos GmbH
in Hamburg, Germany